# Contemporary Anthropological Research in Eastern and North Eastern India

# Contemporary Anthropological Research in Eastern and North Eastern India

*Edited by*

**Sarthak Sengupta**

GYAN

First Published, 2017

*Published by*

Gyan Publishing House
5, Ansari Road
Daryaganj, New Delhi-110002
Phone: 9811692060
E-mail: books@gyanbooks.com

*Printed at:* G. Print Process, Delhi.

**Cataloging in Publication Data—DK**
Courtesy: D.K. Agencies (P) Ltd. <docinfo@dkagencies.com>

**Contemporary anthropological research in Eastern and North Eastern India** / Sarthak Sengupta.
pages cm
Contributed articles.
Includes bibliographical references.
ISBN 9788121213585

1. Physical anthropology—India, Northeastern. 2. Physical anthropology—India. 3. Ethnology—India, Northeastern. 4. Ethnology—India. I. Sengupta, Sarthak, 1955- editor.

DS430.S46 2017 DDC 305.800954 23

In memory of

Professor B.M. Das; Professor M.N. Phookan
and Mrs. Manjurani Goswami
who are no more with us on this beautiful Earth

# Contents

# List of Tables

# List of Figures

# Acknowledgement

Given the expanse and coverage of this volume, I have so many individuals, institutions, and organisations that I want to thank who have made this compilation possible.

I would never forget the inspiring response I received from all the eminent contributors who on my request, contributed research articles in this anthology. Without their unalloyed cooperation and academic support, this volume would not have been in its present form. I have no words to thank them, but I trust this small mention at least records my depth of gratitude for their academic collaboration, patience, and forbearance in making my effort a reality.

I also wish to express my appreciation to my elder son Sushruta, his wife Surovee, my granddaughter Shinjinee, and younger son Samrat, all of them gave me the freedom I needed to remain focused during the strenuous task of editing the compilation. My wife Kaveeta also deserves appreciation for bearing with me as usual.

I shall be failing in my duty if I do not express my heartfelt thanks to the Director and the staff members of Gyan Publishing House, New Delhi for understanding the importance of this book, and honouring my proposal to publish the manuscript, and bringing it out expeditiously.

March 01, 2017 (Sarthak Sengupta)

# Prologue

Diversified culture and people of Eastern and North Eastern India has attracted the attention of many anthropologists from different parts of the globe. This region of our country is a meeting place of so many ethnic groups and customs that it has long been recognised by anthropologists as one of the most dynamic fields of research work. Many scholars in different fields carry out a systematic and detailed investigation on ethnography and human variability in this region. Initially, most of these studies were conducted by administrators, missionaries, travelers and not by professionally trained anthropologists. At present, however, a good number of well-trained scholars from India and abroad had taken up anthropological studies with dedication and had done commendable contributions in augmenting the horizon of the anthropology of the region.

The beginning of Post Graduate teaching in anthropology at Calcutta University will go down in the history of Indian Anthropology for being the first University department in the entire country. At present, the universities offered anthropology at Post Graduate level in this part of our country is around twenty in number.

Post-Graduate Department of Anthropology at Dibrugarh University (established in 1966) completed it's glorious five decades in 2016. Fifty years is a milestone in the life of any institution, not just counting the years passed, but it is an occasion to analyze critically the achievement. The present endeavour is a humble attempt to commemorate its 50 long years of the journey by publishing an anthology of contemporary anthropological research activities in Eastern and North Easter India. It is a combination of disparate research articles written by individual contributors on themes chosen by them, but all of them deserve serious attention of the contemporary anthropologists. Each and every contributor of this volume is closely associated with the Department in its all-round development.

The volume, however, in no way can claim to have thorough coverage of the ongoing anthropological research activities on the people of the region within this limited space by dealing all aspects, but a good cross-section of man, society, and culture of the region is here reflected. The effort expanded in compiling this volume will be well rewarded if this anthology proves to be informative, stimulus and useful to anthropologists besides other social scientists; administrators, planners, policy makers and indeed anyone with a concern about the anthropological research activities in this enchanting region of our country.

March 01, 2017 (Sarthak Sengupta)

# List of Contributors

**Angshuman Sarma**, North Eastern Social Research Centre, Jagriti, GMCH Road, Christian Basti, Guwahati-781005, Assam.

**Arup Ratan Bandyopadhyay**, Department of Anthropology, University of Calcutta, 35 Ballygunge Circular Road, Kolkata-700019, West Bengal.

**Chandrajyoti Sonowal**, Centre for Study of Social Inclusion and Inclusive Policies, Tata Institute of Social Sciences, Deonar, Mumbai-400088, Maharastra.

**D.K. Limbu**, Department of Anthropology, North Eastern Hill University, Mawkynroh, Umshing, Shillong-793022, Meghalaya.

**Debasis Kumar Mondal**, Department of Anthropology, University of Calcutta, 35 Ballygunge Circular Road, Kolkata-700019, West Bengal.

**Debasmita Kar**, Department of Anthropology, University of Calcutta, 35 Ballygunge Circular Road, Kolkata-700019, West Bengal.

**Geetika Ranjan**, Department of Anthropology, North Eastern Hill University, Mawkynroh, Umshing, Shillong-793022, Meghalaya.

**Irengbam Bijeta**, Department of Anthropology, Manipur University, Canchipur, Imphal-795003, Manipur.

**Jintu Kalita**, Department of Anthropology, North Eastern Hill University, Mawkynroh, Umshing, Shillong-793022, Meghalaya.

**Juri Borah**, Department of Anthropology, Dibrugarh University, Dibrugarh-786004, Assam.

**Jyotismita Sharma**, Department of Anthropology, Assam University, Diphu Campus, Diphu, Karbi Anglong, Assam.

**Kh. Narendra Singh**, Department of Anthropology, Assam University, Diphu Campus, Diphu, Karbi Anglong, Assam.

**M.C. Arunkumar**, Department of Anthropology, Manipur University, Canchipur, Imphal-795003, Manipur.

**Madhumati Chatterjee**, Department of Anthropology, Sarojini Naidu College for Women, 30 Jessore Road, Kolkata-700028, West Bengal.

**Manis Kumar Raha**, Revati F/1, Neelachal Abasan, 98 Rajadanga Gold Part, Kolkata-700107, West Bengal.

**Manoranjan Pal**, Biological Anthropology Unit, Indian Statistical Institute, 203 Barrackpore Trunk Road, Kolkata-700108, West Bengal.

**Melvil Pereira**, North Eastern Social Research Centre, Jagriti, GMCH Road, Christian Basti, Guwahati-781005, Assam.

**Mini Bhattacharyya Thakur**, Department of Anthropology, Gauhati University, Guwahati-781014, Assam.

**Nitish Mondal**, Department of Anthropology, Assam University, Diphu Campus, Diphu, Karbi Anglong, Assam.

**Nivedita Som**, Biological Anthropology Unit, Indian Statistical Institute, 203 Barrackpore Trunk Road, Kolkata-700108, West Bengal.

**Premananda Bharati**, Biological Anthropology Unit, Indian Statistical Institute, 203 Barrackpore Trunk Road, Kolkata-700108, West Bengal.

**Queenbala Marak**, Department of Anthropology, North Eastern Hill University, Mawkynroh, Umshing, Shillong-793022, Meghalaya.

**R. P. Athparia**, North Eastern Social Research Centre, Jagriti, GMCH Road, Christian Basti, Guwahati-781005, Assam.

**Ranjana Ray**, Department of Anthropology, University of Calcutta, 35 Ballygunge Circular Road, Kolkata-700019, West Bengal.

**Rashmi Upadhyay**, Department of Anthropology, North Eastern Hill University, Mawkynroh, Umshing, Shillong-793022, Meghalaya.

**Ritu Geu Goswami**, National Institute of Public Cooperation and Child Development, Khanapara, Guwahati-781022, Assam.

**S. Saikia**, Department of Anthropology, Women's College, Shillong, Meghalaya.

**Sarthak Sengupta**, Department of Anthropology, Dibrugarh University, Dibrugarh-786004, Assam.

**Sekh Rahim Mondal**, Centre for Himalayan Studies, University of North Bengal, Raja Rammohunpur, Darjeeling-734013, West Bengal.

**Subha Ray**, Department of Anthropology, University of Calcutta, 35 Ballygunge Circular Road, Kolkata-700019, West Bengal.

**Subrata K. Roy**, Biological Anthropology Unit, Indian Statistical Institute, 203 Barrackpore Trunk Road, Kolkata-700108, West Bengal.

**Surajit Kumar Pal**, Shivam Kumj, Nalini Apartment–5, Flat No. F-1, Barde Nagar, Borgaon (East), Gorewara Rank Road, Nagpur-440013, Maharashtra.

**Susmita Bharati**, Biological Anthropology Unit, Indian Statistical Institute, 203, Barrackpore Trunk Road, Kolkata-700108, West Bengal.

**Tanaya Kundu Chowdhury**, Biological Anthropology Unit, Indian Statistical Institute, 203 Barrackpore Trunk Road, Kolkata-700108, West Bengal.

# Chapter - 1

# Interrogating Cosmopolitanism from Anthropological Perspective

*—Sekh Rahim Mondal*

## Introduction

In contemporary times the term cosmopolitanism has emerged as a viable concept and also a policy/project in the multiethnic urban setting. In the context of neo-liberal globalisation the increasing economic interaction and dependence as well as their consequential growth of industrialisation, and urbanisation there has been a growth of both in and out migration and so also of immigration in all parts of the world. This flow of population *(ethnoscape)* leads to the growth of social heterogeneity and cultural hybridity in wild spaces. Under such a complex social situation the issues of inter-group relations and their identities are very crucial. Managing diversity is the prime concern of a multi-cultural social set up and under such a social context cosmopolitanism has emerged as an important concept and also as a policy for social harmony. But unfortunately, anthropologists have not paid much attention towards the study the cosmopolitan issues, particularly in India.

The present study is a humble attempt to examine and interrogate the concept of cosmopolitanism in an analytical manner from the perspective of anthropology. The chapter is based on facts gathered from a review of relevant literature supported by empirical findings and research experience of the author in the field of anthropology since long.

## Reviewing the Concept of Cosmopolitanism

By cosmopolitanism, we usually mean a space (town, city etc.), the population of which is belonging to all parts of the world or the country thus not restricted to any specific place or its population. A cosmopolitan place is free from national or regional limitations and attachments. In recent times the global cities are becoming more and more cosmopolitan i.e. indifference to ethnicities or religions. A cosmopolitan citizen is one who has no national, regional and ethnic prejudices, hence regarded as cosmopolite.

In contemporary political and social theory, cosmopolitanism is a policy/projects as much as a concept. The cosmopolitan policy is related to the notion of cosmopolitan democracy which would evolve a good governance to allow greater interaction with people for a smooth social solidarity and mobility. The term cosmopolitan is used to indicate a model of political and social organisation in which the citizens (peoples) where even they are located should have a voice, input and even political representation in global affairs in parallel with and independently of their own governments and national identities. The concept of democracy deployed here entails a substantive process rather than merely a guiding rules and working as a transforming politics from a mode of domination/subordination to a mode of service.

Since the intensification of neoliberal globalisation, there has been a trend in increased flow of peoples i.e. migration or immigration (legal, illegal, voluntary, involuntary etc.) followed by capital, technology, ideology and information what Appadurai (1996) designated as *ethno-scape, finance-scape, techno-scape, ido-scape* and *media-scape.* Under such a situation cosmopolitanism has emerged as an important theoretical concept and practical project for towns and cities. In the context of the global economic dependence of economic interaction, there has been a tendency of migration of workers of various skills and categories which has enhanced the claims of citizenship of residents in different countries of places with the country. The social process of such a nature leads to competition between local and non-local population and resulting to ethnic or religious contradictions and clashes. Moreover, the process of cultural globalisation and homogenisation as created by market forces and designed by multi-nationals and superpowers causing serious problems towards identity, dignity and human rights issues. The social situation of such a nature demands a remedial measure by way of cosmopolitan policy as it offers a middle way between unfettered globalisation or universalism and localism or nationalism (Appiah, 2006; Archibugi and Held, 1995; Huntington, 1996; Iqtidar, 2010).

In the context of contemporary globalisation, the emergence of cosmopolitanism is a process which means not only the erosion of borders (physical or social) but also linking markets, states, cultures, religions and civilisation. It also implies interaction as well as confrontation with the alien "other" all over the globe. The world is certainly not politically borderless today, but boundaries are becoming blurred and indistinct, becoming permeable to flows of peoples, capitals, ideologies, technologies and information. This cosmo-politicisation not only helps in developing trans-national, trans-regional, trans-ethnic social relations but also helps in adopting cosmopolitan attitudes with respect to migrants and immigrants. Today the medias and information technology also provides avenues to develop the cosmopolitan attitude and characters. Cosmopoliticisation cannot totally erase the confrontational and intolerant dichotomy between 'self' (ours) and 'others', or 'we' and 'they' distinctions, rather it helps in minimising the degree of such dichotomies. Human groups bear multiple identities. The identity constructions depend on context and situation. The notion of 'power' and 'relation' plays the very crucial role in identity formation and identity perception. A cosmopolitan space is providing the breeding ground of multiple identity constructions as per demands of the local, national and global situation.

In the discourse of cosmopolitanism, there is a danger of fusing ideal with real. How cosmopolitanism actually operates cannot be separated from how cosmopolitanism should be. Cosmopolitanism actually dictated by the forces of 'power' or in other words the relationship between dominant majority and weak minorities.

Philosophically cosmopolitanism has a deeper meaning. Every human being is rooted by birth into two worlds, two communities i.e. (a) in the cosmos (nature) and in polis (the state/place/city etc.), all individuals are rooted in one cosmos (citizen of the nature) but in different states, territories, nations, religious, cities and other settings. This creates a plural membership and identities. Being a part of cosmos every man and woman are equal to nature (in religious world it is equal to God), yet being a member of several states, territories and societies they are varied, distinct, diversified and there by members of the different polis (units). Cosmopolitanism ignores 'either' and 'or' principle but incorporate 'this' and 'that' (Beck, 2006; Held, 1999).

## Cosmopolitanism and Cultural Diversities

Cosmopolitanism is primarily a normative and philosophical concept. Hence, it needs to be conceptualised through social scientific as well as anthropological perspectives. In a social context, the most crucial questions are how is cosmopolitanism dealing with cultural differences of varied ethnic, social and religious groups? Therefore, cosmopolitanism can be distinguished from 'ideal' and 'real' patterns in the ways of dealing with differences and diversities. Cosmopolitanism cannot ignore multiculturalism. In cosmopolitan context multi-cultural or pluri-cultural existence is quite obvious and natural as the cosmopolitan space or setting is inhabited and shared by distinct peoples of varied historical and social backgrounds. The problem is that the ideal universalistic account of cosmopolitanism carries an ethnocentric bias as it desires to operate with 'thin' and 'singular' conception of identity which is reality 'plural' in character thus devoid of relativistic attitude. Its central shortcoming is that it operates not only within an a-historical notion but also ignoring the past (background), thereby seeks to mould (assimilate or galvanise) the particular memories and cultures of past into a universal standard for future. In doing so, it fails to recognise the persistence and significance of particularism. As a matter of fact, this perpetuates exclusion as its central features. Moreover, it tries to simplify the complex relationship between nationalism, pluri-culturalism and cosmopolitanism. Globalisation proposes universalism and cosmopolitanism with a hidden tendency of suppressing diversities. The explicit idea is that the nationalism, particularly the ethnonationalism or religio-nationalism is considered as enemies or problematic for cosmopolitanism. Theoretically, cosmopolitanism attacking all forms of vertical differentiation which bringing social differences into a hierarchical relation of domination (superiority) and subordination (inferiority), but it cannot completely remove the difference. Moreover, it perpetuates, the new forms of distinctions in way of 'insider' and 'outsider', 'in-group' and 'out-group', and 'we' and 'they'. This sometimes reached to the level of 'good citizen' and 'bad citizen'.

Cosmopolitanism affirms 'other' as different and at the same time 'unequal', 'unwanted' and sometimes as 'enemy'. Theoretically, it calls for a new way of integration and amalgamation that facilitate and affirm co-existence through mutual aids and understanding across social boundaries, where differences be sacrificed on the ground of co-existence. In this context, this new notion of integration is actually a form of assimilation or absorption, which is nothing but a different word for hegemony over the unwanted 'others' i.e. majority over the minority (ethnic, linguistic, cultural and religious). True and ideal (normative) cosmopolitanism aware of diversities thus accept differences but does not absolutes it due to 'power' game. Rather it finds out the ways for rendering tolerable situation. Actually, the spirit of democracy acts as a binding force of co-existence and tolerance. It relies and operates on a framework of universally uniting and binding norms that should prevent post-modern particularism (Beck and Grande, 2007; Beek and Sznaider, 2010; Calhoun, 2002).

## Cosmopolitanism and Multiculturalism

Cosmopolitanism has a deep relation with the multiculturalism. Multiculturalism is a fact and also a value in cosmopolitan context. Its central insights are: (a) Human beings are culturally rooted, they grow up and live in a culturally structured world and organise their social relations in terms of a culturally derived system of meaning and significance, (b) Different cultures represent different systems of meaning and vision of good life, (c) Every culture is internally plural and differentiated and reflects a continuing interaction with different traditions and thoughts.

Multiculturalism advocates cultural diversity and exhibits a society in which different communities forge a common identity while retaining their specific cultural attributes and identities. It pictures a society which is characterised not only by multiple cultural solitudes but also by living together and participating as equal partners in local or national economic and political life. From a multicultural perspective, a good society characterises the diversity and encourages a creative dialogue between different cultures and traditions. Modern democratic societies embrace multiculturalism by demonstrating a deeper and more profound egalitarian impulse within them, rather them the mere presence of plural of multiple cultures. Multiculturalism acknowledges the existence of diverse communities, but what is more important is that it accords positive value to the collective identities of all ethnic communities living in a particular place. Multiculturalism represents a new kind of universalism and cosmopolitanism, where the people are included in the state or in the place not only as members of diverse ethnic groups but with equal rights and duties.

Multiculturalism and democracy are closely related. Only democracy can explore the formats of interaction among the diverse groups that prescribes equality and respect. Multiculturalism actually gives democracy its health and vigour. But in a democratic set up the danger of political majoritarianism is now widely noticed. This has become an assimilative ingredient in the metabolism of modern democracies. Multiculturalism creates awareness about the danger of majoritarianism and violation of human rights. It points to the way in which cultural majoritarianism disadvantages the minorities and weaker sections. Moreover, it alienates them and thereby generating conflict between the communities. Safeguarding minorities and disadvantaged sections need policies of inclusion and good governance that ensure full and equal membership to all communities within the cosmopolitan context or the state (Joseph, 1999; Mahajan, 1999; Mondal, 2005).

## Cosmopolitanism and Human Rights

Modern cosmopolitan politics and policies (projects) begin with the principle that sovereignty is not the highest principle. Rather the highest principle is human dignity and well-being, thus the main duty is to prevent the suffering out of exclusion wherever it occurs. As a matter of fact, the leading cosmopolitan ideas today are rooted in the issues of human rights and inclusive policies. The cosmopolitan attitude is to be learned through secular, trans-national and democratic social practices. This is the ideological and political formulation of modern cosmopolitanism. In a normative sense, cosmopolitanism means recognition of 'cultural otherness' and 'diversities' both externally and internally. This is also called moral cosmopolitanism. But in actual practice nowhere in the world at the beginning of the twenty-first century, such conditions being accepted and that has created danger, thereby form the risk society at a functional level. Therefore, the question emerges what can unite human beings of different ethnic, social, cultural, territorial and national backgrounds if not recognition and respect for difference are there? Contemporary cosmopolitan space is suffering from the dilemma between the threat of pluralism and the recognition of otherness (Beek and Sznaider, 2010; Beck and Grande, 2007).

## Concluding Remarks

The word cosmopolitanism derives from Greek word cosmopolites which mean citizen or member of the world (nature), the cosmos is the world and politics is the citizen. Cosmopolitanism has been examining various ways viz. philosophical, political, anthropological and sociological. The anthropological and sociological cosmopolitanism rests upon the fundamental foundation of acknowledging and respecting 'others' who are socially and culturally different. Actually, cosmopolitan debate rests upon the attitude towards the relationship between majority and minority. Cosmopolitanism calls for equal rights and dignity. But the most crucial question emerged here is that whose rights have to be respected and protected and whose rights are to be ignored or not granted.

As like as other social science concepts the concept of cosmopolitanism has also of Western origin. At West, cosmopolitanism deals with the issues of 'good' and 'bad' cosmopolites. A 'good' cosmopolitan is one who has been highly westernised and the bad cosmopolites are those who visibly reject or ignore and not following the western influences i.e. western way of life. In the eyes of the west individuals who embrace western ideas and carries western values and life ways are considered fully cosmopolitan and are more likely to be afforded dignity and protection than those who not only denied the western cultures but also maintain their respective identities. In this regard, cosmopolitanism is linked with westernisation and thus not free from Euro-centric or Western bias.

There is a difference between cosmopolitanism as a concept and cosmopolitanism as a policy. There is a normative difference between the western and non-western version of cosmopolitanism. The former is Eurocentric, Secular (irreligious), modern and highly hegemonic, while the latter is value-loaded, humanitarian, relativistic and post-modern. Again the former is an assimilative project to establish cultural homogeneity, while latter recognise the diversity and heterogeneity.

Cosmopolitanism also needs to be examined both from the perspectives of texts and contexts i.e. ideal and real (empirical). Actually, cosmopolitanism is not problematic, but what make it problematic is how the power looks into it and how the power wants to use and follow it in social and political context. Cultural diversities are the reality and also the natural phenomenon, hence galvanising and suppressing cultural diversities in the name or at the cost of cosmopolitanism is not wise, rather dangerous on the question of human rights, human dignity, and human self-esteem. Therefore, the success of cosmopolitanism depends on the recognition of human and cultural diversities of a particular setting. In cosmopolitanism concept which is moral that may be regarded as a true form of cosmopolitanism, while those are immoral may be called as hegemonic cosmopolitanism.

Managing diversity is the prime concern of a multi-cultural setting and under such a heterogeneous social context cosmopolitanism has a very crucial role both as an ideology and also as a policy.

Anthropology as a holistic science of man has a great scope of examining, interrogating and comprehending the issues of cosmopolitanism both from theoretical perspectives and also from empirical realities. Historically the focus of anthropology is the study of 'others'. Hence the issues' relating to the 'others' (otherness) in cosmopolitan context is an important field of anthropological research, both at urban and rural context. India being a multi-ethnic and multi-cultural country offers a good field of study of cosmopolitanism from the perspectives of Anthropology.

In Anthropological literature of India, the cosmopolitanism issue is not a new one. Professor Oscar Lewis of Illinois University, USA, took up the study of Rampur village near Delhi city in 1951, which was published as a monograph in 1958. Out of this study, Lewis developed the concept of 'rural cosmopolitanism' to indicate the inter-village connections and inter-relationships among the peoples of different villages (Lewis, 1958).

## References

Appadurai, A., 1996, *Modernity at Large: Cultural Dimensions of Globalisation,* London; University of Minnesota Press.

Appiah, A., 2006, *Cosmopolitanism: Ethics in a World of Strangers,* New York; WW. Norton.

Archibugi, D. and D. Held, 1995, *Cosmopolitan Democracy: An Agenda for a New World Order,* Cambridge; Polity Press.

Beck, U. and E. Grandi, 2007, *The Cosmopolitan Europe,* Cambridge; Polity Press.

Beck, U. and N. Sznaider, 2010, 'New cosmopolitanism in the social sciences'. In BS Turner (Ed.) *International Handbook of Globalisation Studies,* London; Routledge.

Beck, U., 2006, *The Cosmopolitan Vision,* Cambridge; Polity Press.

Calhoun, C., 2002, 'Imaging solidarity: Cosmopolitanism, constitutional patriotism and the public space', *Public Culture,* 14, 1: 147-171.

Held, D., A. McGrew, D. Goldblatt and J. Perraton, 1999, *Global Transformation Politics: Economics and Culture,* Cambridge; Polity Press.

Huntington, SP., 1996, *The Clash of Civilisations and the Remarking of World Orders,* New York; Simon and Schuster.

Iqtidar, H., 2010, 'Muslim, cosmopolitanism contemporary practice and social theory'. In BS Turner (Ed.): *International Handbook of Globalisation Studies.* London; Routledge.

Joseph, S., 1999, 'Of minorities and majorities'. *Seminar,* 484: 30-34.

Lewis, O., 1958, *Village Life in Northern India, Studies in a Delhi Village,* Urbana; University of Illinois Press.

Mahajan, G., 1999, 'The problem–A symposium on democracy in culturally diverse societies', *Seminar,* 484: 12-13.

Mondal, SR., 2005, 'Multiculturalism in India: Opportunities and challenges', *Occasional Paper,* No.16, Centre for Himalayan Studies, University of North Bengal.

# Chapter - 2

# The Chitrakars of Eastern India: An Attempt at Interpreting Prehistoric Art

*—Debasis Kumar Mondal, Kakali Bhattacharjee and Ranjana Ray*

## Introduction

Leo Tolstoy had defined art as, *"Art is not, as the metaphysicians say, the manifestation of some mysterious idea of beauty or God; it is not, as the aesthetical physiologists say, a game in which man lets off his excess of stored-up energy; it is not the expression of man's emotions by external signs; it is not the production of pleasing objects; and, above all, it is not pleasure; but it is a means of union among men, joining them together in the same feelings, and indispensable for the life and progress toward well-being of individuals and of humanity"*. This is especially applicable to folk artists, who are the main focus in this chapter.

The ability to make art or artistic objects are one of the most important features of a human being. A 'work of art' means any permanent or transitory object or device that enables the artist and/or the public to have an artistic experience precisely distinguished from those human-made objects which are considered as artificial (Gortis, 2003:1242; Scott, 2006:630).

Art and artists go long way back down in human history. The earliest available evidence of artistic objects in India came from the Acheulian tradition of lower Palaeolithic culture, dating back to 200,000 to 400,000 years B.P (Kumar, 2010:11). The appearance of art and artistic objects in course of human history are important markers for understanding the development of hominid cognitive behaviour. It indicates the development of capacity for abstraction of ideas, beliefs, and perceptions into visuals. It is a form of communication, self-expression and often be associated with ceremonies and rituals (Ranjana *et al.,* 2011). Human history had seen the development of art in various forms. Art is defined as naturalistic and symbolic or abstract. It can most definitely be said that art is a way of communication, where symbols play a vital role. Contemporary society and the universe of the people are expressed through art.

Since its discovery prehistoric art had drawn the attention of the anthropologists and archaeologists and has been studied from various angles and aspects. This was done with multidisciplinary methodologies. Dating prehistoric art is often a difficult proposition. That too had been solved with the help of modern technologies. The most difficult situation arises out of the difficulty in explaining the objective, motivation, function and purpose of the prehistoric art (Renfrew, 2006). For understanding rock art with the help of science of signs are aptly taken into consideration for interpretation (Seglie, 2001; 2011).

A large quantity of prehistoric art, petroglyphs, and rock art had been discovered in India and a lot of work had been done on them (Chakravarty, 1984; Chakravarty and Bednarik, 1997; Sreenathan *et al.,* 2008). Preliterate and living art of the primitive people had also drawn the attention of the scholars, not only for comparative study but for understanding some of the prehistoric art as well. Scholars in India had been fascinated with the similarity in motifs, colour, mode of painting and engravings with the local tribal communities and have taken up study for interpretation of prehistoric art (Chakravarty, 2011). One of the authors of this chapter had made a study of the tribal art and has suggested methodologies for interpretation (Ray, 1984; Ghosh, 1984).

The term tribal is an ambiguous one in India. The terminology is closely linked with the colonial history of the land. The term is rather a political one because there are groups of people living in comparative isolation who cannot be distinguished as much from the tribes. These people are better defined as folk. Folk is rather a generalised term. The authors prefer the term folk for describing a type of art which is not only traditional but has got a long history of persistence in India.

India is a land of vibrant colour and rhythm. The diverse cultural realm of India is reflected in its art, both of the past and the present. Both the tribal and the folk people spend their leisure time in pursuit of art in various forms. They paint their habitations, utensils, make colourful textile and even paint their body with colour and tattoo marks. Decorating the faces with designs made with sandalwood paste at the time of life cycle rituals is an important aspect of culture in India. The art, the designs, the motifs and the colours used have special symbols in individual societies. The mythology of the country has got a close connection with different places and diverse environment. Cosmology is very much a part of the folk art. Rituals and customs are deep rooted and can be traced back to a very early time.

## Patuas or Chitrakars

The present chapter discusses a traditional way of scroll painting, which is associated with storytelling in the form of lyrics and songs. This kind of art involves symbols for mythological deliberations by the folk artists to the folk communities. This kind of art is locally known as *pata.* Those who draw the pictures or in other words the artists preparing the art are known as Patuas or Chitrakars (McCutchion and Bhowmik, 1999). *Chitra* is a Sanskrit word meaning picture. Those who make the *Chitra* are known as Chitrakar. These people are also known as Patuas. The Patuas or Chitrakars form a kind of social order. Patuas are a sect of perambulating artists who go around the villages with their paintings and tell the stories which are mainly connected with local mythologies, gods, goddesses, current events, nature, cosmic events and catastrophes. The paintings are in the form of scrolls, which they go on unfurling as the story progresses. The tales are usually sung by the Patuas. This they do in exchange for alms. The scrolls are not sold. They are means of sustenance to them. In the present chapter, such art, and artists living in West Bengal are described. At present women are engaged in such painting and both men and women go from door to door with their scrolls, especially after the harvest season. Earlier only the male Patuas went with their art to different villages.

A '*pata*' is a roll of multiple scrolls. It is like a moving picture gallery. It contains a series of pictures rolled out one after the other in which the development of a complete story from beginning to end is painted. The art shows wonderful force and vividness. The story of each picture is melodiously chanted by the 'Patuas'. The song and lyric are composed by the artist himself. The moral basis of art has always been kept steadily in view. Each '*pata*' ends with a picture of the court of the King of Death God (*Yama*) and of the last judgment, and the artist invariably ends up chanting the eternal law of ultimate triumph of virtue and the defeat and punishment of vice. This custom, which was an admirable medium of spiritual and moral instruction as well as of art education in ancient and medieval India, survived in an almost unimpaired form until about fifty years ago in the rural areas of Bengal. With the advent of modernisation, the art has gradually lost its charm and the Patuas were thrown to abject poverty and misery. Many of them had to give up the traditional craft and search for alternative means of livelihood, which is a very hard task for the people who are largely landless. In the last few decades, there are endeavours for the revival of the art (Bhattacharya, 2001).

## History of *Pata-Chitra*

'*Pata-chitras'* is a very ancient tradition of Bengal as well as of India. It is evident from the Buddhist literature that *pata-chitra* goes as far back as at least before seventh century BCE. The use of '*pata-chitra'* by the Buddhist preachers for the purpose of popularising Buddhist faith among the common folk suggests that it was a popular and indigenous art form prevalent among the Indians well before the birth of Buddha (Sengupta, 1973).

The archaeological evidence has given the '*pata*' a much older date than suggested by literary sources. The art objects found from Mohenjo-Daro, Harappa, Ajanta, Khajuraho, Paharpur, and Amaravati belong to dates ranging from 3000 BCE to early historic period. The art of these sites bears a close resemblance to *'pata'* art, the folk painting of Bengal. These may be the legacy of the wonderful '*chitralekhas*' so frequently mentioned in classical Sanskrit literature (Sengupta, 1973).

Most Sanskrit dictionaries include the word *'patta'* to mean cloth. It could be any kind of fabric or textile, namely, silk, cotton, dried palm leaves etc. '*Patta*' in fact is originally an Austro-Asiatic word. Two major languages of Austro-Asiatic group are the Santali and Mundari. These are spoken by a broad group of the tribal community known as Kol. Though according to legend, Kols lived in a mythical land called Kolhan, they are largely indigenous inhabitants of the eastern plateau region of Indian sub-continent. In the Kol languages, *'pata'* is not used to mean 'silk' or 'jute'. In Santali language, '*patka*' is a piece of cloth about 16 cubits long which is used as a turban or cummerbund. '*Patkar,* is the Santali word for 'Patua'. '*Pataka,* is a similar word but it means flag in Sanskrit. '*Chitra patta*' similarly means a canvas for painting. The word *'pata'* is quite common in some Dravidian languages (Sengupta, 1973).

'*Pata-chitra*' is folk art because it is produced by such people of villages who do not have any so-called academic training. They inherit their skill from their ancestors. The father trains up his sons and the mother her daughters. Folk arts and crafts could perhaps be better understood in the context of the economic, social and religious condition of the common people of the villages. Through the long period of its evolution from the remote pre-Buddhist past of India, the tradition represented by these scroll painting has always remained a rural art, free from any artificial court influence on the one hand, and any ecclesiastical or monastic influence on the other.

## Patuas of West Bengal

Field work had been carried out in the village Naya, in the district of Medinipur in West Bengal. Work had also been done by Korom (2006) and others in the same village. With recent endeavour of various sectors of social workers and NGOs the village and its occupants and their craft have come into focus.

The standard anthropological methodology is followed in the present work. In the village, Patuas were interviewed with the use of structured schedules. Participant-observation method was followed for understanding the *pata* and the Patuas. Case studies were made of some Patuas for getting in-depth knowledge about the meaning of the symbols represented in the art for the interpretation of the mythological, ritual and other meanings of the art. The total perspective of the art from the viewpoint of the artist and their messages to the rural and folk people of the area was the focus of the study. The study also provided with an idea about the continuity of perception of the universe by the artist and the universality of the symbolism in the abstraction in their art. The final motive was to get a tool for interpretation of the past through the present.

West Bengal is a state in Eastern India. The state is flanked by Bangladesh on the east and Bhutan on the north. Physiographically the state is on the deltaic plain of the River Ganges. It is a part of the Bengal basin. On the north lie the Himalayas. On the west is the plateau, which is an extension of the Deccan plateau to the east. The plateau is undulating in nature and is dotted with hills. A number of easterly flowing rivers drain the plateau and merge on the Gangetic alluvial plain. The district Medinipur is located in the western part of West Bengal. The district is at the junction of the eastern plateau and the Gangetic plains. The land mass is quite old. The plains are of older alluvium of the River Ganges. The plain merges into the rolling plateau. The plateau geologically has a base of Archaean rock topped by Quaternary deposits.

Ample evidence of the presence of early man is there in the form of stone tools (Das and Ghosh, 1966; Ray, 2003). Cultural evidence for the continuous presence of man is coming from the Lower Palaeolithic culture onwards. Earliest date for the presence of man goes back to c. 0.4 m yrs in the region (Ray, 1999). It may even go further back. Rock art in the Eastern plateau region is found in large quantity. These may be of prehistoric, early historic as well as of the present day tribal communities (Imam, 2011).

The village Naya is under the subdivision of Pingla in the district Medinipur in West Bengal, India. The Patuas in this village live mostly in mud houses, huddled together in the form of a hamlet. All the Patuas studied are poor and belong to the economic category of 'below poverty level' according to the standard set by the Government of India. The Patuas of this village has converted to Islam during Mughal rules. Originally they were Hindus belonging to a lower caste group, considered by the higher caste group as untouchable. At various stages of history in India people from marginalised communities had taken up the religion of the ruling groups, such as Mughals and British. This not only enabled the converts to take advantage of the egalitarian system of the respective religions but also get the support of the empire (Ray *et al,* 2002).

However, in the districts of Birbhum, Medinipur, 24 Parganas, Burdwan and Murshidabad, Potua villages or hamlets are situated at the outskirt of Hindu locality. The 'Patuas' occupied a position intermediate between the Hindus and the Muslims (Dutta, 1932). The legend goes that the Patuas were born as a result of mating between *Viswakarma,* the celestial architect, and *Ghritachi*, the celestial courtesan. Potuas used to earn their livelihood by drawing scrolls, which described the glory of Hindu Gods and Goddesses and making idols of gods and goddesses. One day a 'Patua' was drawing the picture of Lord Mahadeva, at that time Mahadeva himself was passing through that way. Seeing the God the 'Patua' became afraid and put his brush into his mouth. Mahadeva said, "you would earn your livelihood by drawing the pictures with polluted brush" and cursed him–"from now onwards you would become 'Yavan', non-Hindu". The 'Patua' cried and begged his mercy. Then Mahadeva said-"you would earn your livelihood by drawing the pictures and making idols of Hindu Gods and Goddesses but follow the rules and regulations of the Muslim".

The Patuas of the village Naya is following Islam religion but still they are marginalised because they cannot enter the general mosque but have got their own special mosque in the village. Marriage takes place within the Patua community. Divorce is allowed according to Muslim law. Although they follow Islam religion they still have retained their Hindu names. Literacy rate among the Patuas of the village is very low. All the people above 35 years of age are illiterate. But they know the mythologies by heart, handed down to them generation after generation through oral tradition and through their art.

Everyone in the village knows to draw on the *pata* and know the stories by heart and can sing them out. All the Patuas of the village participates in preparing the *patas*. Even a child of three years of age is given paint and brush and the child starts learning to draw.

To supplement their earning the adult persons both male and female work as agriculture labour in the paddy fields. After the harvest, they travel from village to village, door to door and supplement their earning with whatever the villagers would pay for seeing the *patas* and listening to the tales. Traditionally the payment is made in kind, mainly in the form of freshly harvested paddy.

In recent times some voluntary organisations, as well as Ministry of Culture; Government of India, has taken interest on the art and artists. It is considered as cultural heritage of India and some form of impetus is given for the promotion of the art. Previously this kind of art was not for sale but recently endeavours are made by way of organising exhibitions and finding markets for the paintings. However, without the accompanied lyrics these are simple pictures devoid of explanation to the symbols.

## The *Patas*, the Art

Although traditionally the *pata* was made on a clay tablet, cotton, silk, jute and handmade paper, the last one is the preferred medium at present since this is readily available now in the market.

There are several stages of making the canvas. Firstly, a kind of glue is made by boiling crushed rice in water. The paper is first washed in water and spread out on a smooth wooden board. The rice starch glue is applied on the surface of the paper. Another sheet of paper is washed and placed on the first one and stuck to it. Rice glue is applied on the free surface of the second sheet. About ten or twelve sheets of paper are successively glued and placed one on another to form a thick pad. When the glue is slightly hardened the pad is rubbed hard with a stone pestle against a wooden board, so that the layers get permanently stuck together and form one compact sheet. Several similar compact pads are prepared and successively joined at the ends so as to form one long scroll. The joints are rubbed hard on the wooden board to make them stick together fast. The scroll is spread out in the open on several successive nights to be soaked with dew and is rubbed hard every morning. In order to secure the scroll against tearing, a strip of cloth is stuck with glue to each long edge on the reverse side. Once the canvas is made they roll it in order to give it the desired shape. The size of the scroll depends on the length of the story. On two ends of the scroll, bamboo sticks are attached breadth-wise for holding the scroll and for slowly unfurling. The Patua sings the stories as he shows the pictures by unrolling the scroll from the bottom and rerolling to the top. The patua goes from door to door collecting alms in the form of cash and rice. Traditionally they do not sell the *Patas*. The art was solely for entertainment and was the property of the 'Patua'. The situation has changed with government intervention and one can purchase the scrolls, especially at fairs arranged for the purpose.

Natural vegetable colours made out of various fruits, flowers, leaves, shoot, and root are used for painting the *patas*. These are often dried, ground, crushed and powdered. Together with the vegetable parts they also use powders made out of conch shell. Shell powders add intensity to the colour. Patuas prepare the colours at home in the traditional method. Colour is usually prepared during the winter season. They avoid the monsoon, because in the rainy season due to high humidity in the air, the colours do not dry easily. They preserve the colours inside covered boxes and use them whenever required. The authors have collected data on the materials used for making colour and have found that they make the colour from locally available plants. Two or three ingredients are mixed to bring out the desired shade and colour. Gum from Green 'Bael' (*Aegle marvelous*) is used as a binder to be mixed with all dyes. It is strained and preserved in bottles. Certain painters use fine powder of 'conch' shell in small quantity for extra binding. The brush is prepared at home by taking far from squirrel's tail.

The potuas start by painting the decorative borders first. The individual frames are demarcated with such borders. The border disguises the seam between frames. Patuas prefer daylight hours for painting.

## Types of '*Patachitras*'

Two types of '*patas*' are usually made. One kind is known as '*Chauka Pata*', is meaning square and single framed ones. These '*patas*' are made in different sizes. The other kind is known as '*Jarano Pat*' or the scroll paintings. The theme of the *patas* is mostly mythological. These are local in nature and had been transmitted orally through songs. There is Hindu and tribal mythologies on respective gods and goddesses and tales related to them. They also make *patas* on Muslim saints, *pirs,* and *gazis.* 'Patua art has always been dynamic, changing to meet the needs and interests of their audiences' (McCutchion and Bhowmik, 1999).

A few *patas* that had been seen by the authors at the village is a picture, drawn by Gorachand Chitrakar is the story of the origin of 'Patuas' and how the tradition of Patuas began in the village. It says that many years back there lived a demon in a cave outside the village. It came out at night stole people from the village and ate them. The villagers lived in fear, stayed home at night, were unable to sleep. They feared the demon would consume everyone if something was not done about him. At a village meeting, a wise person came up with a plan. They built a large mirror to fool the demon. They set the mirror up outside the demon's cave and when he emerged, he saw his own reflection in the glass. Enraged, the demon grabbed a huge stone and hurled it at his reflection thinking it was another demon. The mirror shattered into hundreds of pieces. Each fragment reflected another demon and another and another. Everywhere the demon looked, he found himself surrounded by other demons. Finally, he killed himself in despair. To spread the word of the demon's death, 'patuas' painted and sang the story as they travelled from village to village. They took it up as a profession and started to tell stories about gods and goddesses, such as Shiva Ganesha, and Durga.

One picture illustrates the story about the God Ganesha and how he lost his head and was given an elephant's head. It says that once the goddess Parvati was taking a bath. She took the skin she scrubbed from her body and made it into the shape of a boy, Ganesha. She placed the boy at the door to guard her while she bathed. When Lord Shiva, Parvati's consort, came home, Ganesha wouldn't let him enter. Shiva got mad and cut off Ganesha's head. Parvati was upset and told Shiva that he had just killed their son. Shiva vowed to bring Ganesha back to life by replacing his head with the first creature he saw. With the help of another God, Vishnu, Shiva found an elephant, whose head was transplanted onto Ganesha's body and Ganesha was brought back to life. That is how the god Ganesha got his elephant head.

Another picture is of a devastating flood, a catastrophe. The Mother Ganges, goddess of the sacred Ganges River, was very angry. She released the waters of the river on the land. In the flood men, women and livestock were washed away. The Goddess of the river is shown sitting on a mythical water creature.

## Symbols, Myths and Cosmologies

Work among the Patuas had been done by art historians, museologists, archaeologists, and anthropologists. According to scholars, scroll painting is one of the earliest art forms of Bengal. Buddhist period was the golden age for patuas. Buddhist Monk and Kings made extensive use of scrolls to explain the truth of this world, and of the punishments waited for the sinners. By this time, the scroll painting had spread to Bali, Java, Sri Lanka, Malaysia and Tibet (Dutta, 1932).

Potuas as Chitrakars were reported in the first census of India. Risley (1891) reported that there was a striking ethnical similarity between the Chitrakars of the South India and those of West Bengal (Bhattacharya, 1973:309). Some branches of the Chitrakars have the last name as 'Mal' suggesting that the Patuas have originated as an offshoot of the tribe Malpaharia. In India, the last name is usually the caste name.

At earlier days the 'patuas' had never had a single occupation of scroll painting and singing and of idol making. The male folk had several occupations, such as basket making with bamboo strips, snake charming; taming and training monkeys or bears for shows in the villages. They also acted as quack veterinary doctors. The woman folk used to sell '*Alta*', a red liquid for painting the feet of women. These occupations suggest that they either were an offshoot of a tribal community or they belonged to a lower rank of the society.

However, the Patuas make use of the simplest technique of line and colour to express the varied emotions of humanity as well as supernatural aspects. Symbols in the *patas* represent not only the gods and goddesses but at the same time different fertility aspects of land

and nature. Potuas live a life based on the agricultural economy, which is reflected in their arts and crafts. Folk ballads, myths, legends and any other branches of folklore current among the people are the basic elements in the content of folk art and crafts. The worship of different folk Gods and Goddesses and various rituals also determine the character of theme.

Patuas are often divided into subgroups on the basis of the theme of their *pata*. There is a group in West Bengal known as *Jadu* or *Duari Patuas*. The word *Jadu* means magic. This kind of art had never been used as the vehicle of folk entertainment. *Jadu-patua* is believed to be an undisputed authority on the semi-magical mortuary rites of the deceased. He is supposed to know that a man is put to death by a *pisacha*, an evil spirit. There was a custom among the Santal tribes that when a person died a Patua was to be called. The Patua will draw an effigy of the dead man on a scroll, put eyes on the figure. Without eyes, the person will not be able to leave the suffering in the hell and go to heaven. This was an old ritual of the Santals. The bereaved Santal family used to pay to the Patuas, so that their relatives will be able to see the way to Heaven and be free. At present, the numbers of *Jadu Patuas* are declining. Other Patuas nowadays shun the *Jadu Potuas*.

It is very much apparent from the study of the Patuas and their trade that the art has got a deep philosophical and spiritual significance. They carry the tradition of myths, beliefs, rituals and customs not only in their art but in the oral tradition as well. These people may be considered as carrying the legacy of symbolising belief and customs in the form of art. These people at the same time are bearing the meaning to the symbols. Through their art not only myths but nature and its various moods are put into figures. The Patuas render symbolic character to the abstract and intangible aspects of a culture. For scientific and logical interpretation of prehistoric art role of religion is very important. The ideological connections with ancestors and various gods make very little difference in terms of the time dimension. The long legacy of Patuas and their art is a living tradition bridging prehistory to the present day. The study offers an important instance and methodology for studying prehistoric art and arriving at a plausible interpretation.

## References

Bhattacharya, A., 2001. *Paschimbanger Patachitra*, Loksanskrity O Adibasi Sanskrity Kendra, Tathya O Sanskrity Bibhag, Paschim Banga Sarkar, Kolkata.

Bhattacharya, B., 1973. 'Islamisation of the Patuas'. In S Sengupta (Ed): *The Patas and Patuas of Bengal*. Calcutta; Indian Publications.

Chakravarty, KK and RG. Bednarik, 1997. *Indian Rock Art and its Global Context*. Delhi and Bhopal.

Chakravarty, KK, 1984. *Rock Art of India*. New Delhi; Arnold-Heinemann Publishers (India) Pvt. Ltd.

Das, R and AK. Ghosh, 1966. 'Palaeolithic industries of West Bengal'. *Bulletin of Cultural Research Institute*. 5, 1-2: 83-93.

Dutt, G., 1932. *Folk Arts and Crafts of Bengal: The Collected Papers*. Calcutta; Seagull Books, Reprinted in 1990.

Ghosh, AK, 1984. 'Significance of rock-art in the light of ethnographic parallels'. In KK Chakrabarty (Ed): *Rock Art of India*. pp. 106-111. New Delhi; Arnold-Heinemann Publishers (India) Pvt. Ltd.

Gortis, B., 2003. 'Abstraction and art'. *Philosophical Transactions: Biological Sciences* 358, 1435:1241-1249.

Imam, B., 2011. 'Comparative traditions in village painting and prehistoric rock art of Jharkhand'. *Art and Communication in Preliterate Societies*. XXIV. pp. 70-81. Valcamonica Symposium, Capo di Ponte (Italy). July 2011.

Korom, FJ., 2006. *Village of Painters: Narrative Scrolls from West Bengal*. New Mexico; Museum of New Mexico Press.

McCutchion, D and SK. Bhowmik, 1999. *Patuas and Patua Art in Bengal*. Kolkata ; Firma KLM.

Ray, R., 1984. 'Data retrieval on rock art'. In KK Chakravarty (Ed): *Rock Art of India*. pp. 64-71, New Delhi; Arnold Heinemann Publishers (India) Pvt. Ltd.

Ray, R., 1999. 'A study of Acheulian cultural remains from the gravel beds in Orissa'. In MP Tiwari and DM Mohabey (Eds): *Quaternary of India*. 4: 361-369.

Ray, R., 2003. 'Cultural continuity and its implication on human evolution: A study from Eastern India'. *Human Evolution*, 18, 3-4: 203-212.

Ray, R., N. Bhattacharya and S. Mukhopadhya. 2002. 'Marginalisation: A social reality among some Bengali Christians'. *The Journal of the Anthropological Survey of India*, Special Issue on Marginalised Communities, 51, 1: 201-210.

Renfrew, C., 2006. *Figuring It Out: What Are We? Where Do We Come From? The Parallel Visions of Artists and Archaeologists*. London; Thames and Hudson.

Risley, HH. 1891. *Tribes and Castes of Bengal: Ethnographic Glossary.* Vol. I and II. Calcutta; Bengal Secretariat Press.

Scott, S., 2006. 'Art and the archaeologist'. *World Archaeology* 38, 4:628-643.

Seglie, D., 2001. *Prehistoric Art: Guide to Good Practice.* Euro Pre Art. UE, Pinerolo.

Seglie, D., 2011. 'Rock art: Silhouette figuring on the stage of prehistoric man', *Art and Communication in Preliterate Societies.* XXIV. pp. 397-403. Valcamonica Symposium, Capo di Ponte (Italy), July 2011.

Sengupta, S., 1973. *The Patas and Patuas of Bengal.* Calcutta; Indian Publications.

Sreenathan, MV., R Rao and RG Bednarik. 2008. 'Palaeolithic cognitive inheritance in aesthetic behaviour of the Jarawas of the Andaman Islands'. *Anthropos.* 103: 367-392.

# Chapter - 3

# Study on the Somatotype of Male Oraons of North 24 Parganas, West Bengal

—*Tanaya Kundu Chowdhury*
*and Subrata K. Roy*

## Introduction

Somatotype is a well establish three-numeral rating system which includes endomorphy (relative fatness), mesomorphy (relative musculature) and ectomorphy (relative linearity), to depict the shape and composition of the human body (Carter and Heath, 1990). Somatotype rating helps to visualise the body shape of an individual as well as of a group. The credit for the development of somatotype method goes to Sheldon (1940) but several other scientists contributed in their own way and finally Heath and Carter (1967) proposed a modified somatotype technique using anthropometric measurements with universal rating scales, applicable to both sexes and all ages (Carter and Heath, 1990; Carter *et al.,* 1983), which is widely followed presently.

Generally, the somatotype component of individual is determined by certain genetic factors and as a result, significant correlation occurs in somatotype components between parent-child, sib-sib (Rebato *et al.,*2000; Song *et al.*, 1993) and monozygotic and dizygotic twin within each sex (Song *et al.,* 1994).Therefore, several authors studied somatotype of a particular ethnic group (Ghosh and Malik, 2010; Sidhu *et al.,* 1985), differences in somatotype between two (Chandel and Malik, 2012) or more ethnic groups (Bhasin and Jain, 2007) and sex variation in body shape (Bailey *et al.,* 1982), age changes and variation in somatotype (Kaur, 2009; Buffa *et al.*, 2005; Ghosh and Malik, 2004). However, apart from genetic and demographic factors, somatotype components especially endomorphic component is determined by socio-economic factors (Pelin *et al.,* 2010; Muñoz-Cachón, 2007). Also, several authors has shown somatotype of different occupational groups like the army (Donnan, 1959), sports person (Bandyopadhyay, 2007), agricultural labourers (Chandel and Malik, 2012; Ghosh and Malik, 2010; Singh and Singh, 2006), athletes and non-athletes (Rahmawati *et al.,* 2007). Ozener and Duyar (2008) reported that somatotype component is determined by the level of physical activity e.g. high level of physical activity may increase mesomorphic component whereas endomorphy were significantly higher among sedentary individuals.

Apart from variability in somatotype between individuals, some studies also reported the association of somatotype components especially endomorphic components with risk of cardiovascular disease (Herrera, 2004; Williams *et al.*, 2000) and diabetes (Singh Yadav *et al.,* 2007). Roy (2002, 1990) studied the relationship of somatotype with work performance/productivity among the tea garden and agricultural labourers.

In view of the above, the somatotype component (human body shape) is largely determined by way of living more especially physical activity. In the last few decades, with increasing urbanisation, rural indigenous people have migrated to urban areas in search of jobs, adapted to changing circumstances and have accustomed to urban life leaving behind their traditional occupation and way of living. However, it is not clear whether all these changes have effects on their somatotype components. The objectives of the present study are to (1) compare the somatotypes between rural and urban male Oraon individuals and (2) compare the somatotypes between moderately active and sedentarily active occupational groups.

## Materials and Methods

The present study is cross-sectional in nature; data have been collected from a single ethnic group, Oraon, living in rural and urban

Parganas of West Bengal. In a rural area, three Kuliagarh, Debok and Budhuria, under Naihati .. and in the urban area four settlements namely, Pansila, , annagar, Pairaban and Mohendronagar under Khardah and Ghola police station of Barrackpore subdivision, North 24 Parganas district have been selected for the present study. The areas have been selected purposively considering the higher concentration of Oraon households, not adjacent to any industrial areas and shows respective urban and rural characteristics in terms of communication, population density, etc.

Numerically, Oraon is the second largest tribal population of West Bengal (Census, 2001). Oraon is Dravidian speaking endogamous ethnic group living mainly in Chotonagpur region (Roy, 1915) but in search of jobs they gradually migrated to different states of eastern India, namely, Bihar, West Bengal, Orissa, and so on. They were specialists in agriculture (Roy, 1915) but with time they become engaged in numerous other occupations. Few studies have been done on the health aspects of Oraon mainly on nutritional aspect, body composition (Chakraborty *et al.,* 2011; Datta Banik, 2008) and work productivity (Roy *et al.,* 2005; Roy, 2002).

Total enumeration of all the Oraon households has been done for demographic information. Further data on anthropometric traits have been collected from the individuals who voluntarily participated in the study. Data on female participants have been excluded for the present article as most of them were not engaged in any salaried job and do mainly household work. Also, data on aged individuals (age > 60 years) have been excluded as they were mainly disabled, dependent and pension holders. Finally, data on 250 adult male Oraons have been calculated for the study. The age range of the studied population was 18 to 60 years.

Demographic data includes age, sex and occupation, collected using well-tested questionnaire. Anthropometric data have been collected by single investigator following International Biological Programme (IBP) basic list of measurement using standard instruments and techniques (Weiner and Lourie, 1981). The following measurements were collected from individuals wearing light apparel:

1. Stature (cm)
2. Body weight (kg)
3. Bi-epicondylar diameter of subscapular (mm)
4. Bi-epicondylar diameter of (mm)
5. Mid-upper arm circumferences (cm)
6. Calf circumference (cm)
7. Skin fold thickness, biceps (mm)
8. Skin fold thickness, triceps (mm)
9. Skin fold thickness, humerus (cm)
10. Skin fold thickness, suprailiac femur (cm)
11. Skin fold thickness, calf (mm)

The anthropometric somatotype techniques have been used following Carter and Health (1990).

Endomorphy has been determined by using the following formula (regression equation): $0.0000014 (X^3) - 0.00068 (X^2) + 0.1451 (X) - 0.7182$, where X is the sum of triceps, subscapular and supra-iliac skin fold thickness adjusted for stature i.e. X = sum of the skinfold thickness × (170.18/stature).

Mesomorphy has been determined by using the following formula: [(0.858× bi-epicondylar diameter of humerus) + (0.601 × bi-epicondylar diameter of femur) + {0.188 × (mid-upper arm circumference - triceps skin fold)} + {0.161 × (calf circumference - calf skinfold)}] – (stature × 0.131) + 4.50. As a note of caution, both triceps and calfskin fold thickness have been measured in millimetre scale and at the time of subtraction, this unit has been converted into centimetre scale in order to equalise the unit of measurement.

Ectomorphy has been obtained by using the formula HWR (Height-Weight Ratio) × 0.732 – 28.58. Where HWR= Stature/$(\text{Weight})^{1/3}$. If HWR is less than 40.75 but greater than 38.25, ectomorphy has been determined by using HWR × 0.463 – 17.63. If HWR is equaled to or less than 38.25, a rating of 0.1 has been assigned to the ectomorphy rating.

The X and Y coordinate have been calculated using the following formulae:

X = Ectomorphy – Endomorphy,

Y= 2 × Mesomorphy – (Ectomorphy + Endomorphy).

Studied population have been classified based on occupation as a moderately active occupational group and sedentarily active occupational group. The individuals who worked as labourers have been classified as a moderately active occupational group and service holders in government and private sectors, businessman, students and unemployed individuals have been classified as sedentarily active occupational group based on ICMR classification (Gopalan *et al.*, 1971). Within each occupational group, individuals have been grouped as rural and urban people.

Descriptive statistics and t-statistic have been used for anthropometric traits and somatotype components to show the distribution of the data and differences between groups. All skin fold thickness data have been transformed into $Log_{10}$ values for smoothening of the data and then its descriptive analysis has been done. The Somatotype Dispersion Distance (SDD) for the individual somatotypes have been calculated to measure the distance from the mean somatotype separately for the rural and urban individuals of moderately active and sedentarily active occupational group using the following formula:

$$SDD_i = \sqrt{[3(Xi - X)^2 + (Yi - Y)^2]}$$

where SDD = $X_i$ $Y_i$ represent the somatoplot of a given individual in two dimensions; X and Y are the mean values of X and Y coordinate scores of the individuals of a group.

The Somatotype Attitudinal Distance (SAD) for the individual somatotypes have been calculated to measure the distance from the mean somatotype separately for the rural and urban individuals of moderately active and sedentarily active occupational groups using the following formula:

$$SAD_i = \sqrt{[(ENi - EN)^2 + (MEi - ME)^2 + (EC_i - EC)^2]}$$

where SAD = ENi, MEi, ECi represent the endomorphic, mesomorphic and ectomorphic components of the somatotype of a given individual; EN, ME, EC are the mean values of somatotype components of the individuals of a group.

The difference between mean somatotypes of two groups (i.e. rural and urban individuals within moderately active and sedentarily active occupational group) has been tested both in terms of SDD and of SAD by calculating somatotype t-test using following formula:

$$t = X_{S1} - X_{S2} / \sqrt{[(\Sigma X_1^2 + \Sigma X_2^2) \times (1/n_1 + 1/n_2) / (n_1 + n_2 - 2)]}$$

where X = SDD or SAD; S = mean somatotype

Multivariate Analysis of Variance (MANOVA) has been performed considering somatotype components (endomorphy, mesomorphy, and ectomorphy) as a matrix to determine whether there were any differences between the rural and urban moderately active and sedentarily active occupational groups in somatotype components independently. All the analysis have been performed using SPSS version 16.0 (SPSS Inc., Chicago, IL, USA).

## Results

Descriptive statistics of selected anthropometric traits of rural and urban males in either occupational group have been presented in Table 3.1. Rural moderately active occupational group show lower mean values in all anthropometric traits than an urban group but the differences are significant in the case of all the skin folds thickness. Rural sedentarily active occupational group to show lower mean values in all the anthropometric traits than the urban group and the significant differences exist in the case of a bi-epicondylar diameter of humerus bi-epicondylar diameter of the femur and supra-iliac skin fold thickness.

Somatotype components of moderately active and sedentarily active rural and urban Oraons namely, endomorphy, mesomorphy and ectomorphy have been presented in Table 3.2. In moderately, active rural group the mean values of endomorphy, mesomorphy, and ectomorphy components are 2.03-3.72-2.88 respectively. The values of X (0.85) and Y (2.54) coordinate indicate that rural moderately active occupational group belong to balanced mesomorph position in the somatochart (not presented). Whereas, the somatotype components of the moderately active urban group are 2.58-4.07-2.68 respectively and the group also belongs to balanced mesomorph position in

**Table 3.1: Descriptive Statistics of Selected Anthropometric Traits of Male Oraons**

| *Variables* | *Moderately active occupational group (n=152)* | | | | | *Sedentarily active occupational group (n=98)* | | | | |
|---|---|---|---|---|---|---|---|---|---|---|
| | *Rural (n=96)* | | *Urban (n=56)* | | *t-test (df=150)* | *Rural (n=44)* | | *Urban (n=54)* | | *t-test (df=96)* |
| | *Mean* | *SD* | *Mean* | *SD* | | *Mean* | *SD* | *Mean* | *SD* | |
| Height (cm) | 162.75 | 5.37 | 162.88 | 5.70 | 0.14 | 162.24 | 5.47 | 164.76 | 7.21 | 1.91 |
| Weight (kg.) | 55.03 | 8.08 | 56.50 | 8.63 | 1.06 | 56.47 | 9.47 | 60.75 | 11.58 | 1.97 |
| **Diameters (cm)** | | | | | | | | | | |
| Bi-epicondylar diameter of humerous | 6.40 | 0.53 | 6.48 | 0.36 | 1.02 | 6.42 | 0.36 | 6.63 | 0.52 | 2.29* |
| Bi-epicondylar diameter of femur | 8.99 | 0.49 | 9.14 | 0.59 | 1.69 | 8.92 | 0.58 | 9.26 | 0.61 | 2.84** |
| **Circumferences (cm)** | | | | | | | | | | |
| Mid-upper arm | 25.43 | 3.08 | 26.52 | 2.80 | 2.17* | 26.22 | 2.94 | 27.14 | 3.24 | 1.46 |
| Calf | 31.53 | 2.60 | 31.84 | 2.52 | 0.74 | 32.15 | 2.78 | 32.84 | 3.24 | 1.11 |
| **Skin folds ($\log_{10}$ values) (mm)** | | | | | | | | | | |
| Biceps | 0.41 | 0.13 | 0.50 | 0.16 | 3.51** | 0.54 | 0.19 | 0.57 | 0.19 | 0.77 |
| Triceps | 0.72 | 0.18 | 0.79 | 0.21 | 2.13* | 0.81 | 0.24 | 0.86 | 0.19 | 0.98 |
| Sub scapular | 0.99 | 0.17 | 1.08 | 0.18 | 3.18** | 1.07 | 0.22 | 1.10 | 0.20 | 0.48 |
| Supra-iliac | 0.64 | 0.18 | 0.74 | 0.20 | 3.25** | 0.73 | 0.23 | 0.82 | 0.20 | 2.10* |
| Calf | 0.73 | 0.21 | 0.84 | 0.22 | 2.97** | 0.85 | 0.27 | 0.92 | 0.20 | 1.47 |

*p value ≤ 0.05; ** p value ≤ 0.01.

**Table 3.2: Descriptive Statistics of Somatotype Components of Male Oraons**

| *Variables* | *Moderately active occupational group (n=152)* | | | | | *Sedentarily active occupational group (n=98)* | | | | |
|---|---|---|---|---|---|---|---|---|---|---|
| | *Rural (n=96)* | | *Urban (n=56)* | | *t-test (df=150)* | *Rural (n=44)* | | *Urban (n=54)* | | *t-test (df=96)* |
| | *Mean* | *SD* | *Mean* | *SD* | | *Mean* | *SD* | *Mean* | *SD* | |
| Endomorphy | 2.03 | 0.87 | 2.58 | 1.15 | 3.29** | 2.69 | 1.31 | 2.86 | 1.18 | 0.68 |
| Mesomorphy | 3.72 | 1.09 | 4.07 | 1.20 | 1.83 | 3.94 | 1.17 | 4.26 | 1.31 | 1.28 |
| Ectomorphy | 2.88 | 1.22 | 2.68 | 1.47 | 0.90 | 2.59 | 1.33 | 2.39 | 1.65 | 0.65 |
| X | 0.85 | 1.97 | 0.10 | 2.52 | 2.02* | -0.11 | 2.52 | -0.48 | 2.70 | 0.70 |
| Y | 2.54 | 2.66 | 2.89 | 2.95 | 0.75 | 2.60 | 2.83 | 3.28 | 3.31 | 1.07 |

*p value ≤ 0.05; ** p value ≤ 0.01.

somatochart (not presented). Significant differences exist in endomorphic component and values of X coordinate between rural and urban moderately active occupational groups. In the case of a rural, sedentarily active occupational group the somatotype components are 2.69-3.94-2.59 and 2.86-4.26-2.39 for urban group respectively. The values of X-Y coordinate (rural -0.11, 2.60; urban-0.48, 3.28) indicates that both the group belong to an endo-mesomorphic position in somatochart (not presented).

Somatotype Dispersion Distances, Somatotype Attitudinal Distance and somatotype t-ratio between rural and urban group within moderately active and sedentarily active occupational group have been presented in Table 3.3. Rural moderately active occupational group show 4.97, 1.64 SDD and SAD values respectively and urban group show 5.90, 1.95 SDD and SAD values respectively, but the differences are not significant. Rural sedentarily active occupational group show 5.77, 1.99 SDD and SAD values whereas urban group show 6.25, 2.10 SDD and SAD values respectively and again there was no significant differences.

**Table 3.3: Somatotype Dispersion Distances and Somatotype Attitudinal Distances of Male Oraons**

| *Variables* | *Moderately active occupational group (n=152)* | | | | | *Sedentarily active occupational group (n=98)* | | | | |
|---|---|---|---|---|---|---|---|---|---|---|
| | *Rural (n=96)* | | *Urban (n=56)* | | *t-test (df=150)* | *Rural (n=44)* | | *Urban (n=54)* | | *t-test (df=96)* |
| | *Mean* | *SD* | *Mean* | *SD* | | *Mean* | *SD* | *Mean* | *SD* | |
| Somatotype Dispersion Distance (SDD) | 4.97 | 2.83 | 5.90 | 3.17 | 1.08 | 5.77 | 2.99 | 6.25 | 3.867 | 0.08 |
| Somatotype Attitudinal Distance (SAD) | 1.64 | 0.85 | 1.95 | 1.04 | 0.35 | 1.99 | 0.87 | 2.10 | 1.15 | 0.20 |

Multivariate Analysis of Variance (MANOVA) of somatotype components (endomorphy, mesomorphy, and ectomorphy) have been presented in Table 3.4 considering somatotype components as a matrix between rural-urban males of moderate and sedentarily active occupational groups. The results reveal that the differences (F = 4.886) are statistically significant. Further Post-Hoc (Tukey) test have been performed and findings indicate significant differences exist in endomorphic components between (i) rural moderately active and sedentarily active occupational group ($p<0.05$), (ii) rural and urban moderately active occupational groups ($p<0.01$), (iii) rural moderately

**Table 3.4: Multivariate Analysis of Variance of Somatotype Components between Occupational Groups and Area**

| *Wilk's Lamda* | | *F* | | *df* | *Significant* | |
|---|---|---|---|---|---|---|
| *0.840* | | *4.886* | | *3, 246* | *> 0.0001* | |
| **Post-Hoc test (Tukey) (level of significance)** | | | | | | |
| Somatotype components | RMA# vs. RSA# | RMA# vs. RSA# | RMA# vs. RSA# | RMA# vs. RSA# | RMA# vs. RSA# | RMA# vs. RSA# |
| Endomorphy | 0.005* | 0.017** | >0.0001** | 0.951 | 0.967 | 0.509 |
| Mesomorphy | 0.739 | 0.298 | 0.037* | 0.948 | 0.531 | 0.823 |
| Ectomorphy | 0.664 | 0.833 | 0.169 | 0.988 | 0.896 | 0.694 |

*p value < 0.05, ** p value < 0.01
#RMA = Rural Moderately Active occupational group; RSA = Rural Sedentarily Active occupational group;
UMA = Urban Moderately Active occupational group; USA = Urban Sedentarily Active occupational group

active occupational group and urban sedentarily active occupational group ($p<0.01$). Also, in the mesomorphic component, a significant difference ($p<0.05$) exist between the rural moderately active occupational group and urban sedentarily active occupational group.

## Discussion

The aim of the study is to find out the differences, if any, in somatotype between rural and urban living having similar occupational pursuits. Data were collected from a single ethnic group, one of the numerically dominant scheduled tribe populations of eastern India. Data on females and older individuals (> 60 years) were purposively excluded for this study as they were not involved in salaried jobs. For the present purpose, somatotype components have been determined following Carter and Heath (1990) anthropometric-somatotype method on adult male participants only.

Rural males of each independent occupational group show lower mean values in all the selected anthropometric traits than urban males. The trend of the present finding is partly corroborative with the study of Adediran *et al.* (2013), who reported significantly lower mean values in all anthropometric traits for rural Nigerian population than urban Nigerian population and opine dietary change and environmental influence may cause these differences. In a comparative study among urban, rural and forest living Sabar tribe, Chakrabarty and Bharati (2010) reported urban males show higher values in anthropometric traits than rural and forest dwellers and argued these differences caused not due to genetic dissimilarity rather due to economic and major differences in way of living (e.g. physical activity).

Moderately active occupational group of rural habitat shows significantly low mean values in all the skinfold measurements than urban habitat. A sedentarily active occupational group of rural habitat show significantly lower mean values in bi-epicondyle diameters (humerus and femur) and supra-iliac skinfold thickness than urban habitat. Since the occupation of rural and urban occupation groups are similar therefore, it is hard to obtain a significant difference, however, there is a trend to show lower mean values in rural groups, that may be due to food habits. The present result is corroborative with the findings on Oraon low productive and high productive agricultural labourers (Roy, 2002) as well as low and high skill tea leaf pluckers (Roy *et al.,* 2005). Again, Das *et al.* (2013) reported no significant differences in anthropometric traits between Oraon and Munda agricultural labourers.

In moderately active rural males, the endomorphic component is significantly lower than urban males, but of both the group belong to balanced mesomorph position in somatochart. There is no difference between moderately active rural and urban males in SDD and SAD. Many studies have reported that males involved in moderately active occupation (Labourer) belong to ecto-mesomorphic and balanced mesomorphic position in somatochart (Chandel and Malik, 2012; Ghosh and Malik, 2010; Singh and Singh, 2006) and thus corroborative with the findings of the present study. The finding is also corroborative with studies among Oraon agricultural labourers (Roy, 2002), tea garden labourers (Roy *et al.,* 2005), agricultural and brickfield labourer (Roy and Kundu Chowdhury, 2013). However, contrast with the findings of Singh and Singh (2006).

In sedentarily active rural males, mean values of endomorphic and mesomorphic components are lower than urban males but both the group belongs to the endomesomorphic region in somatochart. There is no difference between sedentarily active rural and urban males in SDD and SAD. The finding is corroborative with the study of Singh and colleague (2013), who reported urban and rural carpenters of Punjab state belong to the endo-mesomorph position. Das and Roy (2013) also reported sedentary Santal population show higher values of the endomorphic and mesomorphic component.

In MANOVA of somatotype components (endomorphy, mesomorphy, and ectomorphy) significant differences exist between somatotype components and occupational groups. Therefore, Post-Hoc test (Tukey) has been performed and findings indicate significant differences exist in endomorphic components between/among all the groups. In mesomorphic component, rural moderately active occupational group and urban sedentarily active occupational group show a significant difference. Therefore, it cannot be claimed that the differences are universal between/ among groups in terms of all the somatotype components rather the differences are due to the endomorphic component, which is primarily an activity and food habit related component. However, there is a complete absence of comparable studies in this regard, although, the argument of Parnell and Somerset (1962) cannot be ignored that, there is a general tendency for men in sedentary and upper social class occupations to be fatter and for those doing hard manual work to be more muscular.

It was expected that individuals of both the area and occupational group would show a significant difference in all the somatotype components because of variation in the way of living. The difference exists only in the endomorphic component which is largely determined by physical activity and food habits as was expected. However, findings failed to indicate a difference in the mesomorphic and ectomorphic component. The possibilities of misclassification due to under or overreporting cannot be ruled out; secondly, relative linearity (ectomorphy) was expected to be similar because the subgroups (rural, urban) were from the same population. Further, physical activity varies across individuals depending on the duration of work, posture, time, etc. Present study failed to consider leisure time activity of all the individuals, which may have contributed a lot in the determination of somatotype component. Therefore, studies with rigorous design, activity scoring and analysis should be considered to get a better insight into the problem.

## References

Adediran, OS., PB. Adebayo and AA. Akintunde. 2013. 'Anthropometric differences among natives of Abuja living in urban and rural communities: Correlations with other cardiovascular factors'. *BMC Research Notes*. 6:123. doi: 10.1186/1756-0500-6-123.

Bailey, DA., JEL. Carter and RL. Mirwald. 1982. 'Somatotypes of Canadian men and women'. *Human Biology*. 54: 813-828.

Bandyopadhyay, A., 2007. 'Anthropometry and body composition in soccer and volleyball players in West Bengal, India'. *Journal of Physiological Anthropology*. 26: 501-505.

Bhasin, MK and S. Jain. 2007. 'Biology of the tribal groups of Rajasthan, India: Physical growth and anthropometric somatotypes'. *Anthropologist*. 9: 177-187.

Buffa, R., V. Succa; D. Garau, E. Marini and G. Floris. 2005. 'Variations of somatotype in elderly Sardinians'. *American Journal of Human Biology*. 17: 403-411.

Carter, JEL., WD. Ross, W. Duquet and SP. Aubry. 1983. 'Advances in somatotype methodology and analyses'. *Year Book of Physical Anthropology*. 26: 193-213.

Carter, JEL and BH. Heath. 1990. *Somatotype–Development and Applications*. Cambridge; Cambridge University Press.

Census of India. 2001. *West Bengal Data Highlights: The Scheduled Tribes*. Census Commission of India.

Chakrabarty, S and P. Bharati. 2010. 'Adult body dimension and determinants of chronic energy deciency among the Shabar tribe living in urban, rural and forest habitats in Orissa, India'. *Annals of Human Biology*. 37: 149-167.

Chakraborty, R., K. Bose and S. Koziel. 2011. 'Use of mid-upper arm circumference in determining under nutrition and illness in rural adult Oraon men of Gumla District, Jharkhand, India'. *Rural and Remote Health*.11:1754.

Chandel, S and SL. Malik. 2012. 'Anthropometric somatotype of Kshatriya and Kurmi of Uttar Pradesh: Population and gender differences'. *Human Biology Review*. 1: 1-15.

Das, BM and SK. Roy. 2013. 'Rural-urban differences in nutritional status and physical body dimensions of adult Santal males of West Bengal'. *International Journal of Anthropology*. 28:237-254.

Das, S., B. Debsharma and K. Bose. 2013. 'Adiposity and health status among adult male Mundas and Oraons of Paschim Medinipur, West Bengal, India'. *Journal of Anthropology*. 2013: Article ID 324264, 6 pages. doi:10.1155/2013/324264.

Datta Banik, S., 2008. 'Nutritional status of adult men from the Oraon tribe in Ranchi district of Jharkhand India'. *Malaysian Journal of Nutrition*. 14: 91–99.

Donnan, F. de S. 1959. 'Physique and hazardous occupations'. *British Medical Journal*. 2:728-731.

Ghosh, S and SL. Malik. 2004. 'A comparative study of age changes in somatotypes of Brahmin and Rajput boys of Sundarnagar, Himachal Pradesh'. *Anthropologist*. 6: 19-23.

Ghosh, S and SL. Malik. 2010. 'Variations of body physique in Santhals: An Indian tribe'. *Collegium Antropologicum*. 34: 467-472.

Gopalan, G., BV. Rama Sastri and SC. Balasubramanian. 1971. *Nutritive Value of Indian Foods*. Hyderabad; National Institute of Nutrition, Indian Council of Medical Research.

Heath, BH and JEL. Carter. 1967. 'A modified somatotype method'. *American Journal of Physical Anthropology*. 27: 57-74.

Herrera, H., E. Rebato, R. Hernandez, Y. Hernandez-Valera and MA. Alfonso-Sanchez. 2004. 'Relationship between somatotype and blood pressure in a group of institutionalised Venezuelan elders'. *Gerontology*. 50: 223-229. http://censusindia.gov.in/Tables_Published/SCST/dh_st_westbengal

Kaur, M., 2009. 'Age changes in somatotype components of rural and urban Punjabi Brahmin females'. *Journal of Human Ecology*. 25: 167-173.

Muñoz-Cachón, MJ., I. Salces, M. Arroyo, L. Ansotegui, AM. Rocandio and E. Rebato. 2007. 'Body shape in relation to socio-economic status in young adults from the Basque country'. *Collagium Antropologicum*. 31: 963-968.

Ozener, B and I. Duyar. 2008. 'The effect of labour on somatotype of males during the adolescent growth period'. *HOMO - Journal of Comparative Human Biology*. 59: 161-172.

Parnellr. W and HCA. Somerset.1962. 'Physique and occupation of men admitted to mental hospitals'. *British Journal of Preventive Society Medicine*. 16: 130-146.

Pelin, C., B. Özener, A. Kürkçüoðlu and R. Zaðyapan. 2010. 'Effect of living conditions on somatotype components of young individuals belonging to different socioeconomic strata: A preliminary study'. *Eurasian Journal of Anthropology*. 1:26-32.

Rahmawati, NT., S. Budiharjo and K. Ashizawa. 2007. 'Somatotypes of young male athletes and non-athlete students in Yogyakarta, Indonesia'. *Anthropological Science*. 115: 1-7.

Rebato, E., I. Salces, J. Rosique, L. San Martin and C. Susanne. 2000. 'Analysis of sibling resemblance in anthropometric somatotype components'. *Annals of Human Biology*. 27: 149-161.

Roy, SK and T. Kundu Chowdhury. 2013. 'Differences in selected health traits between occupational groups among Oraons of Jalpaiguri District, West Bengal'. *Journal of Anthropology*. 2013: Article ID 582036, 7 pages. doi:10.1155/2013/582036.

Roy, SK., 2002. 'Factors affecting the work productivity of Oraon agricultural labourers of Jalpaiguri district, West Bengal'. *American Journal of Physical Anthropology*.117: 228-235.

Roy, SK., A. Mozumdar and S. Kar. 2005. 'Effect of skill on work productivity and physical body dimensions of the Oraon tea garden labourers of the Jalpaiguri district, West Bengal, India'. *Anthropologischer Anzeiger*. 63: 449-460.

Roy, SC., 1915. *The Oraons of Chotanagpur: Their History, Economic Life and Social Organisation.* Ranchi; Crown Publications.

Roy, SK., 1990. 'The concept and method of anthropometric somatotype, with an example from the Oraon tea garden labourers of Jalpaiguri district, West Bengal'. *Journal of Indian Anthropological Society*. 25: 129-149.

Sheldon, WH., SS. Stevens and WB. Tucker. 1940. *The Varieties of Human Physique*. New York; Harper.

Sidhu, LS., P. Singal, DP. Bhatnagar and S. Jain. 1985. 'Sexual dimorphism, physique and body composition of adult Bhotia - A high altitude population'. *Indian Anthropologist*. 15: 115-126.

Singh Yadav, V., S. Koley, JS. Sandhu, S. Nigam and P. Arora. 2007. 'A study on somatotyping of patients with Type$^2$ diabetes mellitus in Amritsar'. *Anthropologist*. 9: 247-249.

Singh, A., SP. Singh and J. Sekhon. 2013. 'Occupational impact on body physique and health status: An anthropometric analysis of carpenters'. *Human Biology Review*. 2: 12-23.

Singh, AP and SP. Singh. 2006. 'Somatotypic Variations: An analysis of some traditional occupations'. *Journal of Human Ecology*. 19: 249-251.

Song, TMK., RM. Malina and C. Bouchard. 1993. 'Familial resemblance in somatotype'. *American Journal of Human Biology*.5: 265-272.

Song, TMK., L. Perusse, RM. Malina and C. Bouchard. 1994. 'Twin resemblance in somatotype and comparisons with other twin studies'. *Human Biology*. 66: 453-464.

Weiner, JS and JA. Lourie, 1981. *Practical Human Biology*. London; Academic Press.

Williams, SR., J. Goodfellow, B. Davies, W. Bell, I. Mcdowell and E. Jones. 2000. 'Somatotype and angiographically determined atherosclerotic coronary artery disease in men'. *American Journal of Human Biology*. 12:128-138.

# Chapter - 4

# Is Menopausal Status Related to Body Fat Distribution and Blood Sugar Level? A Study among Urban Living Bengali Hindu Women

—*Debasmita Kar, Nivedita Som and Subha Ray*

## Introduction

Women's reproductive health is largely determined by their ovarian reserve and the secretion of estrogens and progesterone hormones (Burger *et al.*, 2002). For example, usually premenopausal women remain fully fertile and have an uninterrupted menstrual period because of the normal interplay of pituitary and ovarian hormones. However, chronological aging causes the depletion in both ovarian reserve and endocrinal activity of ovarian follicle (Traub *et al.*, 2010). For example, during peri-menopause, the hormonal levels fluctuate widely causing intermittent menstrual cycles (Sherman *et al.*, 1976; Reyes *et al.*, 1977; Santoro *et al.*, 1996). The hormonal levels finally reach nadir during midlife when the ovary stops producing the hormones, a stage called menopause (Fitzgerald *et al.*, 1998; Chakraborty *et al.*, 2004).

The change in ovarian hormonal balance results in the redistribution of body fat in the form of a relative increase in abdominal fat. Literature reveals that decrease in ovarian hormones increases the chance of a woman to become obese during midlife

(Ley *et al.*, 1992; Tremolliers *et al.,* 1996; Toth *et al.,* 2000; Martins and Marinho 2003; Cervellati *et al.,* 2009; Pasco *et al.,* 2012; Munawar *et al.,* 2012). Precisely, a shift in the fat patterning of the body happens to take place during midlife, from gynoid to android types (Kirchengast *et al.*, 1998; Ghosh and Bhagat, 2010; Kaur *et al.,* 2014). Increased visceral fat causes a progressive elevation in blood sugar level and insulin resistance (Brochu *et al.,* 2000). This enhances the likelihood of developing the risk for metabolic syndrome (such as diabetes, hypertension, and cardiovascular disease) among middle-aged women (Guthrie *et al.,* 2001; Revis *et al.,* 2006; Jouyandeh *et al.,* 2013). It is also well established that lifestyle factors along with socio-demographic characteristics are also responsible for determining the pattern of body fat distribution and the blood glucose level in women (Ryan *et al.,* 2000; Sternfeld *et al.,* 2005). For example, an increase in chronological age could result in a shift towards sedentary lifestyle with a reduced physical activity that possibly increases the adiposity level in women at midlife.

Few studies from Indian subcontinent portray a close relationship of age, menopausal status and lifestyle differentials with the incidence of obesity and metabolic syndrome (Ghosh, 2008; Pandey *et al.,* 2010; Bhowmik *et al.,* 2013; Chaudhuri *et al.,* 2014). But, none of these studies attempted to find out whether the menopausal status has any relationship with body fat distribution and blood sugar level, irrespective of socio-demographic and lifestyle characteristics. Thus, we aimed to find out whether menopausal status alone has any relationship with body fat distribution and blood sugar level.

## Materials and Methods

We conducted this study in the city of Howrah, which is an urban agglomerate of Howrah district of West Bengal, located in the eastern part of India. Further to say, the city of Howrah is in proximity to Kolkata Metropolitan city. The study area is numerically dominated by the people of Bengali-speaking Hindu ethnic group.

The study participants were selected from three municipal wards of the Howrah Municipal Corporation (HMC), under the jurisdiction of Howrah Sadar Subdivision. The selected HMC wards were 45, 46 and 48. These municipal wards were selected for the operational convenience. A total number of 250 women belonging to Bengali-speaking Hindu ethnic group were initially enrolled from the study area. The age range of these women was 25-58 years. A total of 181 women were finally recruited based on the inclusion criteria of this study: presently in wedlock, had at least one surviving child, attained natural menopause in the case of post-menopausal women, and did not have any reported gynaecological and/or other metabolic disorders. The final sample comprised of 78 individuals from the pre-menopausal group, 38 from peri-menopausal and 65 from post-menopausal groups. Women who had a menstrual period in past three months, not experiencing irregularity were considered as pre-menopausal (Sommer *et al.,* 1999). Post-menopausal status of women was defined as those who stopped menstrual bleeding spontaneously at least for the last twelve months (WHO, 1996). Peri-menopausal status was defined as those who experienced irregular menses within the last twelve months or an absence of menstrual bleeding for more than three months but less than twelve months (Dudley *et al.,* 1998). Women, who either failed to satisfy the inclusion criteria (n=19) or denied to participate (n=50) at the time of field work, were excluded from the study. The nature and purpose of the study were explained to the participants and the written informed consent was gathered from them. It is imperative to mention that the participants who volunteered, showed enthusiasm and eagerness to know about their body fat distribution and blood sugar level. The study was conducted during the time period of April to June 2015.

The participants were interviewed in person to gather information on their socio-demographic and reproductive characteristics using a pretested structured schedule. A similar type of schedule was used in earlier studies conducted on the same ethnic group (Som and Ray, 2012; Som *et al.*, 2014). Data on socio-demographic characteristics include the age of the participants at the time of the interview, educational levels and occupational types of participants and of their husbands, and monthly household income (in Indian rupees). Age of the participants at the time of interview and educational levels of both spouses were calculated in completed years. Age at menarche was ascertained by asking the participants to recall the actual date of the incident, if not, then the nearest month. A few of the participants could recall their age at menarche by referring some landmark event (any specific festivals) or any eventful personal moments (like, her own birthday), which occurred around the time of menarche. Additionally, ages at marriage and a total number of conception were recorded. Age at marriage was further cross-checked from their husbands and/or mothers. A total number of conception involved the number of live births, stillbirth, and miscarriages.

We identified eighteen food items that are commonly available within the study area and generally consumed by Bengali-speaking Hindu ethnic group. The participants were asked to report how often they consumed these foods in the past one week starting from the date of interview. Thus, for each of the food items, there were eight categories of responses ranging from 0 (representing never) to eight (all seven days in a week). Later, the consumption pattern of each of the food items were converted into ordinal scale (such as, regular, occasional, and rare/never) on the basis of the following criteria: regular consumption-five to seven days; occasional consumption- two to four days; and rare or never was determined if the foods were consumed either less than two days or never.

The level of physical activities was recorded based on the participants' reported daily chores (such as, cooking, washing dishes and clothes, mopping the floors, dusting, ironing, watching television, listening music, walking in the morning, commuting related to their work and physical exercise). Participants were asked to report the frequency of taking up each of these chores in the past one week prior to the date of interview. The physical activity pattern was recorded and later converted into ordinal scale following the same pattern used for food consumption information.

We measured the random blood sugar level (mg/dl) of all the participants. Blood specimens were drawn from the tip of the second finger of the left hand of all the participants and analysed using Blood Sugar Monitoring Kit ('One Touch Ultra', model no-Milpitas, CA95035).

Body weight (to the nearest of 0.1 kg), visceral fat, subcutaneous and skeletal fat for the trunk and whole body and per cent body fat

(PBF) were measured on each participant. We used Body Composition Monitor (HBF-362) machine for taking these measurements. Anthropometric traits such as stature, waist circumference (WC) and hip circumference (HC) were taken on each individual following standard protocol (Lohman *et al.,* 1988). Stature (to the nearest of 0.1 cm) was measured using a portable GPM anthropometer for each participant standing without shoes on a horizontal surface with the body stretched upward to the fullest extension and the hand in the Frankfurt plane. WC and HC were measured to the nearest of 0.1 cm with a non-stretchable fibreglass insertion tape over light clothing. WC was measured at the minimum circumference of the torso between the iliac crest and the rib cage. HC was measured horizontally at the level of maximum extension of the buttocks. The participants were on light apparel at the time of taking these measurements.

Several anthropometric indices such as body mass index (BMI), waist-hip ratio (WHR), fat-free mass (FFM) and fat mass (FM) were calculated using the standard formulae:

BMI= Weight (kg)/height (m)$^2$

WHR = WC (cm)/HC (cm).

FM= (PBF/100) x Weight (kg)

FFM=Weight - FM (kg)

## Statistical Analyses

We used descriptive statistics to find out the distribution of blood sugar, body fat, socio-demographic and reproductive characteristics, patterns of food consumption and physical activities of pre, peri, and post-menopausal groups. We applied Analysis of Variance (ANOVA) to compare the blood sugar level and body fat distribution among three menopausal groups. Furthermore, Scheffe's test (post hoc test) was conducted for each of these comparisons independently to understand the differences between pre and peri-menopausal, pre and post-menopausal, and peri and post-menopausal groups independently. Further, we used multiple linear regression analyses to find out the factors that were related to body fat distribution and blood sugar level of the participants independently. Measures of body fat that differed significantly among the three menopausal groups (after deriving from ANOVA result) were considered as dependent variables in the linear regression analyses. Menopausal status, socio-demographic, reproductive and lifestyle (physical activities and food consumption) variables were included as independent variables in the model. Similarly, the same set of menopausal status, socio-demographic, reproductive and lifestyle variables and body fat measures were used as independent variables to find out their relation to blood sugar level. Multivariate Analysis of Covariance (MANCOVA) was conducted to show the relation of body fat distribution and blood sugar level with menopausal status after adjusting the effects of covariates (lifestyle variables and age of the participants at interview). In MANCOVA, menopausal status was included as the grouping variable. Body fat measures (such as PBF, FFM, and WHR, skeletal fat of trunk and whole body) and blood sugar level together were incorporated as dependent variables. Further, the variables that showed significant relation to body fat measures and blood sugar levels in multiple linear regression analyses, were only included as covariates. A minimum p-value of d" 0.05 was considered as statistically significant for all inferential statistics. The entire data were analysed with the help of Statistical Package for Social Science version 20.0 (IBM Corporation, 2011).

## Result

Table 4.1 describes that women of three menopausal groups differed significantly in age reported at the time of interview. However, ages at menarche, marriage, and monthly household income failed to differ significantly across the menopausal groups. Furthermore, the majority of women and their spouse in all the three groups attained education below the 10th standard. Almost all the participants were non-working.

Table 4.2 shows that pre-menopausal women had significantly lower levels of blood sugar than peri and post-menopausal groups. Scheffe test (post hoc test) indicates a significant difference in blood sugar level between each of the pairs of menopausal groups, barring the difference between peri and post-menopausal groups.

**Table 4.1: Socio-demographic and Reproductive Characteristics of the Participants**

| *Socio-demographic and reproductive characteristics* | *Menopausal status* | | | | | | *Chi square value* | *p value* |
|---|---|---|---|---|---|---|---|---|
| | *Premeno-pausal women (n=78)* | | *Peri-meno-pausal women (n=38)* | | *Postmeno-pausal women(n=65)* | | | |
| | *n* | *per cent* | *n* | *per cent* | *n* | *per cent* | | |
| **Age of the partici-pants at the time of interview** (years) (±sd) | 36.37±4.17 | | 41.86±3.37 | | 51.70±4.80 | | 7.128 | 0.001 |
| **Educational levels of the participants*** | | | | | | | | |
| Non-literate | 1 | 1.3 | 1 | 2.6 | 20 | 30.8 | - | - |
| Below 10th standard | 60 | 76.9 | 29 | 76.4 | 38 | 58.4 | | |
| Between 10th and 12th standard | 9 | 11.5 | 2 | 5.3 | 7 | 10.8 | | |
| Above 12th standard | 8 | 10.3 | 6 | 15.8 | - | - | | |
| **Educational levels of the husbands** | | | | | | | | |
| Non-literate | 4 | 5.1 | 2 | 5.3 | 8 | 12.3 | 8.130 | 0.228 |
| Below 10th standard | 47 | 60.3 | 22 | 57.9 | 42 | 64.7 | | |
| Between 10th and 12th standard | 11 | 14.1 | 5 | 13.2 | 5 | 7.7 | | |
| Above 12th standard | 16 | 20.5 | 9 | 23.7 | 6 | 9.2 | | |
| **Working status of the participants*** | | | | | | | | |
| Working | - | - | - | - | 1 | 1.5 | | |
| Non-working | 78 | 100.0 | 38 | 100.0 | 64 | 98.5 | - | - |
| **Occupational types of husbands** | | | | | | | | |
| Service | 30 | 38.5 | 18 | 47.4 | 25 | 38.5 | 1.911 | 0.752 |
| Business | 15 | 19.2 | 5 | 13.2 | 9 | 13.8 | | |
| Others** | 33 | 42.3 | 15 | 39.5 | 31 | 98.5 | | |
| **Monthly house-hold income** (in Indian rupees) (±sd) | 15801.28 ±2591.66 | | 10.328.94 ±1683.87 | | 14967.69 ±2987.45 | | 0.878 | 0.417 |
| **Age at menarche** (years) (±sd) | 12.62±1.60 | | 13.00±1.73 | | 12.83±2.14 | | 0.561 | 0.572 |
| **Age at marriage** (years) (±sd) | 19.02±4.07 | | 19.28±4.17 | | 17.46±5.71 | | 2.554 | 0.081 |
| **Total number of conception** | | | | | | | | |
| Once | 35 | 44.9 | 7 | 18.4 | 10 | 15.4 | 33.51 | 0.001 |
| Twice | 26 | 33.3 | 15 | 39.5 | 12 | 18.5 | | |
| More than twice | 17 | 20.9 | 16 | 42.2 | 43 | 66.1 | | |

*chi square test were not conducted due to presence of zero value in the cells.
**labours, retired.

**Table 4.2: Blood Sugar Level and Body Fat Distribution of the Participants**

| *Variables* | *Premenopausal women (n=78)* | *Peri-menopausal women (n=38)* | *Postmenopausal women (n=65)* | *F* | *P value* | *Post hoc test (P value)* |
|---|---|---|---|---|---|---|
| | *Mean±SE* | *Mean±SE* | *Mean±SE* | | | |
| **Blood sugar level (mg/dl)** | 106.18±30.97 | 138.63±63.78 | 126.75±45.55 | 7.727 | 0.001 | Pre vs Peri (0.002)<br>Pre vs Post (0.026)<br>Peri vs Post (0.432) |
| **BMI** | 25.22±0.55 | 27.06±0.67 | 24.84±0.61 | 2.789 | 0.064 | Pre vs Peri (0.153)<br>Peri vs Post (0.077)<br>Pre vs Post (0.892) |
| **PBF** | 33.83±0.55 | 35.78±0.66 | 36.62±0.54 | 6.992 | 0.001 | Pre vs Peri (0.100)<br>Peri vs Post (0.663)<br>Pre vs Post (0.002) |
| **WC** | 80.59±1.37 | 86.33±2.23 | 81.50±1.77 | 2.500 | 0.085 | Pre vs Peri (0.095)<br>Peri vs Post (0.207)<br>Pre vs Post (0.920) |
| **HC** | 93.48±0.96 | 94.88±1.70 | 90.88±1.21 | 2.472 | 0.087 | Pre vs Peri (0.754)<br>Peri vs Post (0.119)<br>Pre vs Post (0.263) |
| **WHR** | 0.85±0.08 | 0.90±0.01 | 0.89±0.01 | 5.858 | 0.003 | Pre vs Peri (0.016)<br>Peri vs Post (0.874)<br>Pre vs Post (0.022) |
| **Visceral fat** | 7.34±0.51 | 9.52±0.75 | 8.69±0.63 | 3.026 | 0.051 | Pre vs Peri (0.073)<br>Peri vs Post (0.694)<br>Pre vs Post (0.247) |
| **FM** | 23.18±3.38 | 22.43±1.05 | 20.58±0.76 | 0.302 | 0.740 | Pre vs Peri (0.982)<br>Peri vs Post (0.904)<br>Pre vs Post (0.745) |

*(Contd...)*

| | | | | | | |
|---|---|---|---|---|---|---|
| **FFM** | 37.64±0.81 | 39.16±0.92 | 34.63±0.68 | 7.130 | 0.001 | Pre vs Peri (0.478)<br>Peri vs Post (0.003)<br>Pre vs Post (0.020) |
| **Subcutaneous fat of whole body** | 29.66±0.60 | 31.72±0.73 | 30.63±0.68 | 2.036 | 0.134 | Pre vs Peri (0.142)<br>Peri vs Post (0.595)<br>Pre vs Post (0.548) |
| **Skeletal fat of whole body** | 23.61±0.22 | 22.63±0.22 | 21.59±0.19 | 25.116 | 0.001 | Pre vs Peri (0.016)<br>Peri vs Post (0.012)<br>Pre vs Post (0.001) |
| **Subcutaneous fat of trunk** | 25.81±0.60 | 27.22±0.97 | 27.48±0.63 | 1.903 | 0.152 | Pre vs Peri (0.426)<br>Peri vs Post (0.971)<br>Pre vs Post (0.187) |
| **Skeletal fat of trunk** | 18.38±0.25 | 16.96±0.28 | 16.18±0.22 | 21.909 | 0.001 | Pre vs Peri (0.002)<br>Peri vs Post (0.167)<br>Pre vs Post (0.001) |

BMI- body mass index, PBF- per cent body fat, WC- waist circumference, HC- hip circumference, WHR- waist-hip ratio, FM- fat mass, FFM- fat free mass.

The same table further describes that the body fat distribution, measured by PBF, WHR, and FFM, skeletal fat of the trunk and whole body differed significantly across the menopausal groups. Scheffe's test (post hoc test) shows that PBF and WHR were significantly greater in post-menopausal women compared to the premenopausal group. However, premenopausal women had significantly greater skeletal fat on the trunk and whole body and post-menopausal women had significantly lower FFM than their respective comparable groups.

Table 4.3 shows that all the participants, irrespective of the menopausal group's consumed cereals regularly. Similarly, the majority of the participants, irrespective of their menopausal groups reported to consume pulses, green vegetables, roots/tubers, fish, and tea/coffee regularly and other food items such as eggs and meat occasionally. More than half of the postmenopausal women hardly or never consumed soya products while the majority of pre and peri-menopausal women consumed soya products occasionally. Further, a few of pre-menopausal women and most of the peri and post-menopausal women reported regular consumption of snacks.

Table 4.4 shows that most of the participants of three menopausal groups were mostly engaged in domestic activities such as, cooking, washing clothes and dishes and mopping the floor and also reported watching television on a regular basis. Further, it is observed that most of the participants, irrespective of their menopausal status were hardly or never engaged in physical exercise, listening music, commuting related to work, dusting, and ironing. However, a large number of women of three menopausal groups regularly went for a morning walk.

In multivariate analyses (Table 4.5), the trend shows similarity with the findings of ANOVA post hoc results (Table 4.2), even after controlling for socio-demographic, reproductive and lifestyle variables. For example, pre-menopausal group tended to have greater skeletal fat on the trunk, but had lower PBF and WHR than their comparative groups; FFM was likely to be lower in post-menopausal women; while skeletal fat of the whole body was likely to be lower among both peri and post-menopausal women.

**Table 4.3 Food Consumption Reported by the Participants**

| *Food items* | *Menopausal status* | | | | | |
|---|---|---|---|---|---|---|
| | *Premeno-pausal women (n=78)* | | *Peri-meno-pausal women (n=38)* | | *Postmeno-pausal women(n=65)* | |
| | *n* | *per cent* | *n* | *per cent* | *n* | *per cent* |
| **Intake of cereals** | | | | | | |
| Regularly | 78 | 100.0 | 38 | 100.0 | 65 | 100.0 |
| Occasionally | - | - | - | - | - | - |
| Rarely/never | - | - | - | - | - | - |
| **Intake of pulses** | | | | | | |
| Regularly | 38 | 48.7 | 22 | 57.9 | 34 | 52.3 |
| Occasionally | 34 | 43.6 | 14 | 36.8 | 18 | 27.7 |
| Rarely/never | 6 | 7.7 | 2 | 5.3 | 13 | 20.0 |
| **Intake of green vegetables** | | | | | | |
| Regularly | 72 | 92.3 | 38 | 100.0 | 63 | 96.9 |
| Occasionally | 4 | 5.1 | - | - | 2 | 3.1 |
| Rarely/never | 2 | 2.6 | - | - | - | - |
| **Intake of roots/ tubers** | | | | | | |
| Regularly | 76 | 97.4 | 37 | 97.4 | 60 | 92.3 |
| Occasionally | 2 | 2.6 | 1 | 2.6 | 3 | 4.6 |
| Rarely/never | - | - | - | - | 2 | 3.1 |
| **Intake of soya products** | | | | | | |
| Regularly | 2 | 2.6 | 3 | 7.9 | 1 | 1.5 |
| Occasionally | 42 | 53.8 | 18 | 47.4 | 28 | 43.1 |
| Rarely/never | 34 | 43.6 | 17 | 44.7 | 36 | 55.4 |
| **Intake of meat** | | | | | | |
| Regularly | 4 | 5.1 | 2 | 5.3 | 1 | 1.5 |
| Occasionally | 57 | 73.1 | 22 | 57.9 | 31 | 47.7 |
| Rarely/never | 17 | 21.8 | 14 | 36.8 | 33 | 50.8 |
| **Intake of fish** | | | | | | |
| Regularly | 57 | 73.1 | 31 | 81.6 | 42 | 64.6 |
| Occasionally | 18 | 23.1 | 5 | 13.2 | 13 | 20.0 |
| Rarely/never | 3 | 3.8 | 2 | 5.3 | 10 | 15.4 |
| **Intake of egg** | | | | | | |
| Regularly | 20 | 25.6 | 10 | 26.3 | 15 | 23.1 |
| Occasionally | 46 | 59.0 | 15 | 39.5 | 27 | 41.5 |
| Rarely/never | 12 | 15.4 | 13 | 34.2 | 23 | 35.4 |

*(Contd...)*

| | | | | | | |
|---|---|---|---|---|---|---|
| **Intake of fruits** | | | | | | |
| Regularly | 16 | 20.5 | 14 | 36.8 | 26 | 40.0 |
| Occasionally | 15 | 19.2 | 8 | 21.1 | 7 | 10.8 |
| Rarely/never | 47 | 60.3 | 16 | 42.1 | 32 | 49.2 |
| **Intake of milk products** | | | | | | |
| Regularly | 12 | 15.4 | 7 | 18.4 | 9 | 13.8 |
| Occasionally | 5 | 6.4 | 3 | 7.9 | 2 | 3.1 |
| Rarely/never | 61 | 78.2 | 28 | 73.7 | 54 | 83.1 |
| **Intake of snacks** | | | | | | |
| Regularly | 9 | 11.5 | 34 | 89.5 | 57 | 87.7 |
| Occasionally | 7 | 9.0 | 2 | 5.3 | 2 | 3.1 |
| Rarely/never | 62 | 79.5 | 2 | 5.3 | 6 | 9.2 |
| **Intake of sweets** | | | | | | |
| Regularly | 36 | 46.2 | 13 | 34.2 | 24 | 36.9 |
| Occasionally | 26 | 33.3 | 11 | 28.9 | 11 | 16.9 |
| Rarely/never | 16 | 20.5 | 14 | 36.8 | 30 | 46.2 |
| **Intake of noodles** | | | | | | |
| Regularly | 5 | 6.4 | 3 | 7.9 | 3 | 4.6 |
| Occasionally | 27 | 34.6 | 11 | 28.9 | 12 | 18.5 |
| Rarely/never | 46 | 59.0 | 24 | 63.2 | 50 | 76.9 |
| **Intake of butter** | | | | | | |
| Regularly | 18 | 23.1 | 11 | 28.9 | 12 | 18.5 |
| Occasionally | 12 | 15.4 | 4 | 10.5 | 8 | 12.3 |
| Rarely/never | 48 | 61.5 | 23 | 60.5 | 45 | 69.2 |
| **Intake of ice cream** | | | | | | |
| Regularly | 8 | 10.3 | 3 | 7.9 | 6 | 9.2 |
| Occasionally | 6 | 7.7 | 1 | 2.6 | 4 | 6.2 |
| Rarely/never | 64 | 82.1 | 34 | 89.5 | 55 | 84.6 |
| **Intake of cold drink** | | | | | | |
| Regularly | 6 | 7.7 | 5 | 13.2 | 5 | 7.7 |
| Occasionally | 9 | 11.5 | 3 | 7.9 | 6 | 9.2 |
| Rarely/never | 63 | 80.8 | 30 | 78.9 | 54 | 83.1 |
| **Intake of tea/coffee** | | | | | | |
| Regularly | 65 | 83.3 | 31 | 81.6 | 55 | 84.6 |
| Occasionally | 2 | 2.6 | - | - | 2 | 3.1 |
| Rarely/never | 11 | 14.1 | 7 | 18.4 | 8 | 12.3 |

**Table 4.4 Physical Activities Performed by the Participants**

| *Physical activities* | *Menopausal status* | | | | | |
|---|---|---|---|---|---|---|
| | *Premeno-pausal women (n=78)* | | *Peri-meno-pausal women (n=38)* | | *Postmeno-pausal women(n=65)* | |
| | *n* | *per cent* | *n* | *per cent* | *n* | *per cent* |
| **Cooking** | | | | | | |
| Regularly | 72 | 92.3 | 38 | 100.0 | 58 | 89.2 |
| Occasionally | 1 | 1.3 | - | - | 1 | 1.5 |
| Rarely/never | 5 | 6.4 | - | - | 6 | 9.2 |
| **Washing dishes** | | | | | | |
| Regularly | 66 | 84.6 | 30 | 78.9 | 49 | 75.4 |
| Occasionally | - | - | - | - | - | - |
| Rarely/never | 12 | 15.4 | 8 | 21.1 | 16 | 24.6 |
| **Washing clothes** | | | | | | |
| Regularly | 61 | 78.2 | 26 | 68.4 | 43 | 66.2 |
| Occasionally | 13 | 16.7 | 5 | 13.2 | 10 | 15.4 |
| Rarely/never | 4 | 5.1 | 7 | 18.4 | 12 | 18.5 |
| **Moping the floor** | | | | | | |
| Regularly | 69 | 88.5 | 31 | 81.6 | 49 | 75.4 |
| Occasionally | - | - | - | - | - | - |
| Rarely/never | 9 | 11.5 | 7 | 18.4 | 16 | 24.6 |
| **Dusting** | | | | | | |
| Regularly | 4 | 5.1 | 1 | 2.6 | 2 | 3.1 |
| Occasionally | 33 | 42.3 | 17 | 44.7 | 19 | 29.2 |
| Rarely/never | 41 | 52.6 | 20 | 52.6 | 44 | 67.7 |
| **Ironing** | | | | | | |
| Regularly | 2 | 2.6 | - | - | 1 | 1.5 |
| Occasionally | 6 | 7.7 | 1 | 2.6 | 2 | 3.1 |
| Rarely/never | 70 | 89.7 | 37 | 97.4 | 62 | 95.4 |
| **Watching television** | | | | | | |
| Regularly | 69 | 88.5 | 31 | 81.6 | 54 | 83.1 |
| Occasionally | 1 | 1.3 | - | - | - | - |
| Rarely/never | 8 | 10.3 | 7 | 18.4 | 11 | 16.9 |
| **Listening music** | | | | | | |
| Regularly | 27 | 34.6 | 13 | 34.2 | 16 | 24.6 |
| Occasionally | 6 | 7.7 | 2 | 5.3 | 2 | 3.1 |
| Rarely/never | 45 | 57.7 | 23 | 60.5 | 47 | 72.3 |
| **Walking in the morning** | | | | | | |
| Regularly | 47 | 60.3 | 24 | 63.2 | 42 | 64.6 |
| Occasionally | 3 | 3.8 | 1 | 2.6 | 2 | 3.1 |
| Rarely/never | 28 | 35.9 | 13 | 34.2 | 21 | 32.3 |

*(Contd...)*

| | | | | | | |
|---|---|---|---|---|---|---|
| **Physical exercise** | | | | | | |
| Regularly | 7 | 9.0 | 7 | 18.4 | 11 | 16.9 |
| Occasionally | 2 | 2.6 | 1 | 2.6 | 1 | 1.5 |
| Rarely/never | 69 | 88.5 | 30 | 78.9 | 53 | 81.5 |
| **Commuting related to work** | | | | | | |
| Regularly | 6 | 7.7 | 2 | 5.3 | 8 | 12.3 |
| Occasionally | 12 | 15.4 | 6 | 15.8 | 8 | 12.3 |
| Rarely/never | 60 | 76.9 | 30 | 78.9 | 49 | 75.4 |

**Table 4.5 Results of Multiple Linear Regression Analyses for Predicting Body Fat Distribution**

| *Dependent variables* | *Independent variables* | *Un-standardized co-efficient* | *T value* | *P value* | *CI at 95 per cent* | | $R^2$ |
|---|---|---|---|---|---|---|---|
| | | | | | *lower* | *upper* | |
| **PBF** | Menopausal status *Pre-menopause* | -1.486 | 2.177 | 0.031 | -2.833 | -0.139 | 0.190 |
| | Age of the participants at interview | 0.032 | 2.468 | 0.015 | 0.006 | 0.058 | |
| | Mopping the floor | -0.332 | 2.713 | 0.007 | -0.573 | -0.090 | |
| | Physical exercise | -0.376 | 2.697 | 0.008 | -0.651 | -0.101 | |
| | Consumption of snacks | 0.279 | 2.020 | 0.045 | 0.006 | 0.552 | |
| **WHR** | Mopping the floor | -0.007 | 3.076 | 0.002 | -0.012 | -0.003 | 0.166 |
| | Menopausal status *Pre-menopause* | -0.033 | 2.598 | 0.010 | -0.058 | -0.008 | |
| | Consumption of cold drinks | 0.009 | 2.847 | 0.005 | 0.003 | 0.015 | |
| | Physical exercise | -0.006 | 2.257 | 0.025 | -0.011 | -0.001 | |
| **FFM** | Menopausal status *Post-menopause* | -3.755 | 4.023 | 0.000 | -5.597 | -1.913 | 0.227 |
| | Mopping the floor | -0.642 | 3.890 | 0.000 | -0.968 | -0.316 | |
| | Consumption of roots/ tubers | 1.059 | 3.130 | 0.002 | 0.391 | 1.727 | |
| | Consumption of milk/ milk products | 0.528 | 2.995 | 0.003 | 0.180 | 0.877 | |
| | Physical exercise | 0.405 | 2.200 | 0.029 | 0.042 | 0.768 | |
| **Skeletal fat of whole body** | Menopausal status *Post-menopause* | -1.756 | 6.070 | 0.000 | -2.327 | -1.185 | 0.282 |
| | Age of the participants at interview | -0.017 | 3.316 | 0.001 | -0.026 | -0.007 | |
| | Menopausal status *Peri-menopause* | -0.871 | 2.652 | 0.009 | -1.520 | -0.223 | |
| | Physical exercise | 0.270 | 2.048 | 0.042 | 0.010 | 0.530 | |
| **Skeletal fat of trunk** | Menopausal status *Pre-menopause* | 1.678 | 5.565 | 0.000 | 1.083 | 2.273 | 0.312 |
| | Age of the participants at interview | -0.019 | 3.262 | 0.001 | -0.031 | -0.008 | |
| | Physical exercise | 0.147 | 2.380 | 0.018 | 0.025 | 0.269 | |
| | Consumption of sweets | -0.094 | 2.023 | 0.045 | -0.185 | -0.002 | |

Table 4.5 further shows that age of the participants at the time of interview was positively related to PBF but had an inverse relation to skeletal fat of both trunk and whole body. The physical exercise showed inverse relation to PBF and WHR but, had a positive relation to FFM, skeletal fat of both trunk and whole body. Apart from these, physical activity type such as mopping the floor was inversely related to PBF and WHR. However, FFM was likely to be lower among the participants who spend more time on watching television. Furthermore, PBF and WHR increased with higher consumption of snacks and cold drinks respectively. Consumption of roots/tubers and milk products were positively related to FFM independently; however, consumption of sweets was negatively related to the skeletal fat of trunk.

Table 4.6 shows that blood sugar level was likely to be lower among a pre-menopausal group of women compared to other two menopausal groups, even controlling for the socio-demographic, reproductive and lifestyle variables. The trend is consistent with our ANOVA result (Table 4.2). Moreover, blood sugar level became higher with an increase in WHR, consumption of tea / coffee and also with an increase in spending time on watching television. On the other hand, higher consumption of roots/tubers had an inverse relation to blood sugar level.

Results of MANCOVA (Table 4.7) reveals that menopausal status was significantly related to blood sugar level, WHR, FFM and skeletal fat (both trunk and whole body) after adjusting the effects of covariates [socio-demographic (age) and lifestyle variables (physical activities and food consumption)]. The corrected model was found to be statistically significant.

## Discussion

Our study participants differ significantly with respect to blood sugar level and body fat distribution across menopausal status. Multiple linear regression analyses reveal menopausal status as one of the factors related to body fat distribution and blood sugar level. At the final stage, the result of MANCOVA reinforces the relation of menopausal status with body fat distribution and blood sugar levels after adjusting the effects of covariates (socio-demographic and

**Table 4.6 Results of Multiple Linear Regression Analyses for Predicting Blood Sugar Level**

| *Dependent variables* | *Independent variables* | *Un-standardized co-efficient* | *T value* | *P value* | *CI at 95 per cent* | | $R^2$ |
|---|---|---|---|---|---|---|---|
| | | | | | *lower* | *upper* | |
| Blood sugar level | WHR Menopausal status | 129.550 | 3.527 | 0.001 | 57.057 | 202.044 | 0.212 |
| | *Pre-menopause* | -17.930 | 2.745 | 0.007 | -30.820 | -5.039 | |
| | Watching television | 6.594 | 2.817 | 0.005 | 1.975 | 11.214 | |
| | Consumption of roots/ tubers | -7.429 | 3.069 | 0.002 | -12.207 | -2.651 | |
| | Consumption of tea/coffee | 2.575 | 2.048 | 0.042 | 0.093 | 5.057 | |

**Table 4.7 Results of Multivariate Analyses of Covariance**

| *Covariates* | *Dependent variables* | *Type III sum of squares* | *F* | *P value* |
|---|---|---|---|---|
| **Age of the participants at interview** | Blood sugar level | 282.31 | 0.147 | 0.701 |
| | PBF | 106.91 | 5.75 | 0.017 |
| | WHR | 0.002 | 0.439 | 0.508 |
| | FFM | 31.27 | 0.878 | 0.350 |
| | Skeletal fat of whole body | 22.50 | 8.259 | 0.004 |
| | Skeletal fat of trunk | 30.76 | 8.446 | 0.004 |
| **Consumption of roots/ tubers** | Blood sugar level | 14451.93 | 7.541 | 0.006 |
| | PBF | 8.04 | 0.432 | 0.511 |
| | WHR | 0.010 | 1.495 | 0.223 |
| | FFM | 186.97 | 5.248 | 0.023 |
| | Skeletal fat of whole body | 0.87 | 0.319 | 0.572 |
| | Skeletal fat of trunk | 1.68 | 0.464 | 0.496 |
| **Consumption of snacks** | Blood sugar level | 2.98 | 0.002 | 0.968 |
| | PBF | 77.53 | 4.17 | 0.042 |
| | WHR | 0.0000572 | 0.009 | 0.926 |
| | FFM | 23.29 | 0.654 | 0.419 |
| | Skeletal fat of whole body | 8.95 | 3.285 | 0.071 |
| | Skeletal fat of trunk | 13.08 | 3.592 | 0.059 |
| **Consumption of sweets** | Blood sugar level | 2828.97 | 1.476 | 0.226 |
| | PBF | 65.35 | 3.514 | 0.062 |
| | WHR | 0.005 | 0.88 | 0.349 |
| | FFM | 62.28 | 1.748 | 0.187 |
| | Skeletal fat of whole body | 3.002 | 1.101 | 0.295 |
| | Skeletal fat of trunk | 10.62 | 2.917 | 0.089 |
| **Consumption of cold drinks** | Blood sugar level | 2624.20 | 1.369 | 0.243 |
| | PBF | 0.12 | 0.006 | 0.935 |
| | WHR | 0.049 | 7.376 | 0.007 |

*(Contd...)*

| | | | | |
|---|---|---|---|---|
| | FFM<br>Skeletal fat of whole body<br>Skeletal fat of trunk | 26.51<br>0.336<br>0.099 | 0.744<br>0.123<br>0.027 | 0.389<br>0.725<br>0.869 |
| **Consumption of tea/coffee** | Blood sugar level<br>PBF<br>WHR<br>FFM<br>Skeletal fat of whole body<br>Skeletal fat of trunk | 10365.85<br>20.25<br>0.0008<br>10.457<br>5.29<br>6.55 | 5.409<br>1.089<br>0.131<br>0.294<br>1.944<br>1.799 | 0.021<br>0.298<br>0.717<br>0.588<br>0.165<br>0.181 |
| **Mopping the floor** | Blood sugar level<br>PBF<br>WHR<br>FFM<br>Skeletal fat of whole body<br>Skeletal fat of trunk | 4851.66<br>100.16<br>0.054<br>442.38<br>1.345<br>10.66 | 2.532<br>5.387<br>8.117<br>12.42<br>0.494<br>2.929 | 0.113<br>0.021<br>0.004<br>0.000<br>0.483<br>0.088 |
| **Watching television** | Blood sugar level<br>PBF<br>WHR<br>FFM<br>Skeletal fat of whole body<br>Skeletal fat of trunk | 727.40<br>11.31<br>0.019<br>27.13<br>0.22<br>0.700 | 0.38<br>0.608<br>2.904<br>0.762<br>0.084<br>0.192 | 0.538<br>0.436<br>0.090<br>0.384<br>0.772<br>0.661 |
| **Physical exercise** | Blood sugar level<br>PBF<br>WHR<br>FFM<br>Skeletal fat of whole body<br>Skeletal fat of trunk | 1125.35<br>127.06<br>0.03<br>149.85<br>8.88<br>22.87 | 0.587<br>6.833<br>4.625<br>4.206<br>3.261<br>6.282 | 0.444<br>0.009<br>0.032<br>0.041<br>0.072<br>0.013 |
| **Menopausal status** | Blood sugar level<br>PBF<br>WHR<br>FFM<br>Skeletal fat of whole body<br>Skeletal fat of trunk | 20434.42<br>05.62<br>10.044<br>660.52<br>86.62<br>95.226 | 5.331<br>2.84<br>3.329<br>9.27<br>15.89<br>13.07 | 0.005<br>0.045<br>0.038<br><0.001<br><0.001<br><0.001 |
| **Corrected model** | Blood sugar level<br>PBF<br>WHR<br>FFM<br>Skeletal fat of whole body<br>Skeletal fat of trunk | 65220.51<br>858.04<br>0.26<br>1654.34<br>201.78<br>282.00 | 3.094<br>4.195<br>3.648<br>4.222<br>6.731<br>7.039 | <0.001<br><0.001<br><0.001<br><0.001<br><0.001<br><0.001 |
| **Intercept** | Blood sugar level<br>PBF<br>WHR<br>FFM | 123704.5<br>5336.50<br>3.855<br>4850.04 | 64.55<br>287.05<br>574.70<br>136.11 | <0.001<br><0.001<br><0.001<br><0.001 |

*(Contd...)*

| | | | | |
|---|---|---|---|---|
| | Skeletal fat of whole body<br>Skeletal fat of trunk | 2310.69<br>1327.48 | 847.81<br>364.53 | <0.001<br><0.001 |
| **Error** | Blood sugar level<br>PBF<br>WHR<br>FFM<br>Skeletal fat of whole body<br>Skeletal fat of trunk | 321971.2<br>3124.06<br>1.126<br>5985.12<br>457.90<br>611.83 | | |

lifestyle variables).

Literature reveals that menopause-related changes indicate an increase in the levels of adiposity, with a relative reduction in skeletal fat and FFM (Pasquali *et al.*, 1994; Ho *et al.*, 2010; Ghosh and Bhagat, 2010). The rapid loss of bone mineral density helps to reduce the density of FFM and causes an increase in PBF in post-menopausal group (Lindsay *et al.*, 1976; Heymsfield *et al.*, 1989). Ovarian hormonal depletion could also deter the lipolytic metabolism in the abdomen and subsequently develop the android type of fat pattern during menopause (Ley *et al.*, 1992; Wang *et al.*, 1994). However, there is one study (Zamboni *et al.*, 1997) which shows a significant relationship between chronological aging and adipose tissue metabolism. Consistent with these findings, our study shows that age of the participants at the time of interview and menopausal status remain significantly related to PBF and skeletal fat of trunk and whole body. It is observed that PBF is increased with increase in age of the participants, while skeletal fat of the trunk and whole body shows inverse relation to age. The study of Wang *et al.* (1994) showed that changes in FFM are mainly menopause-related, and not because of age. Likewise, two follow-up studies demonstrate an increasing trend in WHR during the menopausal transition, independent of age (Björkelund *et al.*, 1996; Poehlman *et al.*, 1995). Our study corroborates to these findings. It is well documented that accumulation of body fat, particularly in abdomen elevates the blood sugar level, thereby increasing the risk for metabolic syndrome in women during midlife (Kannel *et al.*, 1991; Ghosh and Bhagat, 2009). Our study also demonstrates that a greater WHR is likely to elevate blood sugar level in women. But, simultaneously, sex hormonal deficiency could also regulate the pathways of glucose metabolism. For instance, reduced levels of estrogens and progesterone may decrease the levels of sex hormone binding globulin (SHBG) in the blood (Prescott *et al.*, 2012). Subsequently, the likelihood to develop insulin resistance is increased during menopausal transition (Revis *et al.*, 2006). Thus, a reduced level of blood sugar is noticed among the premenopausal group in our study.

Studies show that the lifestyle factors have a significant influence on fatness and blood sugar level (Ross *et al.*, 2000; Ryan *et al.*, 2000; Meigs, 2002). Again, the practice of moderate physical activities could reduce the levels of adiposity in women, independent of the menopausal status (Poehlman *et al.*, 1995). Our study shows that physical exercise has an inverse relation to PBF and WHR. On the other hand, FFM, skeletal fat of both trunk and whole body are likely to increase with an increase in time spent on physical exercise. As a result, the loss of muscle strength that occurs during midlife could be preserved (Gilliat-Wimberly *et al.*, 2001).

Sedentary behaviours are responsible for the increased incidence of insulin resistance that consequently elevates the levels of blood sugar in women (Pinto Pereira *et al.*, 2012). For example, in our study, the time spend on watching television is positively related to blood sugar levels.

Food habits are also responsible for increased body fat and blood sugar in women. The consumption of low-caloric balanced foods helps to maintain the body weight in a normal range and subsequently reduce the levels of blood sugar in women, even after the attainment of menopause (Folsom *et al.*, 2000; Sternfeld *et al.*, 2005). Hence, a greater FFM in relation to the higher consumption of milk and roots/ tubers as found in our study raises the question whether calcium and fibre rich foods could prevent the loss of lean mass in women during midlife.

Significantly, the blood sugar level of our study participants was found to be lower with increase the consumption of roots/tubers. On the contrary, consumption of calorie dense foods could result in excess body fat and also impair glucose metabolism (Ross *et al.*, 2000). Our study reveals a positive relationship of PBF, WHR and blood sugar levels with the consumption of snacks, cold drinks, and tea/coffee respectively. The higher consumption of sweets tends to reduce the skeletal fat of trunk, while the lower consumption of roots/tubers elevates the blood sugar levels.

Finally, our results from MANCOVA reveal menopausal status to be significantly related to body fat distribution and blood sugar level when the covariates such as socio-demographic (age) and lifestyle variables (physical activity levels and food consumption) were adjusted. The result reinforces the dominant role of ovarian hormone in determining body fat distribution and blood sugar level, at least for this study population.

In the Indian subcontinent, there is a trend in the advancement in age at menopause (Syamala and Sivakami, 2005; Dasgupta *et al.,* 2015). Now, if menopausal status alone can be a strong determinant of body fat patterning and blood sugar level, then the chance of Indian women to suffer from metabolic disorders will increase before they reach mid-life. This will certainly jeopardise the post-reproductive life of Indian women. Thus, it becomes imperative to conduct more research on Indian population so that the health planners can take up effective strategies in promoting the midlife health.

We have noticed certain limitations in this study. Firstly, the inclusion of a number of participants would have been of help to provide a generalised scenario about the menopause-related changes on body fat distribution and blood sugar level. Secondly, use of observation technique in the field, at least on a subsample, could have improved the quality of the data on lifestyle variables (for example, observation on the actual daily consumption of food items and / or physical activity undertaken by the participants). Finally, data on multiethnic groups could have substantiated the validity of the findings in the Indian context.

## Conclusion

We conclude from this study that variability in the ovarian hormonal levels owing to differential ovarian reserves at different menopausal stages remain significantly related to body fat distribution and blood sugar level of women at each stage, irrespective of their socio-demographic and lifestyle pattern.

## References


Bhowmick, D., M. Manna and C. Ghosh. 2013. 'Assessment of uric acid and fasting blood glucose level among pre-menopausal and post-menopausal obese housewives in semi-urban areas of West Bengal, India'. *International Journal of Modern Biology and Medicine.*3:1-6.

Björkelund, C., L. Lissner, S. Andersson, L. Lapidus and C. Bengtsson. 1996. 'Reproductive history in relation to relative weight and fat distribution'. *International Journal of Obesity and Related Metabolic Disorders,* 20: 213-219.

Brochu, M., RD. Starling, A. Tchernof, DE. Matthews, E. Garcia-Rubi and ET. Poehlman. 2000. 'Visceral adipose tissue is an independent correlate of glucose disposal in older obese postmenopausal women'. *The Journal of Clinical Endocrinology and Metabolism,* 85:2378-2384.

Burger, HG., EC. Dudley, DM. Robertson and L. Dennerstein. 2002. 'Hormonal changes in the menopause transition'. *Recent Progress in Hormone Research,* 57: 257-275.

Cervellati, C., FS. Pansini, G. Bonaccorsi, G. Pascale, B. Bagni, C. Castaldini, S. Ferrazini, F. Ridolfi, M. Pedriali, A. Guariento and CM. Bergamini. 2009. 'Body mass index is a major determinant of abdominal fat accumulation in pre-, peri- and post-menopausal women'. *Gynaecological Endocrinology,* 25:413-417.

Chakroborty, TR and AC. Gore. 2004. 'Aging-related changes in ovarian hormones, their receptors and neuro-endocrine function'. *Experimental Biology and Medicine,* 229: 977-987.

Chaudhuri, A and AK. Bandopadhyay. 2014. 'Obesity, a burning problem'. *Journal of Pharmacy,* 4: 1-5.

Dasgupta, D., B. Pal and S. Ray. 2015. 'Factors that discriminate age at menopause: A study of Bengali Hindu women of West Bengal'. *American Journal of Human Biology,* 27: 710-715.

Dudley, EC., JL. Hopper, J. Taffe, JR. Guthrie, HG. Burger and L. Dennerstein. 1998. 'Using longitudinal data to define the peri-menopause by menstrual cycle characteristics'. *Climacteric,* 1:18-25.

Fitzgerald, C., AE. Zimon and EE. Jones. 1998. 'Aging and reproductive potential in women'. *The Yale Journal of Biology and Medicine,* 71: 367-381.

Folsom, AR., LH. Kushi, KE. Anderson, PJ. Mink, JE. Olson, CP. Hong, TA. Sellers, D. Lazovich and RJ. Prineas. 2000. 'Associations of general and abdominal obesity with multiple health outcomes in older women: The Iowa women's health study'. *Archives of Internal Medicine,* 160: 2117-2128.

Ghosh, A., 2008. 'Comparison of risk variables associated with the metabolic syndrome in pre- and postmenopausal Bengalee women'. *Cardiovascular Journal of Africa,* 19:183-187.

Ghosh, A and M. Bhagat. 2009. 'Indian diabetes risk score according to menopausal status in Asian Indian women: The Santiniketan women study'. *Journal of Diabetes,* 1: 140-141.

Ghosh, A and M. Bhagat. 2010. 'Anthropometric and body composition characteristics in pre- and postmenopausal Asian Indian women: Santiniketan women study'. *Anthropologischer Anzeiger,* 68:1-10.

Gilliat-Wimberly, M., MM. Manore, K. Woolf, PD. Swan and SS. Carroll. 2001. 'Effects of habitual physical activity on the resting metabolic rates and body compositions of women aged 35 to 50 years'. *Journal of the American Dietetic Association,* 101: 1181-1188.

Guthrie, JR., M. Ball, EC. Dudley, CV. Garamszegi, ML. Wahlqvist, L. Dennerstein and HG. Burger. 2001. 'Impaired fasting glycaemia in middle-aged women: A prospective study'. *International Journal of Obesity and Related Metabolic Disorders,* 25:646-651.

Heymsfield, SB., J. Wang, S. Lichtman, Y. Kamen, J. Kehayias and R.N. Jr. Pierson. 1989. 'Body composition in elderly subjects: A critical appraisal of clinical methodology'. *American Journal of Clinical Nutrition,* 50: 1167-1175.

Ho, S.C., S. Wu, S.G. Chan and A. Sham. 2010. 'Menopausal transition and changes of body composition: A prospective study in Chinese peri-menopausal women'. *International Journal of Obesity,* 34:1265-1274.

IBM Corporation. 2011. *IBM SPSS Statistics for Windows, Version 20.0.* New York; Armonk: 2011.

Jouyandeh, Z., F. Nayebzadeh, M. Qorbani and M. Asadi. 2013. 'Metabolic syndrome and menopause'. *Journal of Diabetes and Metabolic Disorders,* 2013, 12:1.

Kannel, W.B., L. A. Cupples, R. Ramaswami, J. Stokes, BE. Kreger and M. Higgins. 1991. 'Regional obesity and risk of cardiovascular disease: The Framingham study'. *Journal of Clinical Epidemiology,* 44: 183-190.

Kaur, S., P. Meheta and G. Kaur. 2014. 'Anthropometric profile and menopausal age of 40 to 80 year old women of Punjab: A study'. *Journal of Life Science,* 6: 1-5.

Kirchengast, S., D. Gruber, M. Sator, W. Knogler and J. Huber. 1998. 'The impact of nutritional status on body fat distribution patterns in pre and postmenopausal females'. *Journal of Biosocial Science,* 30:145-154.

Ley, CJ., B. Lees and JC. Stevenson. 1992. 'Sex and menopause associated changes in body-fat distribution'. *American Journal of Clinical Nutrition,* 55: 950-954.

Lindsay, R., JM. Aitken, LB. Anderson, DM. Hart, EB. Mac Donald and AC. Clarke. 1976. 'Long-term prevention of postmenopausal osteoporosis by estrogens: Evidence for an increased bone mass after delayed onset of oestrogen treatment'. *Lancet,* 307: 1038-1041.

Lohman, TG, AF. Roche and R. Martorell. 1988. *Anthropometric Standardisation Reference Manual*. Champaign, IL; Human Kinetics Books.

Martins, IS and SP. Marinho. 2003. 'The potential of central obesity anthropometric indicators as diagnostic tools'. *Revista de Saúde Pública,* 37,6: 760-767.

Meigs, JB., 2002. 'Epidemiology of the metabolic syndrome'. *The American Journal of Managed Care,* 8: S283-S296.

Munawar, F., A. Sara., M. Sadaf Munawar and M. Ahmed. 2012. 'Waist hip ratio and body mass index in women of different age groups'. *Pakistan Journal of Physiology,* 8: 49-51.

Pandey, S., M. Srinivas, S. Agashe, J. Joshi, P. Galvankar, CP. Prakasm and R. Vaidya. 2010. 'Menopause and metabolic syndrome: A study of 498 urban women from Western India'. *Journal of Midlife Health,* 1:63-69.

Pasco, JA., GC. Nicholson, SL. Brennan and MA. Kotowicz. 2012. 'Prevalence of obesity and the relationship between the body mass index and body fat: Cross-sectional, population-based data'. *PloS One,* 7: e29580.

Pasquali, R., F. Casimirri, AM. Labate, O. Tortelli, G. Pascal, B. Anconetani, MR. Gatto, R. Flamia, M. Capelli and L. Barbara. 1994. 'Body weight, fat distribution, and the menopausal status in women: The VMH collaborative group'. *International Journal of Obesity and Related Metabolic Disorders,* 18: 614-621.

Pinto Pereira, SM., M. Ki and C. Power. 2012. 'Sedentary behaviour and biomarkers for cardiovascular disease and diabetes in mid-life: The role of television-viewing and sitting at work'. *PLoS One.* 7:e31132.

Poehlman, ET., MJ. Toth and AW. Gardner. 1995. 'Changes in energy balance and body composition at menopause: A controlled longitudinal study'. *Annals of Internal Medicine,* 123:673-675.

Prescott, J., DJ. Thompson, P. Kraft, SJ. Chanock, T. Audley, J. Brown, J. Leyland, E. Folkerd, D. Doody, SE. Hankinson, DJ. Hunter, KB. Jacobs, M. Dowsett, DG Cox, DF Easton and I. De Vivo. 2012. 'Genome-wide association study of circulating estradiol, testosterone, and sex hormone-binding globulin in postmenopausal women'. *PLoS One*, 7:e37815.

Revis, J and S. Keene. 2006. 'Type II diabetes in American women over 40: Obesity and menopause'. *The Internet Journal of Health,* 6: 1-3.

Reyes, FI., JS. Winters and C. Faiman. 1977. 'Pituitary-ovarian relationships preceding the menopause. I. A cross-sectional study of serum follice-stimulating hormone, luteinizing hormone, prolactin, estradiol, and progesterone levels'. *American Journal of Obstetrics and Gynaecology,* 129: 557-564.

Ross, R., D. Dagnone, PJH. Jones, H. Smith, A. Paddags, R. Hudson and I. Janssen. 2000. 'Reduction in obesity and related co morbid conditions after diet-induced weight loss or exercise-induced weight loss in men'. *Annals of Internal Medicine,* 133: 92-103.

Ryan, AS., BJ. Nicklas, DM. Berman and KE. Dennis. 2000. 'Dietary restriction and walking reduce fat deposition in the mid thigh in obese older women'. *American Journal of Clinical Nutrition,* 72:708-713.

Santoro, N., 1996. 'Hormonal changes in the peri-menopause'. *Clinical Consultations in Obstetrics and Gynecology,* 8: 2.

Sherman, BM., JH. West and SG. Korenman. 1976. 'The menopausal transition: Analysis of LH, FSH, estradiol, and progesterone concentrations during menstrual cycles of older women'. *The Journal of Clinical Endocrinology and Metabolism,* 42:629-636.

Som, N and S. Ray. 2012. 'Menopause-specific quality of life of urban women in West Bengal, India'. *Menopause International,* 18: 99-105.

Som, N., P. Roy and S. Ray. 2014. 'Menopause-specific quality of life of a group of urban women in West Bengal, India'. *Climacteric,* 17: 713-719.

Sommer, B., NE. Avis, P. Meyer, M. Ory, T. Madden, M. Kagawa-Singer, C. Mouton, NO. Rasor and S. Adler. 1999. 'Attitudes toward menopause and aging across ethnic / racial groups'. *Psychosomatic Medicine,* 61:868-875.

Sternfeld, B., AK. Bhat, H. Wang, T. Sharp and CP. Jr. Quesenberry. 2005. 'Menopause, physical activity, and body composition/fat distribution in midlife women'. *Medicine and Science in Sports and Exercise*, 37:1195-1202.

Syamala, TS and M Sivakami. 2005. 'Menopause: An emerging issue in India'. *Economic and Political Weekly,* 40: 4923-4930.

Toth, M.J., A. Tchernof, CK. Sites and ET. Poehlman. 2000. 'Effect of menopausal status on body composition and abdominal fat distribution'. *International Journal of Obesity and Related Metabolic Disorders,* 24: 226-231.

Traub, M.L and N. Santoro. 2010. 'Reproductive aging and its consequences for general health'. *Annals of the New York Academy of Sciences,* 1204: 179-187.

Trémollieres, FA., JM. Pouilles and CA. Ribot. 1996. 'Relative influence of age and menopause on total and regional body composition changes in postmenopausal women'. *American Journal of Obstetrics and Gynaecology,* 175: 1594-1600.

Wang, Q., C. Hassanger, P. Ravn, S. Wang and C. Christiansen. 1994. 'Total and regional body composition changes in early postmenopausal women: Age-related or menopause-related?' *American Journal of Clinical Nutrition,* 60: 843-848.

World Health Organisation. 1996. *Research on the Menopause in the 1990s.* Report of a WHO Scientific Group, WHO Technical Report Series, 866. Geneva; World Health Organisation.

Zamboni, M., F. Armellini, T. Harris, E. Turcato, R. Micciolo, IA. Bergamo-Andreis and O. Bosello. 1997. 'Effects of age on body fat distribution and cardiovascular risk factors in women'. *American Journal of Clinical Nutrition*, 66:111-115.

# Chapter - 5

# Biophysical Properties of Human Scalp Hair: A Study on the Variation of Water Absorption Among the Two Ethnic Groups from India

*—Madhumati Chatterjee and*
*Arup Ratan Bandyopadhyay*

## Introduction

Hair is a unique character found in all mammals. As hairs are unique to mammals and do not occur in other amniotes, they might arise specifically within late Triassic therapsid lineage (ancestor of modern mammals/mammalian forms) approximately 200 million years ago (Meng and Wyss, 1997). The potential selective advantages that may be responsible for the origin of a thick coat of hair, the pelage, include the heat-insulating function in primitive homeothermic mammals (Brink, 1956) and their rise to become the dominant terrestrial vertebrate (Maderson, 2003). Darwinists claim that mammals evolved hair primarily as a result of sexual selection and also for protection and heat insulation (Alibardi, 2012). Of the approximately 3,000 living mammals, only a few lack fur, such as pigs, whales, elephants, humans, mole rats, and walruses. With the exception of humans, the absence of fur is consistent with the animal's natural environment—walruses and whales are aquatic, wild pigs are fairly hairy, and mole rats are ground burrowers. Darwin was very emphatic about the importance of sexual selection in primate evolution and tried to explain human nakedness by selection (Darwin, 1871). Others have attempted to continue this line of reasoning, suggesting that as pre-humans continued to evolve into humans, the species lost most of their hair due to sexual selection (Schwartz and Rosenblum, 1981).

Hair is a proteinaceous fibre with a strongly hierarchical organisation of subunits, from the alpha-keratin chains, via intermediate filaments (IF) to the fibre. The chemistry of the different morphological compartments of hair results in exciting physical properties related to the cytoskeleton evolution particularly in IF (Popescu and Höcker, 2009). The major components of hair are alpha keratins and keratin associated proteins, each of which is encoded by multigene families (Rogers, 1998, 2000). In the hair cortex, hair keratins IFs are embedded in an in the interfilamentous matrix, which consists of hair keratin-associated proteins (KATAP, usually abbreviated as KAP; Powell *et al.*, 1991). KRTAP contains two major groups: high/ultrahigh cysteine (HS) and high glycine-tyrosine (HGT) that are considered to have originated independently, and are essential for the formation of rigid and resistant hair shafts through their extensive disulfide bond cross-linking with the abundant cysteine residues of hair keratins or hydrophobic interactions with keratins (Powell *et al.,* 1995; Rogers *et al.,* 2001, 2002, 2004, 2006, 2007; Shibuya *et al.,* 2004; Yahagi *et al.*, 2004). Contemporary study (Fujikawa *et al*, 2012) reported a predominant expression of the KRTAP/KAP2 proteins in the keratinising zone of the human hair shaft cortex and the results further enhanced the crucial roles of KRTAP/KAPs in hair shaft keratinisation in humans. The biophysical features of KRTAP/KAPs, however, have remained largely unknown. The hair keratins form the intermediate filament cytoskeleton of the trichocytes, which are linked to abundant cell-cell adhesion junctions, called desmosomes. Desmoglein 4 (DSG4) is the major desmosomal cadherin expressed in the hair shaft cortex where the hair keratins are highly expressed (Bazzi *et al.*, 2006). In the mammalian hair follicle (HF), the hair shaft is produced during the anagen or growth phase of the hair cycle which continues in repeated cycles throughout life (Hardy, 1992).

Hair as an ectodermal part of the body could also be taken into account for understanding the variation and evolutionary process.

The hair shaft consists of three concentric layers of a cuticle on the outside, a cortex, and a medulla on the inside (Jave-Suarez *et al.*, 2002). A number of studies have been conducted to identify the protein structure of mammalian hair, wool, and, especially, human hair. Keratin is a laminated complex formed by different structures, which gives the hair strength, flexibility, durability, and functionality. Hair is surprisingly strong. Cortex keratin is responsible for this propriety and its long chains are compressed to form a regular structure which, besides being strong, is flexible (Dias, 2007; Robbins, 2003). The physical proprieties of hair involve resistance to stretching, elasticity, and hydrophilic power.

Hair morphology differs dramatically between human populations and had been utilised as a criterion for population classification by a number of naturalists since the beginning of seventeenth century and still remains useful for population variation (McMichael, 2003). Not only hair form but quantitative variables of human hair from different body sites also revealed significantly differential measures (Mistry *et al.*, 2012) has opened up imperative research horizon of evolutionary biology of hair being non-invasive biological materials. But, current studies tend to emphasise the form of hair fibres independent of their racial origins (Franbourg *et al.*, 2003; De La Mettrie *et al.*, 2007; Loussouarn *et al.*, 2007; Nissimov and Das Chaudhuri, 2014). However, studies related to biophysical properties of hair extended appreciable interest regarding water swelling variability depending on the hydrophilic properties of hair Keratin (Juez and Gimier, 1983; Robbins, 1994; Velasco *et al.*, 2009) along with hair diameter and internal viscosity.

In this context, an attempt has been made in the present chapter to understand biophysical properties of hair in terms of hydrophilic nature among two discrete linguistically different ethnic groups, Munda (Austro-Asiatic speaker) and Oraon (Dravidian speaker) from Eastern India.

## Materials and Methods

The present study consist of 250 hair strands, 5 scalp hair strands each from 25 adult males from the two ethnic groups

(Munda and Oraon). Hair samples were collected by cutting as near as possible to the respective base from the occipital region. At first, the subjects were informed and after getting their consent, a hair sample was collected. All hair samples were washed using the standard technique (Sen and Das Chaudhuri, 2001) and subsequently dried at room temperature. Each washed dry hair strand was mounted on microscopic glass slides with 40 x ocular microscope (Binocular: Letiz, WETZLAR, Germany) with 0.65 objective resolutions. To assess the hydrophilic properties, each hair strands were dipped into the distilled water overnight following the standard technique (Franbourg *et al.*, 2003) with slight modification. Eventually, each hair was measured under 40 x 0.65 resolutions (Binocular: Letiz, WETZLAR, Germany). All the measurements have been taken in *mm* by micrometer fitted with the microscope. Descriptive and inferential statistics have been done in appropriate places. Cut off point was set as $p = 0.05$.

## Results and Discussion

Shaft and Medulla diameter revealed significant ($p<0.05$) difference between Munda and Oraon population in dry and wet state as well (Table 5.1 and 5.2). The result also revealed that the Munda hair strands were significantly ($p<0.05$) thicker than those of the Oraons in dry and wet condition as well. Examination of hydrophilic nature of the hair strands of the two groups revealed significant ($p<0.05$) increase in shaft and medulla diameter among the Oraons in comparison to the Mundas (Table 5.1 and 5.2). The hydrophilic nature revealed significant ($p<0.05$) swelling effect due to water absorption in shaft and medulla diameter among the Oraons hair strands, while the hair strands of the Mundas demonstrated no significant swelling effect by water absorption.

**Table 5.1: Distribution of Shaft and Medulla Diameter of the Dry Shaft Hair Strands**

| *Ethnic groups* | *Shaft diameter ( $\mu$ m) Mean ±SD* | *Medulla diameter ( $\mu$ m) Mean± SD* |
|---|---|---|
| Oraon | 32.90 ± 7.52 | 3.12 ± 0.95 |
| Munda | 34.34 ± 5.73* | 3.68 ± 1.48* |

*p<0.05

**Table 5.2: Distribution of Shaft and Medulla Diameter of the Wet Shaft Hair Strands**

| *Ethnic groups* | *Shaft diameter ( $\mu$ m) Mean ±SD* | *Medulla diameter ( $\mu$ m) Mean± SD* |
|---|---|---|
| Oraon | 27.43 ± 3.39 | 2.61 ± 0.24 |
| Munda | 32.58 ± 4.83* | 3.51 ± 1.39* |

$p<0.05$.

The result obtained in the present study for dry hair was found to be in corroboration with an earlier study (Banerjee, 1963). The hair Keratin has special affinity for water (Velasco *et al.*, 2009) and the absorption depends on the air relative humidity rate and greatly interferes on all the proprieties of the hair, as stretching ability, diameter and internal viscosity of the fibres (Juez and Gimier, 1983; Robbins, 1994; Velasco *et al.*, 2009). This absorptive and swelling phenomenon in the hair fibre may be of great application in hair study because it allows a favoured or delayed penetration of certain organic molecules (Juez and Gimier, 1983; Robbins, 1994; Feughelman, 1997; Ishii, 1997). Since the publication of Sarkar (1954) variations in morphological traits between Mundari speakers and Dravidian speakers have been corroborated by Coon (1966). Subsequently, Anthropometry and Body Composition (Chatterjee, 2009) and molecular marker (Kivisild *et al.,* 2003) studies also demonstrated imperative variation between these two linguistic groups. In this context, the present study also revealed variation in biophysical properties of the scalp hair in terms of hydrophilic nature between the two discrete linguistically variable ethnic groups. Nevertheless, the present study envisaged new dimension in hair research in biophysical properties of human scalp hair.

## Salutation

Financial supports have been obtained from UGC fellowship (RFSMS) and BI (8 and 9), University of Calcutta. Thanks are due to the participants of the present study.

## References

Alibardi, L., 2012. 'Perspectives on hair evolution based on some comparative studies on vertebrate cornification'. *Journal of Experimental Zoology Part B: Molecular and Developmental Evolution*. 318:325-43.

Banerjee, AR, 1963. 'Variation in the Medullary structure of human head hair'. *Proceedings National institute of Science* India. 29 B: 306-316.

Bazzi, H., A. Getz, MG. Mahoney, A. Ishida Yamamoto, L. Langbein, JK. Wahl and AM. Christiano. 2006. 'Desmoglein 4 is expressed in highly differentiated keratinocytes and trichocytes in human epidermis and hair follicle'. *Differentiation.* 74: 129-140.

Brink, AS., 1956. 'Speculations on some advanced mammalian characteristics in the higher mammal like reptiles'. *Palaeontologia Africana.* 4: 77-96.

Chatterjee, D., 2009. *Anthropometry and Body Composition in Mundari and Dravidian Speaking Populations of India.* Unpublished PhD thesis. University of Calcutta.

Coon, CS., 1966. *The Living Races of Man.* London; Jonathon Cape.

Darwin, C., 1871. *The Descent of Man, and Selection in Relation to Sex*, London: John Murrey.

De La Mettrie, R., D Saint–Léger, G. Loussouarn, A. Garcel, C. Porter and A. Langaney. 2007. 'Shape variability and classification of human hair: A worldwide approach'. *Human Biology.* 79, 265-281.

Dias, TCS.; AR. Baby; TM. Kaneko and MVR Velasc, 2007. 'Relaxing/ straightening of Afro-ethnic hair: Historical overview'. *Journal of Cosmetic Dermatology* 6: 2-5.

Feughelman, M., 1997. 'Morphology and properties of hair'. In: DH. Johnson (Ed.): *Hair and Hair Care.* New York; Marcel Dekker, 2nd Edn. pp.1-32.

Franbourg, A., P. Hallegot, F. Baltenneck, C. Toutain and F. Leroy, 2003. 'Current research on ethnic hair'. *Journal of American Academy of Dermatology* 48:S115-S119.

Fujikawa, H., A. Fujimoto, M. Farooq, M. Ito and Y. Shimomura, 2012. 'Characterisation of the human hair keratin-associated protein 2 (KRTAP/ KAP2) gene family'. *Journal of Investigative Dermatology.* 132:1806-1813.

Hardy, MH 1992. 'The secret life of the hair follicle'. *Trends in Genetics.* 8: 55-61.

Ishii, M., 1997. 'Objective and instrumental methods for evaluation of hair care product efficacy and substantiation claims'. In DH. Johnson (Ed.): *Hair and Hair Care.* New York; Marcel Dekker. pp. 261-295.

Jave-Suarez, LF., H. Winter, L. Langbein, MA Rogers and J. Schweizer. 2002. 'HOXC13 is involved in the regulation of human hair keratin gene expression'. *Journal of Biological Chemistry.* 277:3718-26.

Juez, JL and L. Gimier, 1983. *Ciencia Cosmética : Sociedad Española de Química Terapéutica.* pp. 98-119. 2nd Ed. Madrid.

Kivisild, T., S. Rootsi, M. Metspalu, S. Mastana, K. Kaldma, J. Parik, E. Metspalu, M. Adojaan, HV. Tolk, V. Stepanov , M. Gölge, E. Usanga, SS. Papiha, C. Cinnioðlu, R. King, L. Cavalli-Sforza, PA.Underhill and R.Villems. 2003. 'The genetic heritage of the earliest settlers persists both in Indian tribal and caste populations'. *American Journal of Human Genetics* 72: 313-332.

Loussouarn, G., A. Garcel, I. Lozano, C. Collaudin, C. Porter, S. Panhard, D. Saint-L′eger and R. De La Mettrie, 2007. 'Worldwide diversity of hair curliness: A new method of assessment'. *International Journal of Dermatology.* 46: 2-6.

Maderson, PFA., 2003. 'Mammalian skin evolution: A re-evaluation'. *Experimental Dermatoglyphics.* 12:233-236.

McMichael, AJ., 2003. 'Ethnic hair update: Past and present'. *Journal American Academic Dermatology*. 48: S127-133.

Meng, J and AR. Wyss, 1997. 'Multi-tuberculate and other mammal hair recovered from Palaeogene excreta'. *Nature*. 20:712-714.

Mistry, Sanchita, Madhumati Chatterjee, Jyoti Ratan Ghosh, NK. Chakrabarti and Arup R. Bandyopadhyay. 2011. 'Variations of scalp, pubic and axial hair'. *Anthropologisher Angeizer.* 69: 117-125.

Nissimov, JN and AB. Das Chaudhuri, 2014. 'Hair curvature: A natural dialectic and review'. *Biological Reviews* 89: 723-766.

Popescu, C and H. Höcker, 2009. 'Cytomechanics of hair basics of the mechanical stability'. *International Review of Cell Molecular Biology*. (Chapter 4):277:137-156.

Powell, BC., A. Nesci and GE. Rogers. 1991. 'Regulation of keratin gene expression in hair follicle differentiation'. *Annals of the New York Academy of Sciences*, 642:1-20.

Powell, BC and GE. Rogers, 1997. 'The role of keratin proteins and their genes in the growth, structure and properties of hair'. In P. Jolles, H. Zahn, H. Höcker (Eds): *Formation and Structure of Human Hair.* Basel; Birkhäuser, pp. 59-148.

Powell, BC., J. Arthur and A. Nesci, 1995. 'Characterisation of a gene encoding a cysteine-rich keratin associated protein synthesized late in rabbit hair follicle differentiation'. *Differentiation*. 58:227-232.

Robbins, C., 2003. 'The cell membrane complex: three related but different cellular cohesion components of mammalian hair fibres'. *Journal of Cosmetic Science.* 60:437-465.

Robbins, CR., 1994. *Chemical and Physical Behaviour of Human Hair*. New York; Springer 3rd Ed. pp. 391.

Rogers, MA., L. Langbein, S. Praetzel-Wunder, H. Winter and J. Schweizer, 2006. 'Human hair keratin-associated proteins (KAPs)'. *International Review of Cytology*. 251:209-223.

Rogers, MA., L. Langbein, H. Winter, I. Beckmann, S. Praetzel and J. Schweizer, 2004. 'Hair keratin associated proteins: Characterisation of a second high sulphur KAP gene domain on human chromosome 21'. *Journal of Investigative Dermatology*. 122:147-158.

Rogers, MA., L. Langbein, H. Winter, C. Ehmann, S. Praetzel and J. Schweizer, 2002. 'Characterisation of a first domain of human high glycine-tyrosine and high sulphur keratin associated protein (KAP) genes on chromosome 21q22'. *Journal of Biological Chemistry*. 277:48993-49002.

Rogers, MA., L. Langbein, H. Winter, C. Ehmann, S. Praetzel, B. Korn, and J. Schweizer, 2001. 'Characterisation of a cluster of human high/ultrahigh sulphur keratin-associated protein genes embedded in the type I keratin gene domain on chromosome 17q12-21'. *Journal of Biological Chemistry*. 276:19440-19451.

Rogers, MA., H.Winter, L. Langbein, C. Wolf and J. Schweizer, 2000. 'Characterisation of a 300 kbp region of human DNA containing the type II hair keratin gene domain'. *Journal of Investigative Dermatology*. 114:464-472.

Rogers, MA., H. Winter, L. Langbein, A. Wollschlager, S. Praetzel-Wunder, LF. Jave-Suarez and J. Schweizer, 2007. 'Characterisation of human KAP24. 1, a cuticular hair keratin-associated protein with unusual amino-acid composition and repeat structure'. *Journal of Investigative Dermatology*. 127:1197-1204.

Rogers, MA., H. Winter, C. Wolf, M. Heck and J. Schweizer, 1998. 'Characterisation of a 190-kilo base pair domain of human type I hair keratin genes'. *Journal of Biological Chemistry*. 273:26683-26691.

Sarkar, SS., 1954. *The Aboriginal Races of India*. Calcutta; Book Land Ltd.

Schwartz, GG and LA. Rosenblum, 1981. 'Allometry of primate hair density and the evolution of human hairlessness'. *American Journal of Physiology Anthropology*. 55: 9-12.

Sen, J and AB Das Chaudhuri, 2001. 'Brief communication: Choice of washing method of hair samples for trace element analysis in environmental studies'. *American Journal of Physiology Anthropology*.115:289-291.

Shibuya, K., I. Obayashi, S. Asakawa, S. Minoshima, J. Kudoh and N. Shimizu, 2004. 'A cluster of 21 keratin-associated protein genes within introns of another gene on human chromosome 21q22. 3'. *Genomics*. 83:679-693.

Velasco, MVR., Tania Cristina de Sá Dias, Zanardi de Freitas Anderson, Vieira Junior Nilson Dias, Aparecida Sales de Oliveira Pinto Claudinéia, Mary Kaneko Telma and Baby André Rolim. 2009. 'Hair fibre characteristics and methods to evaluate hair physical and mechanical properties'. *Brazilian Journal of Pharmaceutical Sciences*. 45:153-162.

Yahagi, S., K. Shibuya, I. Obayashi, H. Masaki, Y. Kurata, J. Kudoh and N. Shimizu, 2004. 'Identification of two novel clusters of ultrahigh-sulphur keratin-associated protein genes on human chromosome 11'. *Biochemical and Biophysical Research Communications*. 318:655-664.

# Chapter - 6

# Child Health in North East India

—*Susmita Bharati, Manoranjan Pal*
*and Premananda Bharati*

## Introduction

Undernutrition is a major public health problem and may be regarded as a principal cause of ill-health and morbidity. Undernutrition, especially during childhood, has a prolonged effect in one's life. The effect of undernutrition may be felt even during middle age (Nandy *et al.*, 2005; WHO, 2002). Chronic undernutrition reduces physical capacity (James, 1994), increases mortality (Harris *et al.,* 1993) and morbidity (Khongsdier, 2002). Though in recent years, many developing countries are experiencing rapid economic changes and nutritional transition. But in India, still more or less fifty per cent under-five children are suffering from under nutrition (IIPS, 2007)) and the major cause of undernutrition is poverty. Besides poverty, child's undernutrition is also influenced by several socio-economic and socio-demographic variation like gender, age, parent's education, occupation and economic condition of the belongings (Som *et al.*, 2006; Mondal *et al.*, 2010; Sen *et al.*, 2012; Cheah *et al.,* 2010 and Roy, 2000).

Anaemia among the children is very common throughout India but a national level study on it is very scanty. A recent study (Bharati *et al.,* 2015) shows that in India, 64.7 per cent of children aged 6-59 months are affected by various degrees of anaemia and it is very predominant during 6 - 23 months. When seen regionally, the north-east zone can boast of having the lowest percentage of children suffering from anaemia, still, it is not negligible (55.6 per cent).

The highest affected zone is the central zone (71.9 per cent). It is known that all cases anaemia is not due to iron deficiency. Lack of other nutrients like Vitamin C, A and folic acid, hereditary disorders, Malaria and infections by helminths are also responsible for causing anaemia. Very recently, it is known that cow's milk may cause intestinal blood loss in non-anaemic infants and results an iron deficiency. Thus, it is necessary to know about the biological causes as well as the degrees of socio-economic development in different regions of India.

Immunisation is the most effective way to tackle various diseases. Lack of immunisation may lead to high degree of mortality and morbidity among children. It is known that measles in a healthy child has a negligible effect, but it increases mortality 400 times greater in an undernourished population. And in India, Universal Immunisation Programme (UIP) for six vaccine-preventable diseases (tuberculosis, diphtheria, and whooping cough, tetanus, polio and measles) were launched in 1985 with the objective to reduce morbidity, mortality and disabilities due to these diseases. It was also aimed that by 1990 all eligible children would be immunised.

Prevalence of undernutrition and morbidity and status of immunisation is interrelated. So these three aspects need to be studied together in order to promote good health among the children. Implementation of immunisation programmes from region to region varies because these are dependent on various socio-economic and socio-demographic factors. So are the prevalence of undernutrition and morbidity. Here our focus of the study is to know the condition of undernutrition, immunisation and morbidity among the pre-school children in North East India which consists of eight different states namely, Arunachal Pradesh, Assam, Manipur, Meghalaya, Mizoram, Nagaland, Sikkim and Tripura. It is accounted for seven to nine per cent of the total land space of India and is characterised by low capital formation, inadequate infrastructural facilities, geographic isolation and communication bottleneck. Besides this, except Assam, and Tripura, the rest six states are predominated by tribal population. In such a scenario our major objectives of the present study are (i) to assess the health through nutritional status; (ii) to assess the health through morbidity pattern; (iii) to assess the immunisation status and lastly and (iv) to assess the most effective socio-economic factor which help children reduce undernutrition, morbidity and increase the status of immunisation.

## Methodology

For this study, we have used the National Family Health Survey (NFHS–III) data conducted by the International Institute for Population Sciences (IIPS), Mumbai, in 2005-06. They collected data from 29 states in India and the population frame was based on 2001 census. The data is cross-sectional and unit-level data. As our focused area of study is North East India, so we have considered here only the data set of North East India. The sample size consists of 8,412 children of 0-3 years of both sexes from eight states in North East India. For making comparison with total India the sample sizes consisting of 43,737 individuals have been considered. For assessing the nutritional status of children, this survey collected data on weight and height of the children as well as computed 'Z' scores of undernutrition through weight for age and height for age indices.

Z-score value '-2' was used as a cut-off point for prevalence estimation (WHO, 2006). Z-score is defined as the deviation of the value observed for an individual from the median of the reference population, divided by the standard deviation (SD) of the reference population i.e.

$$\text{Z-score} = \frac{\text{(observed value) - (median of the reference population)}}{\text{SD of the reference population}}$$

The classifications of Z-score (followed by NCHS/WHO) are "below normal" ($\leq$ -2), "normal" (-2 to $\leq$ + 2) and "above average" (>+ 2).

An infant is considered as fully vaccinated if the infant has taken one dose for BCG, three doses for DPT and Polio and a single dose of measles. Data on immunisation status are verified from vaccination cards and in case, where a vaccination card was not available or a vaccination was not recorded on the card, the mother's recall of vaccination was accepted.

For assessing three morbidity statuses of infants like diarrhoea, fever and cough, mother of children were asked if their children were suffering from those diseases during the two weeks preceding the survey by recall method. It should be noted that the morbidity data collected on the basis of mother's perceptions of illness without validation by medical personnel.

For socio-economic data, places of residence are taken as "rural" and "urban". Sex of the child is also considered. Ethnicity-wise two groups have been taken as scheduled tribes and 'others'. Religions were considered on the basis of four basic religions but grouped into three namely, Hindu and Muslims, Christian and Others. Mother's educational status are grouped into three categories such as illiterate (those who can neither read nor write) and primary (literate up to class IV standard), secondary (class V to class X standard) and the last group is higher (i.e. higher secondary, graduate or post-graduate etc). Wealth index is a measure of the economic status of the household (Rutstein, 1999). Though it is an indicator of the level of the wealth in the household, it is consistent with expenditure and income measures. It is based on 33 household assets and housing characteristics like household electrification, type of windows, sources of drinking water, types of toilet facility, flooring, roofing, cooking fuel and house ownership, material of exterior walls, number of household members per sleeping room, ownership of a bank or post-office account, ownership of a mattress, a pressure cooker, a chair, a cot/bed, a table, an electric fan, a radio/ transistor, a black and white television, a colour television, a sewing machine, a mobile telephone, and any other telephone, a computer, a refrigerator, a watch or clock, a bicycle, a motorcycle or scooter, an animal-drawn cart, a car, a water pump, a thresher, and a tractor. Here each household asset was assigned a weight generated through principal component analysis and the resulting score was standardised in relation to a normal distribution and each household was assigned a score for each asset and the scores were summed for each household and individuals were ranked according to the score of the household and the scores were divided into five quintile groups starting from lower strata to higher strata like poorest, poorer, medium, richer and richest.

To see the relative and effective intervention, the binary variables for under-nutrition, immunisation status and morbidity were separately regressed on socio-economic variables using categorical logistic regression analysis. For undernutrition, children, whose Z-scores are below–2, are coded as '1' and those with Z-scores–2 or higher are coded as '0'. For immunisation status, not-immunised has taken as '1' and immunised is coded as '0'. For morbidity status, morbidity was considered as '1' and others are coded as '0'. An estimated odd ratio of '1' indicates that the nature of dependent variable is not different from the reference category. If the estimated odd ratio is >1, the probability of becoming affected is more in this category compared to the reference category and if it is <1, then it is just opposite to that of >1 case.

## Results

Table 6.1 describes the health, immunisation and morbidity status among 0-3 year children in India and North East India with its eight states. In India, the prevalence of underweight among 0-3 year children is 40.0 per cent, while in North East India, it is 30.6 per cent. State wise variation in North East India is also prominent. The highest percentage is found in Tripura (40.7 per cent) while the lowest percentage is found in Sikkim (21.5 per cent). Percentage of stunted children is 36.3 in India. In North East India, it is 32.5 and state-wise, the highest percentage is found in Assam and Meghalaya (37.5 per cent) and the lowest percentage (28.6 per cent) is found in Manipur. Regarding anaemia, among Indian children, it is 64.7 per cent while in North East India, it is 55.5 per cent. While looking at state-wise picture, the highest is found in Assam (68.3 per cent) and the lowest is found in Manipur (41.5 per cent). Percentage of Immunised children of age 0-3 years is 41.7 per cent in India, whereas, North East India, it is only 32.7 per cent. In India, percentage of children who have been immunised against BCG, DPT triple doses, Polio triple doses, Measles and by all four vaccinations are in the ratio 76.8:55.4:72.9: 53.7:41.7, while in North East India, the same is found as 65.8:46.9:61.5:41.3:32.7. The highest and the lowest percentages of different immunised states are found to be in Sikkim and Arunachal Pradesh respectively. Morbidity status like occurrences of diarrhoea, fever and cough among children in India and North East India are more or less same though it varies state-wise. The highest percentage of diarrhoea occurs in Sikkim (15.7 per cent) while lowest percentage of diarrhoea, fever and cough occur in Meghalaya (5.9 per cent, 6.9 per cent and 7.2 per cent respectively). The highest percentages of a cough (29.0 per cent) and fever (32.6 per cent) occur among the children of Tripura.

Table 6.2 describes the existing condition of different socio-economic variables in India, North East India and its different states as a regulator of health conditions of the children. In India, the rural-urban ratio is 63.1:36.9, while in North East India, it is 67.8:32.2 though there exists a great divergence among all the states of North East India. The gap between rural and urban is the highest in Assam followed by Tripura and the lowest gap is in Mizoram, followed by Nagaland. On the basis of the concentration of tribal and non-tribal populations, the ratio is 16.2:83.8 in India, whereas it is 53.0: 47.0 in North East India. The highest concentration of non-tribal children (91.1 per cent) is noticed in Assam. In Mizoram, it is just the opposite (1.5 per cent). In other words, Mizoram has the highest concentration of tribal children. There is a great difference between India and North East India in respect of religion. In India, religious concentration of 'Hindu and Muslim', 'Christian' and 'Others' are in the ratio 85.1: 10.1: 4.8 respectively, but in North East India, there are about equal proportions of 'Hindu and Muslim' and 'Christian', the rest is 'others' (9.4 per cent). The highest percentage of Hindu and Muslim group is present in Tripura, followed by Assam (96.2 per cent: 82.8 per cent) respectively and concentration of Christians is maximum in Mizoram (93.3 per cent), then it is followed by Nagaland (81.5 per cent). The proportions of illiterate or primary educated children in North East India are less than that of all India level (49.0:54.8). But higher educated mothers are comparatively more in North East India (51.0:45.2). In statewide distribution, the highest illiterate mothers are found in Arunachal Pradesh (70.4 per cent) and the lowest is in Mizoram (31.6 per cent). The percentage of secondary educated mothers is the highest in Mizoram (62.0 per cent). The proportion of poor households in terms of wealth index in North East India (34.3 per cent) is slightly less but very close to that of All India level

**Table 6.1: Health and Morbidity Status of 0-3 year Children in North East India and in India**

| *Zone/ states* | *N* | *Nutritional status* | | | *Immunisation status* | | | | | *Morbidity status* | | |
|---|---|---|---|---|---|---|---|---|---|---|---|---|
| | | *Under-Weight* | *Stunted* | *Anaemia* | *BCG* | *DPT3* | *Polio3* | *Measles* | *All Vaccin-ated* | *Diarrhoea* | *Fever* | *Cough* |
| North East | 8412 | 30.6(2574) | 32.5(2735) | 55.5(3138) | 65.8(5538) | 46.9(3947) | 61.5(5171) | 41.3(3471) | 32.7(2732) | 9.5(797) | 15.4(1296) | 17.8(1499) |
| Arunachal Pradesh | 770 | 34.7(267) | 37.1(286) | 58.1(398) | 47.5(365) | 31.0(238) | 47.7(366) | 25.4(195) | 17.9(137) | 15.5(119) | 21.1(162) | 24.1(185) |
| Assam | 1293 | 37.9(490) | 37.5(485) | 68.3(753) | 57.4(742) | 38.0(491) | 56.7(429) | 30.9(399) | 24.9(320) | 8.1(105) | 13.6(176) | 18.5(239) |
| Manipur | 1668 | 25.7(429) | 28.6(478) | 41.5(357) | 77.1(1287) | 56.1(936) | 71.9(1200) | 47.0(778) | 40.2(665) | 10.5(175) | 13.6(227) | 18.7(312) |
| Meghalaya | 880 | 38.6(340) | 37.5(330) | 64.0(455) | 67.3(592) | 45.6(400) | 58.0(509) | 42.3(369) | 33.7(293) | 5.9(52) | 6.9(61) | 7.2(63) |
| Mizoram | 778 | 24.9(194) | 33.0(257) | 44.7(319) | 86.6(674) | 63.8(496) | 59.9(464) | 64.4(501) | 40.1(311) | 10.9(85) | 17.2(134) | 14.1(110) |
| Nagaland | 1868 | 26.4(494) | 29.9(559) | — | 47.9(895) | 31.8(594) | 56.0(1044) | 27.3(510) | 19.9(371) | 6.7(126) | 13.3(249) | 14.6(273) |
| Sikkim | 573 | 21.5(123) | 29.0(166) | 59.3(293) | 95.8(549) | 80.6(462) | 84.6(485) | 74.3(426) | 65.1(373) | 15.7(90) | 20.6(118) | 22.2(127) |
| Tripura | 582 | 40.7(237) | 29.9(174) | 63.4(325) | 74.6(434) | 56.8(330) | 64.4(374) | 50.4(293) | 45.3(262) | 7.7(45) | 29.0(169) | 32.6(190) |
| India | 43737 | 40.0(17494) | 36.3(15878) | 64.7(23145) | 76.8(33590) | 55.4(24207) | 72.9(31806) | 53.7(23410) | 41.7(18128) | 9.4(4123) | 15.2(6642) | 18.2(7963) |

**Table 6.2: Distribution of Socio-economic Groups by States in North East India**

| *Zone/states* | *Existing condition of different Socio-economic variables (Per cent)* | | | | | | | | | | | | |
|---|---|---|---|---|---|---|---|---|---|---|---|---|---|
| | *Place* | | *Ethnicity* | | *Religion* | | | *Mother's educational status* | | | *Wealth Index of the family* | | |
| | *Urban* | *Rural* | *ST* | *Others* | *Hindu and Muslim* | *Christians* | *Others* | *Illiterate-Primary* | *Sec* | *High* | *Poor* | *Middle* | *Rich* |
| North East | 32.2 | 67.8 | 53.0 | 47.0 | 46.5 | 44.1 | 9.4 | 49.0 | 44.4 | 6.6 | 34.3 | 27.7 | 38.0 |
| Arunachal Pradesh | 28.2 | 71.8 | 73.3 | 26.7 | 34.0 | 30.9 | 35.1 | 70.4 | 27.0 | 2.6 | 52.6 | 21.2 | 26.2 |
| Assam | 19.9 | 80.1 | 8.9 | 91.1 | 92.8 | 6.7 | 0.5 | 56.8 | 39.4 | 3.8 | 58.2 | 20.6 | 21.3 |
| Manipur | 37.6 | 62.4 | 26.1 | 73.9 | 62.9 | 26.6 | 10.5 | 35.9 | 49.6 | 14.5 | 21.7 | 32.8 | 45.5 |
| Meghalaya | 26.7 | 73.3 | 89.2 | 10.8 | 12.4 | 73.0 | 14.7 | 61.8 | 33.8 | 4.4 | 38.2 | 31.2 | 30.6 |
| Mizoram | 43.7 | 56.3 | 98.5 | 1.5 | 1.9 | 93.3 | 4.8 | 31.6 | 62.0 | 6.4 | 12.6 | 25.7 | 61.7 |
| Nagaland | 39.3 | 60.7 | 81.4 | 18.6 | 18.4 | 81.5 | 0.2 | 45.6 | 49.5 | 5.0 | 33.4 | 27.6 | 39.1 |
| Sikkim | 30.5 | 69.5 | 27.9 | 72.1 | 64.7 | 8.9 | 26.4 | 52.2 | 42.1 | 5.8 | 12.7 | 25.3 | 62.0 |
| Tripura | 21.0 | 79.0 | 19.1 | 80.9 | 96.2 | 0.5 | 3.3 | 52.6 | 43.1 | 4.3 | 40.9 | 37.3 | 21.8 |
| India | 36.9 | 63.1 | 16.2 | 83.8 | 85.1 | 10.1 | 4.8 | 54.8 | 37.6 | 7.6 | 36.2 | 20.9 | 43.0 |

(36.2 per cent). The highest percentage of poor is noticed in Assam (58.2 per cent) and the highest percentage of rich families is noticed in Sikkim (62.0 per cent).

The relationship between socio-economy with various aspects of the health status of 0-3 year children in North East India is given in Table 6.3. Percentages of underweight, stunted and anaemic children are found to be more among poor, non-ST or non-Christian households and in rural areas. Children of less-educated mothers are prominently more affected compared to children of higher educated mothers. In the case of the status of immunisation, the picture is expectedly opposite in natures except for Christian community, where the percentage of immunised children is low compared to Hindu, Muslim and Other communities. Surprisingly, the picture on the morbidity status, i.e., the prevalence of diarrhoea, fever and cough, are not so conspicuously different among the socio-economic groups. Mother's education and wealth index of households do not have much effect on the morbidity status. Among urban children, it is found to be more. It is however seen that Christian children are less affected.

The joint effects of the socio-economic variables on under-nutrition, immunisation and morbidity status of children in North East India are seen by carrying out the Categorical Logistic Regressions (Table 6.4). It is seen that anaemia among non-ST children are significantly less, whereas ethnicity do not have much influence on the status of underweight or stunted children. Gender and area of residence do not have much effect on any of the status of under-nutrition, and immunisation and morbidity status of children, except for place of residence on morbidity status. Children in urban areas are more likely to suffer from diarrhoea, fever and cough. In fact, the risk of diarrhoea, fever and cough among the children cannot be explained through the socio-economic factors considered in this chapter. Mother's education and wealth index have pronounced effect on children's immunisation and health status. Children of higher educated mothers or of high wealth index families are less likely to be undernourished or morbid and more likely to be immunised. Religion has highly significant effect only on the immunisation status, non-ST

**Table 6.3: Distribution of Health and Morbidity Status of 0-3 year children by Socio-economic Groups in North East India**

| *Socio-economic variables* | *N* | *Percentage of under nutrition, immunisation and morbidity status in relation to different socio-economic variables* | | | | | | | | | | |
|---|---|---|---|---|---|---|---|---|---|---|---|---|
| | | *Under-Weight* | *Stunted* | *Anaemia* | *BCG* | *DPT3* | *Polio3* | *Measles* | *All Vaccin-ated* | *Diarrhoea* | *Fever* | *Cough* |
| **Gender** | | | | | | | | | | | | |
| Boys | 4205 | 29.8 | 32.6 | 56.4 | 66.5 | 47.8 | 61.6 | 42.4 | 33.2 | 9.9 | 14.8 | 16.9 |
| Girls | 4208 | 31.4 | 32.4 | 54.6 | 65.2 | 46.1 | 61.6 | 40.3 | 32.2 | 9.1 | 16.0 | 18.7 |
| **Place** | | | | | | | | | | | | |
| Rural | 5705 | 33.8 | 35.4 | 57.8 | 60.8 | 42.0 | 57.7 | 36.9 | 28.7 | 9.0 | 14.3 | 16.7 |
| Urban | 2707 | 23.9 | 26.4 | 50.1 | 76.4 | 57.4 | 69.8 | 50.9 | 41.1 | 10.5 | 17.7 | 20.1 |
| **Ethnicity** | | | | | | | | | | | | |
| ST | 4433 | 28.6 | 28.6 | 54.9 | 61.2 | 42.0 | 57.2 | 38.8 | 28.3 | 9.1 | 13.8 | 14.3 |
| Others | 3928 | 32.8 | 32.8 | 56.0 | 71.1 | 52.5 | 66.6 | 44.3 | 37.6 | 9.9 | 17.3 | 21.8 |
| **Religion** | | | | | | | | | | | | |
| Hindu and Muslim | 3887 | 33.0 | 31.1 | 58.0 | 69.6 | 51.0 | 65.2 | 43.5 | 36.7 | 9.7 | 17.5 | 21.4 |
| **Christians** | 3692 | 28.2 | 33.5 | 50.8 | 60.5 | 41.5 | 57.3 | 38.1 | 27.2 | 8.5 | 13.3 | 14.2 |
| Others | 786 | 30.2 | 34.8 | 57.8 | 72.1 | 52.7 | 64.2 | 46.2 | 38.0 | 12.5 | 15.2 | 17.0 |
| **Mother's education** | | | | | | | | | | | | |
| Illiterate and primary | 4103 | 38.0 | 39.3 | 60.5 | 52.5 | 33.7 | 52.6 | 29.2 | 22.3 | 9.2 | 15.5 | 17.1 |
| Secondary | 3715 | 24.9 | 27.7 | 51.7 | 76.4 | 57.4 | 69.0 | 50.8 | 40.7 | 9.8 | 16.2 | 18.9 |
| Higher | 546 | 13.6 | 13.6 | 42.6 | 93.8 | 75.7 | 78.9 | 68.6 | 56.0 | 9.3 | 9.8 | 16.0 |
| **Wealth Index** | | | | | | | | | | | | |
| Poor | 2885 | 41.2 | 41.7 | 65.8 | 42.7 | 24.7 | 45.6 | 20.9 | 15.6 | 9.2 | 14.7 | 16.9 |
| Middle | 2329 | 33.2 | 35.6 | 53.2 | 68.7 | 48.6 | 64.1 | 43.4 | 33.8 | 9.6 | 16.7 | 18.2 |
| High | 3196 | 19.1 | 22.0 | 47.8 | 84.6 | 65.9 | 74.3 | 58.4 | 47.3 | 9.6 | 15.0 | 18.4 |

**Table 6.4: Categorical Logistic Regression between Socio-economic Variables and Health and Morbidity Status of 0-3 year Children in North East India**

| *Socio-economic variables* | *Percentage of morbidity status in relation to different socio-economic variables* | | | | | | | | | | |
|---|---|---|---|---|---|---|---|---|---|---|---|
| | *Under-Weight* | *Stunted* | *Anaemia* | *BCG* | *DPT3* | *Polio3* | *Measles* | *All Vaccin-ated* | *Diarrhoea* | *Fever* | *Cough* |
| **Gender** | | | | | | | | | | | |
| Boys | 1.00 | 1.00 | 1.00 | 1.00 | 1.00 | 1.00 | 1.00 | 1.00 | 1.00 | 1.00 | 1.00 |
| Girls | 0.932 | 1.023 | 1.085 | 1.033 | 1.050 | 0.977 | 1.072 | 0.927 | 1.024 | 0.917 | 0.878 |
| **Place** | | | | | | | | | | | |
| Rural | 1.00 | 1.00 | 1.00 | 1.00 | 1.00 | 1.00 | 1.00 | 1.00 | 1.00 | 1.00 | 1.00 |
| Urban | 0.942 | 1.111 | 0.957 | 0.842** | 0.876* | 0.987 | 0.909 | 0.927 | 1.232 | 1.361** | 1.199**** |
| **Ethnicity** | | | | | | | | | | | |
| ST® | 1.00 | 1.00 | 1.00 | 1.00 | 1.00 | 1.00 | 1.00 | 1.00 | 1.00 | 1.00 | 1.00 |
| Others | 1.225* | 1.025 | 0.709** | 1.394** | 1.346** | 1.442** | 1.026 | 1.155 | 1.006 | 1.019 | 1.468** |
| **Religion** | | | | | | | | | | | |
| Hindu and Muslim® | 1.00 | 1.00 | 1.00 | 1.00 | 1.00 | 1.00 | 1.00 | 1.00 | 1.00 | 1.00 | 1.00 |
| Christians | 0.955 | 1.161 | 0.558** | 0.763** | 0.774** | 0.922 | 0.750** | 0.663 | 0.878 | 0.738** | 0.846 |
| Others | 0.965 | 1.186 | 0.799* | 1.436** | 1.316** | 1.218* | 1.166 | 1.180 | 1.365 | 0.876 | 0.969 |
| **Mother's education** | | | | | | | | | | | |
| Illiterate and primary® | 1.00 | 1.00 | 1.00 | 1.00 | 1.00 | 1.00 | 1.00 | 1.00 | 1.00 | 1.00 | 1.00 |
| Secondary | 0.742** | 0.768** | 0.896 | 1.742** | 1.644** | 1.379** | 1.599** | 1.575** | 1.087 | 1.018 | 1.087 |
| Higher | 0.456** | 0.404** | 0.695** | 4.837** | 2.548** | 1.671** | 2.453** | 2.110** | 0.963 | 0.523** | 0.783* |
| **Wealth Index** | | | | | | | | | | | |
| Poor® | 1.00 | 1.00 | 1.00 | 1.00 | 1.00 | 1.00 | 1.00 | 1.00 | 1.00 | 1.00 | 1.00 |
| Middle | 0.788** | 0.827** | 0.627** | 2.705** | 2.660** | 1.998** | 2.649** | 2.551** | 0.991 | 1.141 | 1.068 |
| High | 0.441** | 0.493** | 0.550** | 5.579** | 4.667** | 2.859** | 4.097** | 3.877** | 0.920 | 0.974 | 1.024 |

® Reference category; <0.01: 1 % level ** and 0 .01 - 0.05 : 5 % level *

children being more immunised especially for BCG, DPT3 and Polio3. Christian children are least affected by anaemia.

## Discussion

The immunisation status of pre-school children is a major public health issue in India. We, however, focus our study in North East India only; and along with immunisation status; we also investigate health and morbidity status of pre-school children, because they are interrelated. Prevalence of underweight and stunted among 0-3 year children in North East India is 30.6 per cent and 32.8 per cent respectively. When seen state wise, high percentages of underweight children are noticed in Tripura (40.7 per cent), Meghalaya (38.6 per cent) and Assam (37.9 per cent). The low percentages are found in Sikkim (21.5 per cent) and Manipur (25.7 per cent) respectively. Meghalaya and Assam have the same highest percentage of stunted children (37.5 per cent). Regarding anaemia, the highest percentage is found in Assam (68.3 per cent) and the lowest is found in Manipur (41.5 per cent). The overall status of different immunisations is very high in Sikkim which is followed by Mizoram and Manipur. Arunachal Pradesh and Nagaland have very low immunisation status. So far as morbidity is concerned, Meghalaya has uniformly the least percentages of children affected by diarrhoea, fever and cough. The most affected state is Tripura followed by Sikkim and Arunachal Pradesh.

While comparing the status of health among the children of North East India and all India, it is seen that North East India is in a better position compared to India as a whole. It is very surprising note that though the immunisation services in India are being offered free of cost via public health facilities, yet nearly 45 per cent Indian children are deprived of the recommended vaccination (IIPS, 2010).

Regarding the relationship between socio-economy with various aspects of health status, it is seen that the proportion of underweight, stunted and anaemic children are more in rural areas, non-ST ethnic groups, and non-Christian families, families with illiterate or less literate mothers and with poor wealth index. This may be due to the effect of immunisation, since the status of immunisation has a reverse relation, compared to the status of health, with these socio-economic groups. Thus, more is the status of immunisation; less is the percentage of undernourished children. Also, it is unanimously seen through logistic regression that mother's education and family wealth condition is very much related with less undernutrition and more immunisation.

Since undernutrition is a function of both food deprivation and disease, which cause morbidity and mortality; immunisation is an important preventive measure to bring good health.

The study reveals that, unlike India, under-nutrition among 0-3 year children is not related to gender differences in North East India (Bharati *et al.,* 2008). The study also reveals that undernutrition in North East India is less than that of India as a whole. One of the reasons, we guess, is that the highest percentages of ICDS beneficiaries are seen in Manipur, Mizoram, Nagaland and Sikkim (Gragnolati *et al.,* 2005). Percentages of immunised children are remarkably low in Arunachal Pradesh and Mizoram. The reason for low occurrences in Mizoram and Arunachal Pradesh are possibly due to a geographical feature of these states. Otherwise, in Sikkim, the condition is very good and in the rest states, it is more or less same to India as a whole.

From this study, it becomes clear that mother's education is the most effective factor to enhance immunisation and to reduce underweight and morbidity among the children. Education makes a person aware of the necessity of taking immunisation and maintaining hygienic conditions. The economic condition of the family is also responsible for bringing good health for the family. To prevent anaemia among children, family and community must be aware of hookworm infection because hookworm is very much responsible for increasing anaemia among children, mainly in rural areas (Osazuwa *et al.,* 2011). So along with the individual effect, health infrastructure of the state is also responsible for bringing good health among children.

## References

Bharati, S., M. Pal, S. Chakrabarty and P. Bharati. 2015. 'Socio-economic determinants of iron deficiency anaemia among children aged 6 to 59 months in India'. *Asia Pacific Journal of Public Health.* 27: 1432-1443.

Bharati, S., M. Pal and P. Bharati. 2008. 'Determinants of nutritional status of pre-school children in India'. *J Biosocial Science* 40:801-814.

Cheah, WL., WA. Wan Muda, ZA Mohd Hussin and CC. Thon. 2010. 'Factors associated with under-nutrition among children in a rural district of Kelantan, Malaysia'. *Asia Pac J Public Health*. 24:330.

Gragnolati, M., M. Shekar , M. Das Gupta , C. Bredenkamp and YK. Lee. 2005. *India's Undernourished Children: A Call For Reform and Action*. HNP Discussion Paper. Washington, DC; World Bank.

Harris, TB., R. Ballard-Barbasch, J. Madan, DM. Makuc and JJ. Feldman. 1993. 'Overweight, weight loss, and risk of coronary heart disease in older women. The NHANES I Follow up Study'. *American Journal of Epidemiology,* 137: 1318-1327.

International Institute for Population Sciences (IIPS) and ORC Macro. 2007. National Family 5 Health Survey (NFHS-3), 2005-2006, Vol.1: India, Mumbai; International Institute for Population Sciences.

James, WPT., 1994. 'Introduction: The challenge of adult chronic energy deficiency'. *European Journal of Clinical Nutrition*, 48 (Suppl 3): S1- S9.

Khongsdier, R., 2002. 'Body mass index and morbidity in adult males of the War Khasi in North East India'. *Eur. J. Clin. Nutr.* 56: 484-489.

Mondal, N and J. Sen. 2010. 'Prevalence of under nutrition among children (5–12 years) belonging to three communities residing in a similar habitat in North Bengal, India'. *Ann Hum. Biol*. 37:198-216.

Nandy, S., MD. Irving, D. Gordon, SV. Subramanian and GD. Smith. 2005. 'Poverty, child under nutrition and morbidity: New evidence from India'. *Bull World Health Organ.* 83: 210-216.

Osazuwa, F., MA. Oguntade and I. Paul. 2011. A significant association between intestinal helminth infection and anaemia burden in children in rural communities of Edo-state, Nigeria. *N Am J Med Sci*. 3: 30-34.

Roy, NC., 2000. 'Use of mid-upper arm circumference for evaluation of nutritional status of children and for identification of high-risk groups for malnutrition in rural Bangladesh'. *J Health Popul. Nutr*. 18:171-180.

Rutstein, S., 1999. *Wealth Versus Expenditure: Comparison between the DHS Wealth Index and Household Expenditures in your Departments of Guatemala*. Calverton, Maryland: ORC Macro.

Som, S., M. Pal, B. Bhattacharya and P. Bharati. 2006. 'Socioeconomic differentials in nutritional status of children in the states of West Bengal and Assam India'. *J Biosocial Sci*. 38:625-642.

World Health Organisation.1995. *Expert Committee on Nutrition and Physical Status: Uses and Interpretation of Anthropometry*. Geneva: WHO.

World Health Organisation. 2006. *WHO Child Growth Standards, Weight-for-Age*; 2006.

# Chapter - 7

# Hunting Ethnography: Narratives of Hunting from Bolung Village, Arunachal Pradesh

*—Queenbala Marak and Jintu Kalita*

Wildlife is an important resource for those communities that live in and around forests and is exploited for various reasons, including food, additional income, cultural practices and as a sport (Aiyadurai, 2011). In the life of a tribal people, hunting not only becomes a source of acquisition of food but is also considered as a favourite activity among individuals as well as groups. Furthermore, the primacy of hunting is that, while it does not bring in the most food, it produces the kind of food that most people like it best. Thus, among Garos of North East India, hunted meat is considered a 'prestige' food (Marak, 2014). As a practice, hunting is known to all parts of the world. But due to different geographical locations, climates and resources, the application of the techniques and methods of killing or catching of animals using traps and other methods differ (Marak and Kalita, 2013).

This chapter is ethnography on hunting of the Padams, a tribe of the Adi group, from Arunachal Pradesh who possess a rich repertoire of traditional know-how in methods of hunting. It discusses hunting through narratives of the existing hunters of the studied village. This chapter is based on a field study undertaken in January 2013 in Bolung village in Lower Dibang Valley district of Arunachal Pradesh. The Padams are a sub-tribe of the Adi group formerly known as the Abor; and along with the Millangs, Komkars, Pasis, Pangi, Shimong, Bokar Palibo Ramo, Karko, Bori and Minyongs they collectively call themselves the Adi. The Adi constitute a major group and inhabit the lower part of Lower Dibang Valley district especially Roing and Dambuk areas. These groups perform and celebrate the same rituals and festivals, though they speak different dialects. The Padams residing in the study area believe that they originated from Pedong Nane the creator of the universe and mother of all, the earliest ancestor being Keyum. It is said that from Keyum came Yumka, from Yumka came to Kasing, followed by Siang, Abo, Bomuk, Mukseng, Sedi, Dilling, Litung, Tuye, Yepe, and Pedong. The Padam believe Sedi or Sedi-Melo as the creator. Pedong Nane gave birth to vegetations, rivers, insects, birds, animals, spirits and Tani (*Nibo*) the youngest son from whom the Padams sprang.

In Bolung village, every house has or once had a hunter. Compared to a decade ago, they have fewer places to hunt, but more hunters and lesser animals. There are fifteen hunters out of 100 in the village who are considered 'good' and 'experienced' hunters. Some of the animals hunted include deer, porcupines, bears, wild pigs, elephants, squirrels, snakes, tigers, rats, and birds.

## II

Ojing Kartek is one of the experienced hunters in Bolung. He has reportedly hunted more than 200 animals, such as deer, elephant, bear, etc. In the following stories (Narratives 1 and 2), he describes, some of his hunting expeditions.

### Narrative 1

On 15th January 2013, Ojing Kartek decided to go for a hunt for three nights and four days with a friend. They left on their motorcycles with some light bedding along with items like a torch, battery, different kinds of a bullet for deer, bear, tiger, elephant etc., one and a half kg of rice, mug, one pot for cooking, plate, glass, and one bottle of whisky. They went to a private hunting ground owned by a friend. In that area maize grew abundantly, so wild pigs, deer, and porcupine usually came to graze. They decided to build a *chang* (raised bamboo platform) with locally available bamboo. After deciding the place and tree (by checking the direction of the wind) they returned to the base camp which was outside the jungle (30 minutes walking distance) where they built the *chang*.

Ojing Kartek set up vigil from 3.30 pm onwards. Around 6 pm, three wild pigs came to the area where they were. 'There is a rule of animals', says Ojing Kartek. 'Always the female animal goes first otherwise if they have a child, the child will go first'. He first saw a small one and prepared to fire with the LD sera, and then he saw the bigger one. He changed the bullet without making any sound by safety-catch and got ready, and shot. The bigger wild pig was spot dead. The big one was about 150 kg, and the teeth were about five inches long. He cut one nerve from the pig's upper leg. It is believed that if they cut it, then other wild animals will not come near the carcass for 4-5 hours.

When he came back to the camp, the cook enquired about the hunt. When he narrated, the cook was very happy and started preparing for an eventual meal. When Ojing Kartek's friend returned after 9 pm, they went to the spot of the hunt, cut into the wild pig, took out the kidney, liver, heart, intestine etc. weighing over 15-20 kg, and carried it back to the camp where they feasted. Early morning they went back, and cut up all the meat in large chunks and carried to the camp with the help of bamboo in three batches. They then smoked it over the fire. On the 2nd night, his friend killed another wild pig. All the meat was transferred in a similar manner, smoked over the fire, and taken to their respective homes.

They have a tradition that all hunters have to eat the head of that hunted animal together. So they invited the neighbour hunters and they had a feast together. Some relatives were also invited. However, they did not come empty-handed and brought *apong*, rice, chicken, whisky etc. That night they regaled each other with hunting stories.

**Narrative 2**

Fifteen years ago Ojing Kartek asked one of his friends, a relative of his wife, to come along for hunting. They had a plan for hunting for one night. He asked his friend to bring rice only for one night. The hunting ground was Balijaan forest, about

20 km away from Bolung village. They separated out and decided that if they could find an old *chang* they would use that; otherwise they would climb the trees. They also decided to meet at 7 pm at the base camp outside the forest with or without a game.

Ojing Kartek walked towards the bathing place of the wild pigs that he already knew. It was a small waterfall where he saw a big pig, but it ran away and he missed it. As he waited for thirty minutes, he heard some sound above him, which he thought was a monkey. He loaded LD sera and two balls and got ready to fire. Then he noticed that actually it was a huge pig and it pressed the bamboo for which the bamboos moved and touched the other bamboos at that top and made some sound. That was why he mistook the sound as coming from the top of the trees. He immediately changed his bullet without any sound. As the pig turned around to go to the water, he pressed the trigger very carefully without wasting time and that pig was spot dead. He stepped up to the pig and cut the nerve in the upper limb and left the place.

After walking for an hour, he came across *ngipong belang*, a tree whose seeds are relished by pigs and deer. Near the tree, there was an old *chang*. A rubber tree was also nearby. He had some rope with which he repaired the old *chang*. After waiting for some fifteen minutes he heard a sound and saw a huge wild pig, with teeth three inches long. He knew that the wild pig will leave that place in a few seconds, so he immediately fired below the ear. The pig ran away and hit the bamboo. In a few minutes, it lay prostrate.

Next, as he was waiting for deer, Ojing Kartek had an incident with *Robo* (See Narrative 4). He, therefore, ran to the base camp. In the morning as he and his friend were moving out, they met a team of six Nepali labourers, whom they decided to engage in carrying the hunted meat. When they all returned to the hunting spot with the labourers, they saw two wild elephants. They could not any longer wait another night, so they decided to chase off the wild elephants by making fire. With the help of some bamboo, they made a fire and chased the elephants away. Then they cut the two pigs in large chunks and brought it to the camp with the help of the six people.

**Narrative 3**

Ruling Tali around 50 years of age is a resident of Bolung village. He has hunted deer, elephant, wild pigs, porcupine, pythons etc. He usually goes to Bomjir Ghat on the way to Dambok for hunting.

Last winter, he went with his friends for three days hunt. They left with some light bedding and some *apong*, guns, bullets, tea, sugar etc. After a proper study of the area, they made a *chang*. The height of the *chang* depends on the animals, and so is different for every animal. Wild pigs are familiar with the smell of humans. So for making the *chang* of hunting pigs, they studied the air direction. They used some sand on their fingertips and slowly they let it fall in the air. After observing the direction of the air, they made the *chang* in the opposite direction from where the wild pigs would be. After a long wait of about an hour, they saw one large wild pig approaching the area. Ruling Tali shot it with his gun.

The next day they moved to another area where they built a *chang* at 15-20 feet above the ground. They then mixed salt with hot water and kept it on the ground near the *chang*. The deer came to that place to drink the salty water as they were waiting. Ruling Tali shot between the two upper limbs where the heart is situated. That deer was spot dead. He cut that deer in a systematic way in the jungle and brought it to the camp with the help of his friends. They dried it on fire and brought it back home and distributed to the neighbours and relatives.

The above narratives reveal the traditional know-how associated with hunting among the Adi Padams.

## III

Hunting is an important constituent of the Padam food procuring practice. What stands out from the different communities living around them is that it is also intrinsically connected to various rituals and festivals. Mainly two types of hunting can be differentiated–(a) Communal hunting which takes place on certain occasions, and usually has a ritual component to it. (b) Individual hunting in which a hunter alone or with friends go for a hunt, and does not require any occasion, and is devoid of rituals.

Interestingly the Padams have different hunting strategies for different animals. For example, deer are said to be the most intelligent of all animals, and thus it is difficult to hunt a deer. For hunting one, they observe the position where the deer mostly graze and accordingly they construct the *chang* (platform above the trees) out of bamboo. This *chang* is made wide enough because it might be used as a sleeping place at night while waiting for the deer(s) to appear. At other times, they have to shoot in a standing position, and even slight touching off a leaf will create some sound. Thus, the 'correct' construction of this platform is rather important. They also make a bamboo implement for urination at night called *chunga* so that they do not have to descend the platform. Salty water is an attraction to deer, so the Padam hunters boil some water with salt, and using a stick to make a long empty space on the ground, they place the boiled salty water. The selection and location of this pit are made within the range of the hunter. The seeds of the rubber tree are also a favourite of deer; therefore the hunter sometimes makes the *chang* on the rubber tree. Some deer go to the river side to have algae called *helei* and so the *chang* might be set up near the river. Deer (s) can see 100 metres away in such type of open space and when they bend their heads then they can see up to a height of 15 to 20 feet. So, in the open spaces the hunter makes the *chang* above the trees beyond the range of the deer' vision.

There are other important strategies adopted by the Padams when they hunt. Hunters while scoping, placemark some locations in the forest (trees, the direction of stars, the sound of river etc.). It is said that whilst hunting, the men should 'walk like the elephant'. While walking they should place their steps very carefully, and if possible walk barefoot and not with shoes. After one or two steps they should wait two to three minutes and observe the movements of the jungle, and listen to the sound of the tree leaves. At the time of hunting the hunters have to reload the gun with bullets. While doing so the safety-catch in the gun produces some noise, which can alert the prey. Therefore, the hunter has to take utmost care when reloading the gun. After shooting they have to follow the animal by their footprints. If the animal is still alive then the hunter has to be careful while approaching it; otherwise, the animal can attack the hunter.

The Padams use different implements to hunt. They generally use traps, many improvised and manufactured from locally available materials. Some of the traps used include *nnkig* (pit), *etku* (noose trap), *sankit* (noose trap), *egum*, and elephant trap (Marak and Kalita, 2013). They traditionally use bow and arrows, along with the *dao* (iron chopper). Today however guns have become popular due to its efficacy in the killing.

Hunting is a cultural tradition for the Padams. Most of the men in the studied village either hunt or have hunted in the past. It being a part of their tradition, they follow certain norms, values, and ritual activities connected to hunting. Most of these ritual activities are done before hunting. After the hunt is complete, the procured meat is distributed and either consumed immediately or stored through preservation methods to be consumed in the future.

Distributions of meat are different in community hunting and individual hunting. In community hunting, earlier the meat was distributed according to one's age and status. The 'elders' got the 'best' meat while the others got the 'low' quality of meat. Today this process of meat distribution is not followed. Rather meat is distributed equally. In individual hunting too if there are two or three hunters then meat is distributed equally. If a gun had to be borrowed for the hunt, then the hunter who borrowed had to give a part of his share to the owner of the gun. Once a successful hunting party returns then some relatives and friends are invited for a celebration. The invited guests should come carrying some gifts such as chicken, pork, beef, other meat, rice beer etc., failing which it is considered ill-mannered and a great shame. If sufficient meat remains after the celebration, some might be distributed among the neighbours; if not then none is distributed. In the case of deer and wild pigs, the first part carved out is the *mishi*. *Mishi* is a part of meat which is from the limbs and has to be given to the eldest hunter. *Kolkol* is a part of meat which belongs to the chest and is given to the next hunter in rank. *Tarong* refers to the meat of the hip bone and is given to the next hunter. *Kebyak* is that part of meat which belongs to the stomach and is given to the younger hunter(s). *Gasi* is the long meat of the backbone and shared among the younger hunter(s). The method followed while cutting the head of the hunted animal is called *Tuk Yo* (*Tuk* meaning 'skull' and *Yo* meaning 'skin'). *Tuk Yo* refers to the method of cutting off the head and removal of skin before the rest of the meat is cut. Excess meat is usually preserved for later use. First, the meat is cut into chunks and dried over the fire. After it is semi-dried, it is placed in a *beyen*, a bamboo structure over the fireplace. At times they also use *apey*, a small bamboo container where they store the meat. In this manner, meat can be preserved up to two years even though in actual practice it is not kept for so long.

## IV

Traditionally hunting was a part and parcel of festivals among the Padams. The Adis, of which the Padams are a sub-tribe, have three important festivals-*Aaran*, *Peme* and *Solung* (Marak and Kalita, 2013).

The festival of *Aaran* is called the 'rat hunting' festival, celebrated in the month of March (*Ginmur-Kombong*). It is celebrated after the completion of house construction, to mark the change of seasons and the beginning of the seasonal *jhum* cultivation. In *Aaranpidum*, one of the rituals, men go on the communal hunt searching for rats, deer, wild boar etc., after which the hunted animals are brought to the *ganggin* (temple). The hunters offer rats and other animals hunted to female relatives who in turn offer *apong* (rice beer). In the festival of *Peme* held after harvest in November, *Kiinenaane* (Goddess of paddy) is worshipped. During this festival *duar* (youth) of the village go for five days hunting from the second day of November and return on the seventh day. The hunted meat forms the main meal during this festival. After the hunt on the eighth day, all members of the family are restricted from going out of their house or to do any heavy household work, as they observe it as the day of rest. From the twelfth to the fourteenth day of November, the men go for community hunting (*kiruk-ruk dung*). The animals hunted are given to the *pathormuching* (village elders) as gifts and *apong* is taken during the festival which is prepared by the women.

Wild squirrels besides being considered a delicacy are also of socio-cultural significance. Traditionally, a young man desirous of asking for the hand of a maiden in marriage had to gift squirrels to the maiden's guardians. Thus, young men would go out in groups to catch as many squirrels as possible with the help of traps. This custom is still seen in Bolung village.

The Padams believe that there is a malevolent 'lord of the jungle' who is the lord of all animals living in the jungle and the caretaker of all the animals. Padam lore narrates that in the past, *Niibo* and *Robo* were two brothers, and from *Niibo* descended the human beings and from *Robo* the spirits including malevolent spirits. The descendants of Niibo is Tani, i.e. humans and from Robo is Epom a malevolent spirit. Robo and Epom are invisible spirits dwelling in the jungle and are the lords of the animals and cause harm to human beings. These spirits have to be appeased before every hunt so that the hunters are not harmed when they enter the jungle. When the Padams go for a hunt, they offer eggs, areca nut, betel leaf, *apong*, ginger, ginger juice, chicken, *beedi*, cigarette etc to the 'lord' of the jungle on a banana leaf. For daily use, the Padams use the banana leaf on the side where the colour is darker, but the hunter when making an offering to the power in the jungle places all items on the opposite side of the banana leaf. They divide it into three pieces and place it in such a way that it points towards the direction where they will go for the hunt. If that invisible power accepts all the offerings then they will be successful in the hunt and will return safely from the hunt. Otherwise, there could be accidents leading to death. The following story narrates the story of how a hunter fled from the attack of the 'lord of the jungle'.

**Narrative 4**

Ojing Kartek of Bolung village went hunting fifteen years ago to Balijaan with a friend. He successfully hunted two wild pigs and was waiting for one more game, when he suddenly noticed a shining light above him at a gap of about 15-20 feet. He heard an unnatural sound too and realised that it was the spirit of Robo. He was scared for he knew that humans lose their mental stability after experiencing this so he desperately tried to think of a way to leave the place. He then remembered his grandfather telling him as a child that there is an invisible power in urine, and that it can fight this invisible power of the jungle. So he urinated and made a circle around him with his urine. He removed his gun and sword and smeared it with urine. It was for his safety for according to their belief no invisible power can attack him within that circle, but beyond that, the power can harm him. He knew he could not stay the whole night in that place, so he came down from the *chang* and after trying out three times the right direction back to the camp, he immediately ran as fast as he could.

There is another ritual which some of the older generation talked about in traditional hunting. In traditional hunting, they use bows and arrows, and some of the arrows were usually poisoned. In olden times, this poison (*emo*) was collected from Alang Pahar near Mariang town in Upper Siang District. The Padams believe that an invisible power resides in the places where *emo* is found. That power does not allow easy access to *emo* and so in olden times they had to follow some rituals to procure it. First, they would pray at the village temple, and approach a priest who knew how and in what manner to pray to the spirit of the jungle. Then, along with him they would go towards the jungle but would not enter it before the ritual. They believe that at the boundary the invisible power uses a language which is known only to the priest. They also believe that if the Padams use their local language there, then they would suffer in different ways. Sometimes as punishment the head of the person might rotate, sometimes the weather would change, and sometimes they would fall sick and never recover. At this place, the priest prays to the power to let them enter the jungle. Once the rituals are over, the hunters enter and collect the raw *emo* which looks like a yam. They then proceed to mash it up and collect the juice. At this juncture, it is simply juice and if someone drank it, nothing will happen. Then the priest prays over this juice, and after three to four hours a strange smell emanates from it which indicates that the poison has formed. The party then returns to the village temple and again the priest prays. Thereafter an arrow head is immersed in the poisoned liquid and covered with a banana leaf. Today, however, there is no use of bows and arrows in the village.

## V

Hunting for Padams is a part of culture and tradition followed by men and boys. It is a male activity, and women are not allowed to hunt. The Padam society does not allow women to hunt with guns, bows, and arrows etc., and this labour distinction is very strictly maintained. Today, compared to ten years ago, there are fewer places where one can hunt. Not only has population pressure and modernisation impacted the hunting grounds and the wild animals, but there are more hunters and fewer animals to hunt as well.

If there are three or four boys in a family under the age of 18 years, one or two of them are prepared by the village elders for hunting in their childhood. However, they do not allow their children to go hunting alone because of their young age. First, they accompany the elders and learn the different ways and means of hunting by following the elders. Thus, the elders teach the youngsters the use of various weapons and traps, and the young are always eager to accompany hunting parties whenever they get an opportunity. Roy (1960: 141) says, 'young children are also allowed to join in group hunting parties by beating the forest and they always carry bows and arrows'. There are different strategies of hunting which have to be first learned by all hunters when they are young. For hunting, they have to know how to make camp, how to make a *chang* and where they have to make it on a tree and on which tree. They should know how to make a proper plan for hunting. But young boys would not know any of these, so they would have to go with their elders for quite a number of times before they can actually learn.

**Narrative 5**

When Ojing Kartek was in his early teens, he did not have any experience of hunting, or how to identify the animal from its footprint. His first expedition was with his uncles. He along with his elders went to scope the hunting area. He noticed that the maize cobs were eaten by some animal, but he had no idea what animal it was. One of his relatives asked him to sit and wait, while they would collect bamboo to make the platform (*chang*). The constructed platform was then brought and set up, and they left him alone there (on the platform) with a gun, asking him to keep watch till 8 pm, when they would return.

Ojing Kartek had no idea about the jungle directions, so he stayed put at the place where he was left. At 4.15 pm he heard a sound a little far away. After a little moment, he noticed that the sound was approaching him. At that time the leaves of the trees were moving, and so he thought it was a big wild pig. The *chang* where he was waiting was at a height of 15-20 feet above, so he knew that the animal could not notice him. He decided that if the animal notices him he would fire on that animal. He was almost ready for the firing when he noticed the face of the animal looking up at a tree near the maize plant. The face of the animal was long and it was not a wild pig, but a bear.

However, seeing the bear he was not afraid. He took aim and fired just below the ear of the animal and it fell down. He again reloaded the gun and fired at the same spot. His uncles heard that two shots and immediately returned. As they approached, they made a cooing sound, to which Ojing Kartek responded with a louder coo.

His uncles were impressed to see the big bear lying dead, and said that they had never hunted such a big bear in their lives. They cut a big bamboo and tried to carry with the help of six other people, but the bamboo broke due to its weight. Ultimately they managed to carry the dead bear with two bamboos. The length of the bear was over 10 feet.

Hunting is of great significance. It is considered a male activity prestigious only next to war. It has social significance because a good hunter enjoys special status. Thus, Ojing Kartek enjoys an unparalleled status in Bolung village today which he acquired while he was still a young boy.

## VI

From the foregoing sections, it is clear that among the Padams there are different strategies for hunting. Even the setting up and construction of a *chang* (bamboo platform) on which to lay in wait for the animal depends on many factors. For tigers and deer, the platform has to be higher–so that the former cannot jump up and reach, and the latter cannot spy the hunter for it is said to be longsighted. For hunting a wild pig, they take care not to stand in the way of the airflow for a small whiff of human odour will make the pigs bolt. However, they also use a number of locally made traps to catch animals such as the squirrels and rats which are not only a delicacy but also an important part of their rituals and ceremonies. Squirrel hunting in traps still remain a significant game among the Padams for squirrels are not only eaten regularly but are also gifted as presents to the father-in-law by the bridegroom in marriage.

Today the hunting areas have dwindled, but are still public land. Hunting areas near Bolung include Gator, Barok, Pasum, Sukanala, Solong, Lotung, Kirim etc. These places are forest areas near the village. Beyond this, Balijaan, on the way to Tezu, is another hunting ground, which is larger than the area of Bolung village and is a popular area. Most of the hunters from Bolung as well as from Mizu-Mismi Hills go for hunting there. However recently, some areas have been captured by the Mishmi community. Therefore, when they go for hunting in those areas the Adi Padams have to inform the people of that community.

Most men in the village continue to do some form of hunting. Interestingly, there is at least one hunter in each house. Generally, whenever they get free time in the winter and whenever they feel the need to, they go for hunting. However, in real practice and according to traditions, hunting is connected to their lives and therefore undertaken during certain rituals and celebrations. The above narratives reveal richness in the hunting strategies of the Adi Padams. For example, the cutting of the nerve from the upper limb of a dead animal deters other predators from approaching the dead animals; hunters communally consume the head of the hunted animals bringing in solidarity and strength; and how urine can be used to escape from the attack of the 'lord of the jungle.'

It is beyond doubt that hunters and his hunting prowess are intrinsically linked to social prestige. The hunters not only display their trophies in their homes, and their respective *moshups* while they are alive, but continue to revel in these trophies even in death. These trophies decorate their graves after death too and it is believed that these trophies will elevate their status even in their afterlife.

Despite efforts of the Forest Department hunting still, continues though it has reduced to a large extent. This reduction is likely not due to the efforts of the Forest Department or NGOs but rather due to the fact that the number of animals has gone down in the forests and there are very few animals available for the hunt. Another reason could be that meat is now readily available in the market as well as at home since many rear pigs, chicken, buffalo etc at home. The Forest Department organises meetings and awareness programmes on the conservation of wildlife time to time. But during the Adi festivals, the hunters always go for a hunt in the jungle. This fact is known to the Forest Department but our study revealed that they do not interfere much since they know the significance of these hunts.

## References

Aiyadurai, A., 2011. 'Wildlife hunting and conservation in Northeast India: A need for an interdisciplinary understanding'. *International Journal of Galliformes Conservation*, 2: 61-73.

Marak, Q and J. Kalita. 2013. 'Indigenous knowledge systems associated with hunting among the Padams of Arunachal Pradesh, India'. *Antrocom Online Journal of Anthropology*, 9, 2: 237-245.

Marak, Q., 2014. *Food Politics: Studying Food, Identity, and Difference among the Garos*. Newcastle, UK: CSP.

Roy, S., 1960. *Aspects of Padam-Minyong Culture*. Shillong: North-East Frontier Agency.

# Chapter - 8

# History of Religion of Indigenous Population of Brahmaputra Valley

*—Chandra Jyoti Sonowal*

## Introduction

Religion is one of the most widely deliberated aspects in human history. Despite this fact, the definition of religion has never been complete despite scores of such attempts have so far been made. Thus, it is very essential to understand and accept the definition of religion in its conceptuality, rather than its universality. Like many other components of human society, religion also undergoes changes over time. Forces of change in religion sometimes emerge internally while in most cases it remains an external force and people's response to the changing socio-cultural and political and environmental aspects of the concerned population.

The indigenous population living in and around the Brahmaputra valley mostly migrated to this region in remote historical and pre-historic past from South East Asia region. They brought along with them a culture very much different from the culture and tradition of people living in the political mainland India. Over the period of time, a lot of giving and take occurred in the cultural and social domain. The traces of mainland religious components entered the domain of this population at different time and intensity. Similarly, the components of indigenous religion and practices also got infused in the dominant religion like Hinduism when it ventured into the land of these populations.

It is very interesting to note here that while a lot of practices of these indigenous populations of Brahmaputra valley got infused into the localised Hindu norms, very few of their traditional gods and goddesses could secure a place in the mythology of the Hindu religious texts and verses. Rather, it has been observed that traditional entities were either equated with Hindu deities or they were simply discarded. A new mythology and history have been created for most of these population groups so that they could be adapted within the legacy of Pan-Indian Hindu tradition (Sonowal, 2014).

This chapter tries to delineate the nature of Hinduism practiced among the indigenous population of the valley and critically examine the underpinning of the change process in religious practices among this population from various perspectives. This chapter deals, in brief, with the definition of religion, various perspectives/theories used to study religion, the changing aspects of religion, nature of Hinduism that was present in the studied area and infusion of tribal components in it, changes of religious aspects of indigenous population and finally a critical discussion on the underpinnings of changing aspects of indigenous religion.

## Religion Defined

E.B. Tylor's definition of religion can be seen as the initial basis for religious discourse which defines religion as the 'belief in spiritual beings' (Tylor, 1871; 1920). Frazer (1958:58-59) sees religion as 'a propitiation or conciliation of powers superior to men which are believed to direct and control the course of nature and human life'. James (1958:34) defines religion as 'the feelings, acts, and experiences of individual men in their solitude, so far as they apprehend themselves to stand in relation to whatever they may consider as divine'. Durkheim (1965:62) defines religion as a unified system of beliefs and practices relative to sacred things, that is to say, things set aside and forbidden – beliefs and practices which unite into one single moral community called a Church, all those who adhere to them. Radin (1954:3) opines that religion consists of two parts: the first and easily definable, if not precisely, specific feeling; and the second certain acts, customs, beliefs, conceptions associated with this feeling. The beliefs most inextricably connected with the specific feelings is a belief in spirit outside of man, conceived as more powerful than man and as controlling all those elements in life upon which he lays most stress. Wallace (1966:107) sees religion as 'a set of rituals, rationalised by myth, which mobilises supernatural powers for the purpose of achieving or preventing transformation of state in man and nature'. Ortner (1978:152) sees religion as a system that solves problems of meaning generated in large part, though not entirely, by the social order within a theoretically ultimate reality within which those problems will 'make sense'. Geertz (1973:90) quotes religion as: (i) a system of symbols which act to, (ii) establish powerful, pervasive and long-lasting moods and motivation in men by, (iii) formulating conceptions of general order of existence and (iv) clothing these conceptions with such an aura of faculty that (v) the moods and motivations seem uniquely realistic.

These definitions thus go on explaining mostly that religion is a necessity for physical and spiritual survival, an outcome of the quest for unknown and an instrument for social cohesion and continuity.

## The Study of Religion

The systematic and analytic study of religion basically emerged in Europe. In medieval Europe, a certain kind of unity of thought regarding religion could be located–it was the belief in the existence of God and the just claims of secular authority. Enlightenment has challenged the basic assumption of medieval thoughts about religion. For instance, Hume (1711-76) emphasised an empirical input of social facts for experiences and observations while Kant (1742-1804) holds that knowledge is constructed and that we cannot know 'the world in itself'. Stating Christianity as an illusion, Feuerbach (1804-72) holds the view that the proper object of theology and philosophy should be the human beings, rather than metaphysical and speculation concerning the nature of God. Despite such out of turn and innovative ideas were widely debated, people mostly were attached to traditional Christian beliefs and values. These values remained the foundation of many later age anthropologists and sociologists who delineated about religion.

The studies of religion gave rise to diverse theories of religion, mostly dealing with its origin and functions. The modern theories of religion emerged from social sciences like anthropology, sociology, psychology to name a few. Generally speaking, the nineteenth-century theories have focused on the origin of religion; origin here means the historical origin, while the twentieth-century theories have focused on the function of religion. Nevertheless, these were the trends only. Both origin and function were always there in their interpretation.

The social scientific theories of religion hold that the origin and function of religion are mostly non-religious. Religion arises to fulfil either physical or intangible need of human beings. Contrary to this view, the theories from religious studies hold origin and function of religion as religious.

Historical and Evolutionist theory talks about the way religion evolved and grew in time and space. Hagel (1770 - 1831) proposed a comprehensive historical system of progression from the age of religion to the age of philosophy to the final age of science. Comte (1798 - 1857) described the same three staged history by the means of Theology, Metaphysics, and Science or Positivism. Spencer (1820 - 1903) also echoed this idea finally replacing religion and superstition by science. Tylor (1832-1917) schemed religion in 'nature worship' to monotheism through intermediary polytheism. Among the diffusionist (thus, anti-evolutionists), Grabner (1877-1934), Schmidt (1868-1954) and Elliot Smith (1871-1937) traced the diversity of the world religions back to a few–or in Smith's case, one (Ancient Egypt)–Souras, the common origin explain the similarities, and the subsequent historical development of each independent spin-off explained the differences. Psychological theories talks of 'experience and thoughts' pertaining to individuals. Hobbes (1588–1679) proposed that religion was invented to lessen inescapable fear out of awful things happened to people. For Malinowski (1884-1942) religion came into play when individuals needed a feeling of reassurance, control, and of course, relief from fear. Freud (1856-1939) tried to reduce religion as a 'symptom' or manifestation of our mind. Frazer's (1854-1941) input was that religion is an answer to a question or problem, just not a rational answer. The functional theory of religion talks about the inherent functions accomplished by religion. Durkheim (1965:257) put emphasis on the function of religion in terms of enhancing a group of people with a certain identity. The perspective of Historical Materialism in studying religion is based on 'mode of production', 'relation of production'. Marx's (1818-83) opines that Religion reflects the on-the-ground realities of social life. Perhaps the purest version of this idea is the 'Divine Rights of Things'. Harris (1974) opines that religion created an aura of supernatural significance around the materials living and non-living, to encourage people to preserve them or castigated them. In whatever case, a practical, non-spiritual reason for the belief or behaviour can be found, which is the wrapped in a shroud of religious meaning as a form of legitimating and compulsion. Structural Functionalists emphasise that the function of religion is rather social, not individual. Contradicting the functional view of Malinowski and others, Redcliff Brown (1881-1955) argued that function was the central issue for the needs of the group or of society. He saw society and its groups and institutions as having their own needs and therefore, perceived the function of any item of culture or society to be 'contributions that they make to the formation and maintenance of a social order (1965:154)'.

## The Changing Aspects of Religion

Change in socio-cultural components, including religion, is inevitable in human socio-cultural history. 'Secularisation theory' points an overall decline of religion and religious influences because of a set of specific conditions emerging in a particular social domain. According to Bell (1980: 326-327), the enlightened people of the late eighteenth and mid-nineteenth century thought that religion will end in the twentieth century as a result of rationalism and scientific thinking as against the traditional base of religion which was superstition, fetishism, improvable beliefs etc. But such unilinear process of religious events has been challenged by Stark and Bainbridge (1985). They argue that secularisation is a self-timing process and that new religion develops to fill the void when the traditional knowledge loses its influence in a society. James *et al.*, (1989) rather denies the importance of secularisation theorists' four assumptions and points out that there are five components of any religious changes: These are (i) religious changes is sometimes cyclical rather than linear; (ii) religious reformation and attempt to strengthen religion occur frequently; (iii) when a dominant religious tradition declines in influence, it is almost always replaced by another religious tradition; (iv) religious change is found in virtually every society in the world and is evident in the earliest historical accounts and (v) religious change almost inevitably accompanies other (especially political) social changes.

Through a global study, they indicated that religious changes and its process are a complex matter. There has always been some sort of discontent or different views even on established religion. Thus, there is always a section of thinkers or believers straying away from any traditional or established religion. This section may either proceed towards secularisation or may go through some sort of renewed and reform in the established religion. Thus, the reform is for the most different form from established religion that may lead to a new faith. Otherwise, the new things may be adjusted in the old religion making it more widely acceptable one. The authors proposed the stages of religious transformation: decline-dominance-sustained growth- a transition which is a cyclical process. Here decline denotes the decline of traditional religion and/or loss of influence and new religion emerge. Dominance denotes that the emerging religion gains dominance by displacing the old religion or by overpowering other religion. Sustained growth denotes that it consolidates its gain (base) and increase influence. And finally, transition denotes a stage at its peak and begins declining again (to complete the cycle).

The transition of primitive societies starts and heads towards modernity as and when they come into contact with non-traditional societies. As a result of such contact, the traditional religion tends to lose its hold on the lives of its members and a process of religious change sets in. This weakening of the dominant religion has been seen very early in the history of a society, even before the emergence of enlightenment negating the proposition that secularisation of religious domain was influenced by the reasoning intellect emerged out of enlightenment (Bell, 1980).

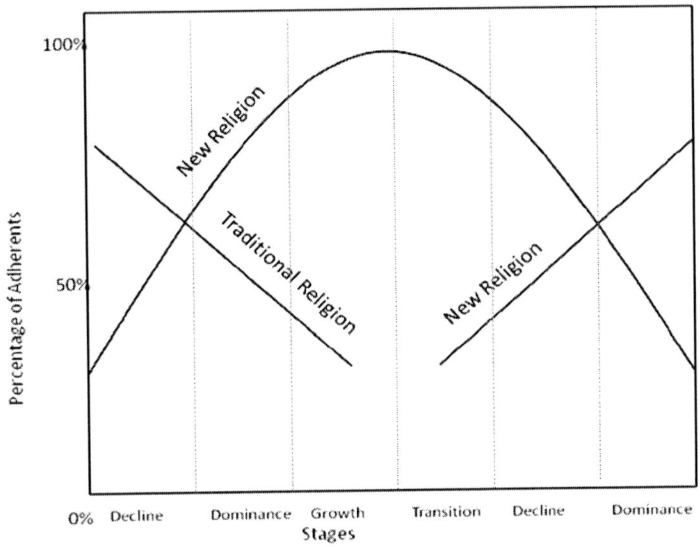


(*Source*: Duke and Johnson 1989).

***Figure 8.1: Stages of Religious Transformation.***

## Parochial Form of Hinduism in Assam

It has been quite often asserted that the indigenous populations in the Assam plains have been Hinduised at different intensities at different point of time in the history. It has also been conceived that by imbibing Hinduism, the tribal people lost their traditional religious practices to a great extent. This seems to be a blanket statement while talking about the influence of Hinduism on tribes of this region. Scholars of religion and culture who studied these aspects in this region have found that the so-called Hindu religious practices existed in this region differ a lot from that of the classical Hindu religion of the mainland India. Probably, due to geophysical constraints this region was mostly left out of the classical Hindu tradition. History also reveals that the rulers of the region often brought Hindu priests and intellectuals from the west to serve the purposes of the rulers. A critical review of all mythology created and the genealogy traced reveal that these are meticulously fabricated pieces of such imported priests and intellectuals at a much later period when a group of indigenous population entered into a structured political arrangement as rulers and kings etc. Another important aspect of the history of the religion of indigenous population of the region is that a vast majority of these populations adapted Vaishnavism starting from the fifteenth century onwards under the direct initiatives of the Vaishnava preachers, some influenced by charismatic stories and some were lured by the opportunities open to the Vaishnavite arrangement. Vaishnavism is far more different from classical Hindu practices and liberal in nature where the tribal people could be adjusted well. It is interesting to note that we do not see any organised initiative taken by none-Vaishnavite Hindu religious authorities to convert indigenous masses to Hinduism as has been seen in the case of conversion to Vaishnavism. Vaishnavism in this region is identified with monotheism, salvation to one god and devoid of any extensive ritualism.

Eliot (1910) observes that a special feature in these aboriginal regions (North East India) was the cult of goddesses who were worshipped with human sacrifices and immoral rites. Gait (1898) indicates the human sacrifice in this region similar to a tradition present in ancient Mexico. Such sacrifices were also performed by Tipperas (tribes in Tripura), Kacharis, Koch, Jaintias, and others. In India, we come across such goddess in Hindu mythology and religious practices who are named as Kali, Vairabi, and Chinnamastaka etc. Social scientists try to see the influence of tribal faith in such mythology and practice because the pure Vedic Hinduism does not reveal the presence of such goddesses. There is every possibility that these entities are the later inclusion in Hindu faith as a result of absorption of local and tribal faith into greater Hindu mythology and tradition. Uses of meat, liquor, blood etc are mostly in contrast to the mainland Hindu ritualistic domain which is far widespread in North East and Bengal even in Hindu faith.

The Hindu God Lord Siva has a specific link with the Hinduisation of the tribal and indigenous peoples in the region. The tantric legend of Assam relates Lord Siva and his spouse goddess Sati. It indicates that Sati ended her life at the place of ritual organised by her father King Daksha for; he insulted Siva denoting him as a savage. Lord Siva started circuiting the universe taking her corpse on his shoulder. At this Lord Vishnu cut the body of Goddess Sati into several pieces. It is believed that the sacral part of Sati's body fell in some parts of Assam (Kamakhya), Jaintia Hills (Falijur) and in Bengal (Kalighat), and emerged as the sacred place for Hinduism and Saktism. This legend, as per knowledge, is a late inclusion in Sanskritic Hindu mythology indicating tribalisation or parochialistic of Hindu beliefs and practices in the region.

Eliot *(ibid)* and many other social scientists and historians have perceived that rites related to these sacred places were initially conducted by local tribal priests. But in due course of time, these sacred places were ritualised by Brahman priests following their superior intellect and capability to relate locals with the universal entity. Thus, in return for such opportunities, the Brahman elites/priests supported the authority of the tribal chiefs and kings and assigned them the divine link of pan-Indian nature, and making them different from their subjects. There are ample instances of such kinds.

The Koch (an indigenous population mostly found in western part of Assam and its adjacent areas of West Bengal) chief Biswa Singha was declared as son of Lord Siva, a Kshatriya (a caste group holding second position in caste hierarchy) who lost sacred thread while fleeing to get rid of the furry of Parasurama (believed to be a reincarnation of Lord Vishnu who vowed to make the earth Kshatriya free). The story says that one tribal person called Hariya Mech, who was a Mech Kachari (a tribal community of Assam) once, was tilling his land. While his wife went to provide him breakfast in the field, Lord Siva got engaged in sexual act with her in the disguise of her husband. The son born to her became King Biswa Singha in due course of time and established Koch kingdom (Sarkar, 1991). Biswa Singha's son Nara Narayan was the most powerful king and he patronised Nava-Vaishnavism propagated by Sri Sankardeva during the sixteenth century. Numerous tribal people converted to new religious ideology leaving their traditional tribal practices and became Koch community.

There are many other legends that get parochial, linking local tribal communities to the greater Hindu culture. One of such legends links all Kachari tribes to the legendary hero of Mahabharata–Ghototkoch, the son of second Pandava, Bhima. The Kacharis feel proud to be called themselves Kshatriyas (Endles, 1911; Pulloppillil and Jacob, 1997; Pegu, 2004; Roy, 2002). Contrary to such localised story the popularly (also nationally) known Hidimba temple is situated in Himachal Pradesh. In North East India such stories were probably recreated when the tribal kings were Hinduised. It has been revealed that as late as 1790 the Kachari Raja of Khaspur and his brother entered the body of a copper effigy of a cow. On emerging from it they were proclaimed to be Hindu of the Kshatriya caste, and a genealogy of a hundred generation reaching to Bhima, the hero of Mahabharata, was composed for them by the Brahmanas (Gait, 1906:351). Saktism (a way to propitiate gods offering blood and magical activities etc.) remained the religious code of Rajas and aristocracy in this region. It was probable that the common mass was not Hinduism to the same tune till the emergence of Vaishnavism in the sixteenth century.

Two other contemporary legends link the remote north-eastern part of the country to the mainland culture of the country. One of these legends talks about the marital relation between princesses Usha of Agnigarh (now Tezpur in Assam) with Aniruddha, the grandson of Lord Krishna. Contrarily, similar kinds of stories are also heard in other parts of the country. It is known that Bana is a *gotra* (clan) of Jats found in Rajasthan and Uttar Pradesh in India. Banas are believed to be the descendants of King Banasura. Their capital was at Bayana in Bharatpur. Usha temple, at Bayana, was built during the reign of Raja Laxman Sen, by his wife in memory of Usha. There is mention of Bana Chieftains along with Pallavas and as feudatories of Cholas in Tamil Nadu. Thus, the authenticity of such stories is always in doubt and there is every possibility that such stories were the medium of Hinduisation of local people in remote areas.

Another legend talks about the marriage of Lord Krishna with princess Rukmini. It is said that Rukmini was the daughter of king Bhismaka who ruled a kingdom Kundil in Sadiya of upper Assam (Gait, 1906). The Chutiya community and the Deori tribes of Assam claim themselves to be the descendants of king Bhismaka. But it is widely believed at the national level that king Bhismaka's kingdom was in Vidarbha, the north-east part of Maharashtra. Considering the difficult location of Sadiya in Assam no rational people will believe that there could be any marriage relation between the places like Sadiya and Dwaraka in those days.

The Ahom royal history is full of accounts of Hindu influence right from the days of King Sudang pha or Bamuni Konwar (the king was born to an Ahom queen who gave to a baby boy in a Brahmin's house who rescued her from the river). Ahom king Dihingia Raja took the Hindu names as Swargadeo or Swarga Narayana in 1497. Ahom history was re-created giving Hindu names or equated Ahom deities with Hindu deities and assigning Ahom kings heavenly status. Brahminic tradition has come in as Saktaism and lots of localised Hindu rituals penetrated Ahom domain. The influence of Sakta faith was quite evident in this region. The Koch king Naranarayana rebuilt the Kamakhya temple which was destroyed by Kalapahar, a Mughal army captain, sacrificed 140 men there, protected the rising Vaishnava sect, offered refuge to Sri Sankaradeva and seven Satras were built in Koch kingdom.

The history of Assam shows that this extensive country has been brought almost wholly within the pale of Hindu orthodoxy by effective methods of propagating the faith called Saktism – a hybrid of Hinduism and local tribal culture, based on passion, fear and aimed at giving authority, power and recognition for kings and princes. It attracted the people and tribal chiefs mainly. It is quite important here to delineate the nature of Hinduism practiced or was practiced by the local tribes and other indigenous peoples to examine the view that the traditional tribal communities are basically Hindus. Urban (2011) has rightly observed that while we talk about religion, especially in Assam, we talk of Hinduism of relatively different from mainland Hindu religion. In Assam, we see two divisions of Hindu practices, the Vaishnavism based on pure salvation and the Brahmanic Hinduism, mostly attached with a form of Saktism and based on tantric ideology. One can observe inclination of traditional tribal communities more towards tantric practice if they are relatively more attached to tradition. The ancient Kamrupa (Assam) has been known for Tantric activities which are justified by the tribal peoples' animistic and Tantric practices. Strictly speaking, Hinduism among tribes in the region is mostly inclined, in practice, towards Tantric practices. Urban *(ibid)* opines that the emergence of Tantric tradition as found in North East India is a more complex process. It involves a more subtle interaction, negotiation, and mutual transformation between Brahmanic and local non-Hindu traditions. He argues that the Sakta, Tantra in Assam largely the result of a long historical negotiation between Sanskritic tradition and the indigenous kings who patronised them. Proposing a concept of social transformation, Doniger (2010:6) suggests that the development of Hinduism as a whole in South Asia was not simply a process of Sanskritisation, rather it was a process of '*desification*' that is the influence of local (*desi*) and indigenous culture on Brahmanic religion. He terms the process also as organisation or popularisation or desification.

The complex negotiation between Sanskritic and tribal tradition has been indicated by historical as well as by mythical narratives of Kamrupa indicating the interaction between the two domain since the time of epic age. Among the early texts, *Kalika Purana* stores a lot of information about such links and interactions. It says that the origin of name Kamrupa emerged due to the fact that the god of love, Kamadeva, regained his beauty, which was otherwise defaced by the curse of Lord Siva for disturbing him in his eternal meditation. The same text also indicates that Kamrupa came under the rule of Naraka, a Hinduised and half-divine son of Lord Vishnu and Goddess Earth and he drove out the tribal ruler and established Vedic worship. The text suggests that Kamakhya as 'Mother Goddess' was in existence in Kamrupa even before Naraka established Vedic Hinduism here. It also indicates that Naraka confined worshipping Goddess Kamakhya in its pristine form. That the existence of worship to Mother Goddess among the traditional tribal people of this locality is a fact has been proved by the religious faith present among the tribes like the Kacharis, Deories etc who worship their goddess in the name of Bhoroli (by Kacharis), Kechaikhaiti (by Chutiyas / Deories), Ka Blei Synsar (by Khasis) etc. Scholars like Mishra (2004:5), Bareh (1967:37-38) and Dold (204:96) established the fact that Goddess Kamakhya was a tribal deity. This complex process of interaction between local tradition and Hinduism can be accessed from historical accounts of local kings of the region. The Varman Dynasty to whom the Kacharis trace their link is supposed to emerge in fourth century AD. The Pala kings of Assam along with Varman dynasty tried to relate themselves to the mythical king Naraka. Likewise, as has already been mentioned the Koch kings relate their origin to Lord Siva and the Ahom kings to Lord Indra.

One important point to mention here is that the Hinduisation process never assigned the local kings a dignified or equal status to the caste hierarchy. There is always a clash between Brahmanic superiority and tribal (local) inferiority present in the mythology and history of kings of this region. Though the kings and chiefs of tribal origin may be assigned the highest order sometimes equal to God (at least at the local level), in terms of purity of blood or origin they are seen cursed for being born to partly impure blood or non-Hindu origin. There are ample instances of such stories fabricated by elite Brahmanic domain in the region. For instance, it is said that Naraka was conceived during a menstruating period of the Earth, and therefore, he could not hold high the Vedic way of life and turned inimical to gods, destroyed heaven, even wanted to marry goddess Kamakhya. Thus, he was cursed for this insanity and finally was killed by Sri Krishna. King Bana of Shonitpur was a great devotee of Lord Siva, but finally, he also got cursed and was destroyed by Sri Krishna. Likewise, the Salastambha dynasty was cursed to become a non-Hindu barbarian dynasty. Koch king Biswa Singha was a half-divine tribal king, according to Yogini Tantra, which indicated that his mother, who was actually a beautiful Yogini was cursed by a Brahmana to be born as a Mleccha women. In her Mleccha life, she coupled with Lord Siva and King Biswa Singha was born. His son Naranarayana also was cursed by Goddess Kamakhya in the event of his adventurous wish to behold the goddess. The Goddess beheaded the priest Kendukalai through whom the king wanted to behold the Goddess and in this event, the Goddess warned the king that henceforth no one of his dynasties should visit the temple lest they get destroyed. Similar sort of stories is there for Ahom kings also. The forefather of Ahom king Khunlung and Khunlai were said to be born out of a union between Lord Indra and a Mleccha women called Sama. All these stories and legends indicate the complex nature of interactions, adjustment, and conflict of interest and maintenance of religious superiority etc. throughout pre-historic and historic past in the region.

The ritualistic observances of so perceived Hindu religious followers irrespective of the affiliation to tribe or non-tribes indicate the admixture of Brahmanic and tribal traditions. Yogini Tantra of seventeenth century Assam describes the religion of the region as *Kirati* (tribal) religion - which includes the consumption of alcohol, and all manners of wild animals. Blood sacrifice is one of the primary ritualistic performances of Kirati Dharma. Sacrifice has been a part of Hindu ritual. But it remained symbolic in many ways. If at all animal sacrifice is made it is always made with pure one, that is domestic, non-wild animals. While in North East India, sacrifice of ducks, hens, pigeons, *Mithun*, and buffalo and to some extent the human being remained the tradition. The Vedic rites call solely for the offering of pure which the *Satapatha Brahmana* suggests to include horses, cows, goats and sheep etc. According to this text, the impure non-domestic animals include the *gaura* (a kind of buffalo), the *gavaya* (a species of ox) and the barbarians of the jungle. The Hindu gods and goddesses are offered with semi-pure or impure sacrifices by locals in Kamarupa. In Vedic rituals sacrifice of animals is performed by un-blooded suffocation of the animal, while in Sakta rites, the animals are beheaded, the blood and the severed heads are offered to the deities purified by Mantras.

At the highest extent, human sacrifice was very much in practice until the fifteenth century in this region. As mentioned earlier, the temple of Kechaikhati, Tamreswari, Kamakhya etc was a centre for such performance. Human sacrifice has been termed as the supreme kind of sacrifice to please the goddess. But this act was meant for the king who performs it for victory in war, success against enemy, welfare of the kingdom, for the want of political power etc. The sacrifice of some British officials by the king of Gova, a Jaintia king, perhaps was the last known human sacrifice for such purpose, the consequences of which resulted in the annexation of Jaintia kingdom by the Colonial ruler.

All the above delineation makes it clear that the tribal religion of the plains we see nowadays and also the greater Hindu religion in the region is not in its pure form. All there is the emergent nature of religions transformed through lots of negotiations, adaptations, and transformations.

## Changes of Religious Faith Among the Indigenous Population

It has been mentioned at the very beginning of the chapter that components of religion are not static. They keep on changing depending upon some factors. If we look at the indigenous population of the region we find that the religious beliefs and practices of these people are no longer in their traditional form. Some of them have lost almost all of their traditional religious practices while some of them are able to retain certain components in a pristine or changed form. Now, it is very important to deliberate as to why these indigenous populations had to change their traditional religious practices. What function of the society was unable to perform by their traditional religious norms for which they had to adapt new religious components.

It is important to note that change of religion of the kings and rulers did not necessarily require a change in the religious practices of their subjects. It is quite evident that when the Ahom king and the Koch and Kachari kings were recognised as descendants of Hindu gods and goddesses or other legendary entities, the common masses were not converted to the same line of religious faith. Thus, conversion to the religious faith of common masses has to be examined in a different perspective as compared to the conversion of the religion of the kings and rulers.

It has been pointed out that accepting universal or dominant religious components by the rulers and kings of the indigenous/tribal origin were the necessity of these entities. This is because; a king or a ruler cannot be a common person. He must have something different from his fellow men. Thus, attaching him to a divine blood or origin was one of the most appropriate strategies to draw the difference. So we see the recreation of divine mythology relating the genealogy of the kings to the gods or mythological hero of a dominant religion. In this way the Ahom royal groups were portrayed as the descendants of Lord Indra, the Koch kings were portrayed as the descendants of Lord Siva; Kacharis were portrayed as the descendants of Bhima etc.

Contrary to such smooth process of conversion, common masses have a separate reason for accepting a new religious faith. Studying the religious history of the indigenous people of the region, it becomes evident that drives for the necessity of change in religious components have never come from within the people. Rather, it was always the initiative of some charismatic outsiders who tried to infuse new ideas among the people. This conversion enterprise used diverse incentives to lure people to the new faith. Needless to say that people must have beheld something exotic which their traditional religion was lacking in.

Horton's extensive study among the African tribes provides an opportunity to understand the process of religious conversion among the tribal people worldwide. His 'Intellectual Theory' (1971) seeks to explain the religious change in terms of changing experience of social relation–a movement from an ethnic to world religion in the context of a society's incorporation into wider social and economic relations through colonialism. This, they argue, that the cosmologies of indigenous African religion typically have two tires: an upper tier consisting of a high god who rules the macrocosm, or the world beyond the local communities; and a lower tier consisting of numerous lesser superuman beings who watch over and participate in communities' immediate natural and social worlds. The high god is seldom approached and vaguely elaborated while the lower gods intensively interact frequently. But as and when the community venture into the wider world beyond their traditional domain, they have to pay greater attention to the high god as he is the controller of that outside world. Thus, until and unless the high god is not affected, the interaction with non-traditional religious components hardly likely to affect a drastic change in their beliefs and practices. Horton argues that in the case of interaction between an ethnic religion and world religion there is every possibility of absorption of high god of indigenous religion. The intellectual theory thus emphasises that it is not the activities of the proselytisers that mostly influence so-called religious conversion; rather, it is the framework of indigenous religion and the challenges they face in an alien or new situation they encounter with.

This theory of religious conversion find ground in the study of the indigenous population of the Brahmaputra valley, for those whose migration history is unknown, and those whose migration history is known. For instance, the Ahoms, who came to Assam plain by the early part of the thirteenth century (1228 AD) brought with them their unique religious components and *Chumdeo* as their high god. Their first social interaction in the plains was with the Morans, Borahi and Kacharis who were the earliest known population of the region. Ahom's state policy helped grow a social assimilation between the Ahoms and these earlier settlers. Ahoms continued with their traditional practice of economic activities, infused the wet rice cultivation etc in the region. The geophysical condition they entered into was also mostly similar to their original homeland. Thus, probably the Ahom commons did not feel the need of a change in their immediate cosmology and high god. But, there were fusion and fission of beliefs and practices between Ahoms and non-Ahom locals due to social co-existence and marital relations etc. Ahom ruler's adaptive mechanism in terms of religious policy did not favour the traditional religion of the ruler group to proliferate among its subjects. Rather it was a reverse process.

A dual process worked in Ahom kingdom in religious domain. While in the royal court the king was converted to Hinduism by the process of rationalising the Ahom gods and goddesses equating them with Hindu gods and goddesses, the Ahoms commons were exposed to the wave of Nava-Vaishnavism. While the royal court felt its necessity adopt Hinduism for the want of separating itself from the fellow people with the help of re-created mythology whereby divine blood has been assigned to them, the commons were lured towards Vaishnavism for its simplistic way to relate oneself to god and liberal characters that hardly recognised social hierarchy. The Vaishnava preachers did not put any strict restriction upon the new converts in terms of the continuation of their traditional rites. Thus, most of the new converts could continue some of their very core rites and rituals. A similar situation was also seen in royal court where the influence of tantric Hindu rites got the upper hand under the initiatives of Brahmin priests and traditional practices got subordinated. In both cases, the high god of the Ahoms had to compromise with the Hindu gods and goddesses. Fall of Ahom king and subsequent colonial rule and changed the equation in the political and demographic arrangement, the traditional Ahom religion lost its ground and the entrepreneurs of Ahom ethnic reconstructionist had to revive and recall those forgotten and sometimes obsolete components to build up Ahom resurgent ethnic movement.

In most of the conversion cases, the driving force remains non-political. For instance, the Sonowal Kacharis of upper Assam adopted Vaishnavism by seventeenth century AD. It is important to note that the story that links Ghototkoch to the Kacharis was a politically motivated recreation of mythology-making the route for the Kachari Kings of western Assam to enter into the domain of Hinduism and thereby having Kshatriya blood to be eligible to rule a kingdom. But there is hardly any historical record how Sonowal Kacharis got separated from the ambit of the well established Kachari kingdom of the west.

It is believed that the Sonowal Kacharis of Sadiya region adapted Vaishnava tradition from Satradhikar Keshavananda Deva Goswami who took refuge in that area when the Ahom king started atrocious action against the Vaishnavite preachers at the behest of the Brahmin priest patronised by the kings. His personality and charismatic action attracted the Kachari people. It is said that at his trickeries the Kacharis burnt the body of their traditional god man *Gojai* who in turn cursed the Kacharis to be servant of the alien Vaishnavite gurus. It is important to note here that the Sonowal Kacharis did not have to change their high god, but at the act of the *Gosain*, his importance diminished to a great extent. They continued their traditional practices simultaneously with Vaishnavite rites. The primary motive of the Vaishnava preacher in this region was not to civilise the indigenous people, but to amass wealth by means religious taxes called *Kar Bhar*, which was collected annually by the *Pachoni* (workers of the Satra) or fetched by the devotee themselves at regular intervals. At present the religious taxes of indigenous population possess no significance because the revenue bases of the Satras are now changed to other sources. The political and demographic situation after the colonial rule changed a lot; Sonowal Kacharis had to interact with non-tribal people around them. By the time the caste infested notion on hierarchy and social distance entered the Assamese society. Sonowal Kacharis did not found their traditional identity and customs suitable to cope with the changing situation. Thus, accepting Vaishnavism and becoming a cleaner population became the need of the hour. Thus, we see the whole of Sonowal Kacharis took initiation with the Aoniati Satra and became Vaishnavite.

Mishing, the second largest tribal population of Assam, also imbibed Vaishnavite tradition to some extent. Migrated from the hills of Arunachal Pradesh, the Mishings had to adapt a lot of social and economic components of the plains of Brahmaputra valley. In the plains, the Mishings had to interact with the Kacharis, Chutiyas and the Ahoms and Bodos to a great extent. They were unable to keep their religious tradition in their pristine form due to change in geophysical condition in the plains. But having being intact with their traditional language, they could preserve most of their rites and rituals unaffected by other forces.

Acceptance of Vaishnavite tradition by the Mishing follows an incident which says that a group of Mishing people was about to slaughter a gilt for she was barren. Incidentally, a Vaishnava preacher was passing by them who told them not to kill the gilt and assured that she would give birth to piglet soon. To their surprise, she gave birth to piglets after a few days. At this, the Mishing people got convinced that the preacher has divine power. So they took initiation under him. This way Vaishnavism entered into the domain of the Mishing. The system of religious tax was also imposed on the Mishing which continues till now.

Like the Sonowal Kacharis, the Mishings also follow dualism in religious domain. In one hand they follow the monotheistic Vaishnavite tradition, on the other; they follow their traditional animistic tradition. The high god of the Mishings was not changed by the Vaishnavite preacher. Rather, it was the recent adventure of the Mishing people themselves to equate Lord Indra and Lord Varuna with two supreme gods of the Mishings. People in general hardly tend to equate them. But, it is important to note that due to changing geophysical condition, as they migrated from hills to plains, their cosmology and mythology landed into a mismatch for which they lost their credentials to some extent in the changed environment. Acceptance of non-traditional customs also was a necessity because they were surrounded by a population which had a different set of belief and practices. In their day-to-day interaction, they had to venture through such alien culture. So, acceptance of Vaishnavism opened a way to negotiate with the requirement.

Contrary to such dualism, indigenous communities like Moran, Muttak and Chutiya accepted Vaishnavism under the Moamoriya *Gosain*. It is said that Sri Aniruddha Deva was abandoned by Sankaradeva on a river island in the Brahmaputra River for, he venture into a forbidden text *Dhatu Tamrakshari*, dealing with magical power. While wandering around the island he saw some local people throwing nets in water to catch fish. They were about to stop fishing as they did not get a single fish when Aniruddha Deva insisted them to try once more and assured that this time, they would get fish. They did it reluctantly and to their surprise, the nets came up with full of fishes. At this, the people present there realised that he was not an ordinary person. They took him to their village and accepted him as their religious teacher. This way Moamoria religious sect was established. Morans, Muttak, Chutiyas and some Ahoms and Kaivarttas became a follower of this Vaishnavite sect. It is interesting to note that contrary to the process followed by other Vaishnavite indigenous groups; these people were so absorbed by the new religion that they abandoned almost all of their traditional deities and faith. It is interesting to note that the geophysical condition and economic base of these people did not change drastically. Then, what was the necessity of these people to get separated from their traditional deities and cosmologies? The Moamoriya Satras, in general, are located in the vicinity of the villages of its subjects. Thus, interaction of the religious authorities with their subjects was very much direct and face to face. This resulted into the strict monitoring of religious activities of the subjects by the religious preachers. Next, it was learnt that the religious preachers of Moamoriya Satra were not given equal status in a religious fraternity for; they preached the people of the lower social ladder like tribals and other non-Hindu locals. This created zeal among the Moamoriya gurus to impose strict norms to be followed by their subjects who reflect purity and cleanliness in terms of rites and rituals, customs and traditions. This resulted in the total banishment of traditional gods of these communities–be it the higher or the lower gods.

## Conclusion

The delineation made above reveals that religion has served the purpose of adaptive mechanism among these societies. Contrary to the general belief that dominant religion absorbs local religion, in North East India, the Hindu religion emerged as the amalgamation of local components with the Hindu religious traditions giving rise to a unique character to the Hinduism in the region. This is also one of the reasons for which the expansion of Hinduism did not affect Tribal religion in a drastic manner. This was because the tribal people could find the places of tradition and custom in the Hindu rites and rituals existed in the region. Adaptation of Vaishnavism by the local communities, at the first place, was based on the charismatic act of preachers, which later on emerged as adaptive mechanisms of these people in changing situations. One of the most striking differences of the recreation of mythology and religious history between Brahmaputra valley and many other parts of the country is that all the non-traditional religious traditions do not talk about parochial legendary hero and gods that took birth or reincarnated in the valley. The narratives about the birth and reincarnation of those gods and goddesses, their range of activities, the places where, and the people on whom they performed the divine activities are situated outside the territorial limits of the region. The mythology of this land talks about the defeat of the local heroes, demonisation of local rulers and punishment for following traditional practices etc. There is nothing to feel proud about the past of these people when one relate them to the text and mythology of Hindu and Vaishnavite tradition. It does not mention about the rivers, hills, and forest of the land they venture. The mythology of non-traditional religion does not relate to their day-to-day activities and entities they encounter with. Thus, those indigenous populations who discarded their traditional gods and goddesses have lost their roots to the land in terms of mythological and historical perspective. Contrarily, those who are still attached to their traditional high and low gods, are able to relate themselves to the nature and culture of their past. This particular aspect finds its importance in terms of the contemporary emerging ethnic resurgence of various indigenous population groups in the region.

## References


Anthony, Wallace, 1966. *Religion: An Anthropological View*. New York; Random House.

Bareh, H., 1967. *The History and Culture of the Khasi People.* Kolkata.

Bell, Daniel, 1980. 'The return of the sacred'. In *The Winding Passage*. pp 324-354, New York; Basic Books.

Clifford, Geertz., 1973. 'Religion as a cultural system', In Michael Banton (Ed.): *Anthropological Approaches to the Study of Religion*, ASA Monograph.

Dold, P., 2004. 'The Mahavidyas at Kamrupa: Dynamics of transformation in Hinduism', *Religious Studies and Theology*, 23:89-122.

Doniger, Wendy, 2010.*The Hindus: An Alternative History*. Penguin Books.

Duke, JT and BL. Johnson. 1989. 'The stages of religious transformation: A study of 200 nations', *Review of Religious Research*, 30, 3: 209-224.

Durkheim, E., 1965. *The Elementary Forms of Religious Life.* Trans. Joseph Ward Swain, New York; Free Press.

Eliot, Charles NE., 1910. 'Hinduism in Assam', *Journal of Royal Asiatic Society of Great Britain and Ireland*: 1155-1186 (October).

Endles, S., 1911. *The Kacharis*. Calcutta; McMillan.

Frazer, James, 1958. *The Golden Bough: A Study in Magic and Religion*, New York; McMilan.

Gait, EA., 1898. 'Human sacrifices in ancient Assam' *Journal of Asiatic Society of Bengal:* 56.

Gait, EA., 1906. *A History of Assam*. Calcutta; Thacker Spink and Co.

Harris, Marvin, 1974. 'Reply to Corry Azzi'. *Current Anthropology* 15: 323.

Horton, Robin, 1971. 'African conversion', *Africa:* 41, 2: 85-108.

Hutton, JH., 1921 (1969). *The Angami Nagas*. London; Oxford University Press.

Mishra, NR., 2004. *Kamakhya: A Socio-Cultural Study*. New Delhi; D.K. Print World.

Ortner, Sherry, 1978. *Sherpas through their Rituals*, London; Cambridge University Press.

Pegu, Jadav, 2004. *Reclaiming Identity: A Discourse on Bodo History*. Kokrajhar; Jwngsar.

Pulloppillil, Thomas and Jacob Aluckal. 1997. *The Bodos: Children of the Bhullumbutte*. Guwahati; Spectrum Publications.

Radcliffe-Brown, AR., 1965. 'On social structure'. In *Structure and Function in Primitive Society*. New York; The Free Press.

Radin, Paul, 1954. *The Evolution of an American Prose and Epic*, Bollingen Foundation; Sp. Publication.

Roy, Babul, 2002. 'Descent groupings, belief system and social structure among the Dimasa Kacharies of Assam'. *Man in India*, 82, 1-2: 73-99.

Sarkar, JN.,1992. 'Early rulers of Koch Bihar'. In HK. Barpujari (Ed.): *The Comprehensive History of Assam,* pp. 70, Vol. II. Assam; Publication Board.

Sonowal, CJ., 2014. *Religion and Ethnic Reconstruction among the Tribes of Northeast India,* New Delhi; Akansha Publishing House.

Stark, Rodney and James Chirico. 1985. 'Humanity, globalisation and worldwide religious resurgence: A theoretical explanation'. *Sociological Analysis.* 46 (Fall): 219-242.

Terwiel, BJ., 1996. *Recreating the Past: Revivalism in North East India* (http://www.jstor-org/stable/27864746.

Tylor, EB., 1871, 1920. *Primitive Culture.* London; Murray.

Urban, HB., 2011. 'The womb of Tantra: Goddess, Tribes, and Kings in Assam'. *The Journal of Hindu Studies*, 4:231-247.

William, James, 1958. *The Varieties of Religious Experience.* New York; New American Library.

# Chapter - 9

# Fragile Peace and Travesty of Justice: The Case of the BTAD in Assam

*—Melvil Pereira and Angshuman Sarma*

For decades, one of the problems that stubbornly challenged the policy-makers in North East India has been the demand for autonomy bordering on secession by various indigenous communities of the region. With the apprehension that their identity and culture were at stake, the indigenous communities demanded that they are protected from policies and plans that adversely affected their way of life. They felt that people not belonging to their community were settling in their land in increasing numbers. They demanded that they are allotted a homeland exclusively for themselves where they could practise their traditional way of life and remain faithful to their ancestral heritage. While some pleaded for autonomy at various levels within the framework of the Constitution of India, others demanded absolute sovereignty and threatened with secession from India.

The Government of India has addressed these concerns of the indigenous communities in various ways and means, chief among them being the granting of territorial autonomy leading to the creation of new states and formation of autonomous district councils (ADCs) as articulated in the Sixth Schedule of the Indian Constitution (Syiemlieh, 1989; Hansaria, 2010). The creation of new states and ADCs in North East India has provided a secure atmosphere for dominant indigenous communities to practise their way of life and develop along the lines of their own genius (Elwin, 1988: IX).

However, scholars have drawn attention to the consequences of such a policy framework which, while addressing the concerns of a dominant indigenous community, threatens the well-being of minority communities in a particular state or an ADC (Barooah, 2013). For instance, the creation of the state of Mizoram has addressed the concerns of the Mizos but has threatened the way of life of other minority communities (Vijukumar, 2013: 30-31). Similar is the situation in the ADCs (Barbora, 2008).

This chapter looks at the creation of Bodoland Territorial Area Districts (BTAD) and unravels the anomalies hidden in the political package that addresses the demands of the Bodos while neglecting the citizenship rights of the non-Bodo population in BTAD. It argues that while the creation of BTAD upholds the group rights of the Bodos, it denies similar rights to other groups in the region. Such an arrangement results in the denial of justice to non-Bodo individuals and groups.

## Creation of BTAD

BTAD came into existence as a result of a complex historical trajectory. One of the major factors responsible for its creation was the rampant in-migration that took place during the latter half of the nineteenth century and the early decades of the twentieth century. When tea plantations mushroomed in Assam during the nineteenth century, the tea garden owners, who were primarily British, ran short of the labour force. They found an easy supply of labourers from central India, mainly people from tribal communities inhabiting the Chotanagpur plateau. Tens of thousands of indentured labourers were transported to Assam to work in the Brahmaputra valley tea plantations in the latter half of the nineteenth century (Karotemprel and Datta Roy, 1990). This immigration of workers from central India continued during the twentieth century and even after India gained independence.

The second wave of immigration to Assam took place during the early decades of the twentieth century, encouraged and promoted by the British mostly for the purpose of generating revenue for the colonial government (Choudhury, 2015). There followed a systematic migration of people from the densely populated districts of East Bengal to the sparsely populated districts of Brahmaputra valley of Assam. Workers were also needed to undertake road construction work, mining of coal and extraction of oil. This meant an inflow of migrants from different parts of the country. The unabated immigration and settlement of people in Assam resulted in changing the population composition of Assam. The natives of Assam became increasingly worried about their lessening number. Such a scenario continued even after India gained independence leading to the 'anti-foreigners' movement in Assam during the 1980s *(ibid).*

Tribal communities were one of the groups that were severely affected by immigration. Despite the creation of tribal blocks and tribal belts which protected tribal land, the immigrants managed to legally settle down in tribal land in connivance with the local administration (Barbora, 2008: 331). The Bodos, one of the affected tribal communities of Assam, increasingly felt threatened by this continuous flow of immigrants. This set the stage for the Bodoland movement which demanded an ethnic homeland for the Bodos of Assam which in due course resulted in the creation of BTAD.

The creation of BTAD was preceded by over a decade long violence that resulted in the killing of hundreds of people and displacement of thousands of persons (Fernandes, 2012). In a desperate bid to stop violence in the Bodo inhabited areas, BTAD was awarded to the Bodo tribe in exchange for the Bodoland Liberation Tigers Force surrendering their arms and dropping their demand for a separate state for the Bodos (Misra, 2012). At a historical event that took place on the 10th, February 2003 the Bodo Liberation Tigers (BLT) surrendered their weapons and signed the Memorandum of Settlement.

After a series of tripartite talks between the Government of India, Government of Assam and Bodo Liberation Tigers, a Memorandum of Settlement was signed on February 10, 2003 in New Delhi by Mr Hagrama Basumatary, the BLT Chairman, Mr R C A Jain, secretary to the Ministry of Home Affairs of the Government of India, Mr P.K. Dutta, Chief Secretary to the Government of Assam, Sri Tarun Gogoi, Chief Minister of Assam and Shri L.K. Advani, Deputy Prime Minister of India. (Choudhury, 2015: 82).

The main objectives of the agreement were to create an autonomous self-governing body to be known as Bodoland Territorial Council (BTC) within the state of Assam and to administer a territory covering 3,082 villages in four districts–Kokrajhar, Chirang, Baksa and Udalguri–under the provisions of the Sixth Schedule of the Constitution of India, to abolish the Bodoland accord of 1993, to fulfil economic, educational and linguistic aspirations and the preservation of land rights, socio-cultural and ethnic identity of the Bodos; and to speed up the infrastructural development in the newly formed BTC area *(ibid)*.

## Demographic Profile of BTAD

The inhabitants of BTAD can be broadly divided into three categories- tribals, non-tribals and the Scheduled Castes. Communities like Bodos, Rabhas, Garos, Sonowal Kacharis, and Meches represent the tribal population. Non-tribal ethnic groups include Assamese, Koch-Rajbanshis, Adivasis, Bengalis, Nepalis, Marwaris and other tea garden workers some of whom are OBCs. Baniyas and Dhobis and so on constitute the Scheduled Caste population. Apart from Hindus, who are the dominant religious group, there is a sizeable proportion of Muslims inhabiting the BTAD and Christians. A noteworthy proportion of Bodos and a number of other communities still practice their ancestral religion.

According to the Census of India 2011, the total population of BTAD is 31,51,047 individuals which constitute 10.10 per cent of the total population of the state of Assam. Among them, 16,00,712 (50.8 per cent) are males and 15,50,335 (49.2 per cent) are females. The sex ratio for the total population of BTAD is 969 and the literacy rate is 66.25 per cent. The ST sex ratio is 999 which could be an indicator of the higher status enjoyed by women in tribal communities compared with women in non-tribal communities.

Table 9.1 shows the demographic profile of BTAD by districts according to Census 2011. It also displays the population of SC and ST in BTAD. The total population of BTAD is 31,51,047. The ST population is 10,55,732 (33.50 per cent) and SC population is 1,75,632 (5.57 per cent). The rest of the population, that is 19,19,683

(60.93 per cent), constitutes the non-tribal communities. Thus, nearly one-third of the population belongs to tribal communities while two-thirds of it are non-tribal.

**Table 9.1: Population of BTAD by Districts**

| *District* | *Total Population* | *SC Population* | *ST Population* |
|---|---|---|---|
| Kokrajhar | 8,87,142 | 29,570 (3.33) | 2,78,665 (31.41) |
| Chirang | 4,82,168 | 35,135 (7.28) | 1,78,688 (37.05) |
| Baksa | 9,50,075 | 73,083 (7.69) | 3,31,007 (34.84) |
| Udalguri | 8,31,668 | 37,844 (4.55) | 2,67,372 (32.14) |
| BTAD | 31,51,047 | 1,75,632 (5.57) | 10,55,732 (33.50) |

Figures within brackets indicate percentages; *Source*: Census 2011.

## Population by Tribes in BTAD

Table 9.2 displays data on the tribal communities in BTAD. The majority tribal community in BTAD is the Bodo. Among the 9,95,983 tribal people, 8,99,907 are Bodos (90.35 per cent). The remaining 96,076 (9.65 per cent) of the tribals belong to the Rabha, Garo, Hajong, Sonowal Kachari, Barman, Mishing (Miri), Tiwa (Lalung), Deori and other tribal communities.

**Table 9.2: Population Pattern of ST Communities in BTAD**

| *Names of ST* | *Total* | *Male* | *Female* | *Per cent to Total ST Population* |
|---|---|---|---|---|
| Boro, Boro Kachari | 8,99,907 | 450,122 | 449,785 | 90.35 |
| Rabha | 75,177 | 37,750 | 37,427 | 7.55 |
| Garo | 16,171 | 8,083 | 8,088 | 1.62 |
| Hajong | 2,370 | 1,208 | 1,162 | 0.24 |
| Sonowal Kachari | 1,738 | 886 | 852 | 0.17 |
| Barmans | 199 | 93 | 106 | 0.02 |
| Other STs | 421 | 213 | 208 | 0.04 |
| **Total ST** | **9,95,983** | **4,98,355** | **4,97,628** | **100.00** |

The demographic data displayed in Table 9.1 and Table 9.2 shows that just one-third of the population is tribal while the rest is non-tribal. The non-tribal segment consists of people belonging to SC, OBC and general categories. Among the tribal people, Bodos are the predominant group with over 90.00 per cent of the tribal population.

BTAD has the presence of religions like the Hindu, Muslim and Christian. Among tribal communities, some people still practise their traditional religion.

One notices an immense diversity of population by ethnic groups, religion and language. While diversity is an asset, it can also become a liability when it is abused by vested interests. BTAD is caught up in such a situation. Very often such diversity is used by leaders to gain political mileage which in the long run creates divisions in society (Fernandes, 2012).

## Uneven Representation of Communities in BTC

The BTAD has a Council comprising a maximum of 46 members. As many as 30 of the 46 total seats are reserved for STs. Five seats are reserved for non-tribal communities and another five seats are open to all communities. Six members are to be nominated by the Governor of Assam (Siddique, 2015). Some hold that the Memorandum of Settlement that gave rise to BTAD itself is undemocratic towards the non-Bodo population in BTAD. For instance, for 60.93 per cent of the non-ST population in BTAD less than 25.0 per cent seats are reserved in the Bodoland Territorial Council (BTC). Major non-Bodo communities in BTAD, namely, the Adivasis, Nepalis, Muslims and Koch-Rajbanshis, do not have a fair representation in BTC.

There have been three elections in BTAD: in 2005, 2010 and 2015. Table 9.3 presents community-wise representation of elected candidates. In 2010, 78.0 per cent of the members of the BTC were from the Bodo community. This became reduced to 65.0 per cent in 2015. In 2010, even the two unreserved seats (No. 20 Mothanguri constituency and No. 2 Guma constituency) were represented by candidates belonging to Bodo community.

Religious minorities are a sizable portion of BTAD population. But only two members of that community were elected in 2010. Their representation was marginally increased to three in 2015. Two OBC candidates were elected in 2015. There was no direct representation for them in 2010.

**Table 9.3: Elected Candidates to BTC from Different Communities**

| *Community* | *Candidate elected in 2010* | *Candidate elected in 2015* |
|---|---|---|
| Bodo | 31 | 26 |
| Non-Bodo ST | 2 | 5 |
| Adivasi/Tea tribe | 3 | 2 |
| Minority | 2 | 3 |
| Hindu Bengali | 2 | 1 |
| OBC | 0 | 3 |

*Source*: As provided by BTC authority.

Article 2.3 of the BTAD Accord says that 30 out of total 46 seats should be reserved for ST candidates. However, it does not specify tribe-wise representation in BTC. As can be seen in Table 9.2, apart from the majority Bodos, there are Rabhas, Garos and other STs in BTAD. The BTAD Accord is ambiguous in clearly indicating tribe-wise representation of candidates in BTC. During 2010 and 2015 BTAD elections, very few non-Bodo tribal candidates were elected. Non-Bodo tribal communities constitute nearly 10.00 per cent of BTAD tribal population (see Table 9.2) but had only 2.0 per cent representation in 2010. Rabhas have 7.0 per cent population in BTAD. But there is only one candidate elected from Rabha community in 2015. Thus, in reality, the ST category seems to be coterminous with the Bodo community. As the data shows, the fruit of ST reservation is largely cornered by the Bodo candidates.

## Anomalies in BTAD Accord

There are some basic anomalies in the BTAD Accord of 2003 that created the ground for the current situation. In 2003, ST population did not constitute the majority in many development blocks brought under BTAD. Table 9.4 shows the percentage of ST population in those Development Blocks as per the 2001 census.

Table 9.4 provides information on the percentage of ST population in various Development Blocks prior to the creation of BTAD. Of the 21 Development Blocks, only in three the percentage of ST population was more than 50. In seven Development Blocks, the ST proportion was less than 10 per cent. Thus, some leaders from non-Bodo communities point out that the very signing of the BTAD Accord was on undemocratic grounds. They are puzzled by the fact that the ST population which is around one-third of the BTAD population was given two-thirds of representation in BTC. They hold that the over-representation of ST communities, which is *de facto* the Bodo community, is a travesty of justice.

**Table 9.4: Scheduled Tribe Population in Development Blocks**

| *Development block* | *Per cent of ST population* | *Development block* | *Per cent of ST population* |
|---|---|---|---|
| Kokrajhar District | | Bongaigaon District | |
| Chidli-Chirang part | 3.68 | Baitamari | 3.90 |
| Gosaigaon | 8.86 | Barobazar | 54.06 |
| Kachugaon | 44.50 | Manikpur | 7.34 |
| Kokrajhar | 51.90 | Sidli-Chirang | 25.95 |
| Dotama | 51.80 | | |
| Nalbari District | | Darang District | |
| Baksa | 44.39 | Kalaiogaon | 12.60 |
| Tamulpur | 29.65 | Khairabari | 33.41 |
| Barigog-Banbhaag | 9.45 | Udalguri | 41.93 |
| East Nalbari | 2.13 | Dalgaon–Shiyalmari | 7.30 |
| Tihu –Barama | 25.66 | Maazbat | 13.48 |
| Barpeta District | | | |
| Govardhana | 13.24 | | |
| Jalah | 45.70 | | |

*Note*: The data in Table 9.4 is according to Census 2001, prior to the creation of BTAD.

Some leaders speak about the constant threats they are experiencing. At times they are pressurised to vote in favour of the Bodo candidates. Some recalled the violence let loose on the non-Bodo communities for not voting for the Bodo candidate in elections. Back in 2003, there were newspaper reports that mentioned about the armed Bodo militants forcefully taking signatures from *gaonburhas* (village leaders) of villages like Paahla-Shimalubari and Xathixaamukaa pressurising them to include their villages in BTAD (*Asomiya Pratidin*, 30 April 2003).

Article 3.2 of BTAD Accord says ‘A committee comprising one representative each from the Governments of India and Assam and BLT will decide by consensus on the inclusion of additional villages and areas in the BTC from out of 95 villages and areas on the basis of the criteria of tribal population being not less than 50.0 per cent'. BLT was the only non-governmental agency authorised to decide the fate of those 95 villages. The non-inclusion of non-Bodo communities is an aberration of democratic values. Till today, no activity of that tripartite committee has been published in the media.

Table 9.5 identifies the revenue circles in BTAD whose ST population is less than 50 per cent of the total. The leaders of non-Bodo communities question the grounds on which these circles were included in the BTAD. Table 9.5 shows two circles in which the ST population is less than ten per cent. All the circles mentioned in the table actually have less than 30 per cent ST population. The inclusion of these circles within ST population has bewildered many non-Bodo community members in BTAD.

**Table 9.5: Revenue Circles in BTAD**
**Where Population Share of ST is Very Low**

| *Name of circle* | *Name of District* | *Per cent of ST population* |
|---|---|---|
| Kokrajhar (part) | Chirang | 7.70 |
| Barnagar | Baksa | 15.83 |
| Rangia | Baksa | 28.50 |
| Pathorighat | Baksa | 20.45 |
| Bhowraguri | Kokrajhar | 9.31 |
| Dalgaon | Udalguri | 21.75 |
| Majbat | Udalguri | 19.98 |

According to Article 4.1 of BTAD Accord, 'Provision of paragraph 1(2) of the Sixth Schedule regarding Autonomous Regions will not be applicable to BTC'. But the demand for ST status for Koch Rajbongshi is still a burning issue within the BTAD. If they get ST status in the future, would they be able to form an Autonomous Regional Council? The BTAD Accord does not provide for the formation of Regional Councils for minority communities. Further, whether Koch-Rajbongshis will get a share in those thirty ST reserved seats is also not clear.

In a situation when Koch Rajbongshi, who are a sizeable proportion of the population in BTAD are given ST status, the provision of paragraph 2.1 of the Sixth Schedule regarding

Autonomous Regions within an Autonomous District could have been a wise solution. But the Accord has already eliminated that possibility. What will be the position of Koch Rajbongshis will be a big uncertainty if they are given ST status in the future.

The proponents of Bodo Movement deny the fact that Bodos are a numerical minority on the ground that most of the land in BTAD region actually belongs to the tribal belt and blocks. It is true that historically the tribal belt and blocks were encroaching upon by non-Bodo communities. As of now 3,49,505 *bighas*, four *kothas* and eight *lessas* of land (approximately 1,16,502 acres) in the tribal belts, blocks and sub-plan areas have been encroached upon illegally in the BTAD area alone according to the data provided by the Bodoland Territorial Council (The Telegraph, 4 July 2014).

However, what is perceived by the Bodos as the encroachment of their land by immigrants is contested by non-Bodo communities. Some of them, like the Koch Rajbongshi, consider themselves as natives. Some others hold that they have settled down in BTAD for more than a century and are legitimate land owners who have documents and records to back their claim. Moreover, the BTAD Accord itself gives protection to the land rights of the non-tribals in the region under the jurisdiction of BTC. Article 4.3 of the Accord says:

> Safeguard for the settlement rights, transfer and inheritance of property, etc. of non-tribals will be suitably incorporated in para three of the Sixth Schedule. Any such law as may be made by the BTC in this regard will not, in particular:
>
> 1. Extinguish the rights and privileges enjoyed by a citizen of India in respect of their land at the commencement of BTC.
> 2. Bar any citizen from acquiring land either by way of inheritance, allotment, settlement or by way of transfer if such citizens were eligible for such bonafide acquisition of land within the BTC area. (BTAD Accord).

Further, Article 4.8 says: 'The Amendments to the Sixth Schedule shall include provisions in such a manner that non-tribals are not disadvantaged in relation to the rights enjoyed by them at the commencement of BTC and their rights and privileges including land rights are fully protected'.

So far we have identified some of the anomalies in the BTAD Accord. The main among them is the over-representation of Bodos in the BTC at the cost of other communities. The major groups like the Adivasis, the Koch Rajbongshi and the Muslims are under-represented in the BTC. The non-implementation the provision of the Sixth Schedule which allows for the creation of Regional Council is another anomaly. The denial of equal rights to all individuals and groups comes with the heavy cost of sacrificing democratic rights which threatens the very existence of smaller ethnic groups.

## Democratic Values and Fragile Justice

As discussed in above sections, one of the ways in which the Government of India has addressed the concerns of ethnic minorities is by granting them autonomy which is known by various names like self-rule, self-determination and minority rights. These political arrangements provide ethnic minorities with the power to control a part of the natural resources in their territory and to live a life according to their customs and traditions. Going by the experience in North East India, this arrangement has helped the dominant ethnic community in a state or an ADC to enrich its culture and strengthen its identity. However, such an arrangement has also led to tensions and conflicts. This chapter has shown that the gain and enhancement of a dominant ethnic group is at the cost of the democratic rights of smaller ethnic groups which are present in that territory and have similar goals of protection and preservation of their culture and identity. The rights of the smaller communities are trampled upon while upholding the rights of the dominant ethnic group (Baruah, 2008: 16; Baruah and Rouleau, 2011: 184). The provision of autonomy and self-rule comes at the cost also of another democratic principle which upholds equal representation.

The idea of autonomy, ethnic homelands and self-rule were part of a package that tried to address the legitimate concerns of indigenous communities of North East India. But, has the creation of ethnic homelands solved the problem of alternate nationalisms? In the three

Sixth Scheduled Districts of Assam, the solution of ethnic homeland and greater autonomy has not worked. The ethnic minorities in these districts have resented the step-motherly treatment meted out to them. While the rights of some were given Constitutional recognition, the rights of other sections were marginalised and even ignored leading to further conflict.

Should the Government of India continue creating ADCs and ethnic homelands in a bid to address demands of ever increasing small nationalities in North East India? Should the state provide space to engage with the demands that insist on exclusive land rights for a dominant ethnic group? It is argued that such arrangements and negotiations result in the denial of democratic rights and justice to smaller ethnic groups. These political packages created more areas of tension and conflict than they tried to resolve (Baruah and Rouleau, 2011: 184).

To many political thinkers, making space for community rights within the framework of liberal democracy is fraught with problems both for the state and for the affected parties (Holder and Jeff, 2002; Benhabib, 2002; Riley, 2007; Misra, 2014). Most democratic governments confront the challenge of plotting a course between upholding the ideals of justice, fairness, equality while making space for community rights. When the balance is tilted in favour of either group rights or individual rights, justice is denied either to the individuals or to the groups. The challenge to liberal democratic governments today lies in creating models where the rights of individuals or small groups are not jeopardised while accommodating the demands of a dominant indigenous community.

## References

Barbora, S., 2008. 'Autonomous districts and/or ethnic homelands: An ethnographic account of the genesis of political violence in Assam (North East India) against the normative frame of the Indian Constitution', *International Journal on Minority and Group Rights*, 15: 313-334.

Barooah, VK., 2013. 'The killing fields of Assam: Myth and reality of its Muslim immigration', *Economic and Political Weekly*, 48, 4: 43-52.

Baruah, P and NM. Rouleau, 2011. 'Democracy, representation, and self-rule in the Indian Constitution', *Law and Politics in Africa, Asia and Latin America*, 44, 2: 177-195.

Baruah, S., 2008. 'Territoriality, indigeneity and rights in the North East India', *Economic and Political Weekly*, 43, 12-13:15-19.

Benhabib, S., 2002. *The Claims of Culture: Equality and Diversity in the Global Era*. Princeton; Princeton University Press.

Choudhury, T., 2015. 'Bodoland movement: A study'. *International Journal for Humanities and Social Science Studies,* 1,4: 78-84.

Fernandez, W., 2012.'Violence in Kokrajhar'. Retrieved from http://www.countercurrents.org/fernandes180812.htm on 20 January 2016.

Hansaria, V., 2010. *Justice B.L. Hansaria's Sixth Schedule to the Indian Constitution (3rd edition). New Delhi;* Universal Law Publishing Company.

Holder, CL and JJ. Corntassel., 2002. 'Indigenous peoples and multicultural citizenship: Bridging collective and individual rights', *Human Rights Quarterly*, 24, 1: 126-151.

Karotemprel, S and B. Datta Ray, 1990. *Tea Garden Labourers of North East India*. Shillong; Vendrame Institute.

Misra, U., 2012. 'Bodoland: The burden of history', *Economic and Political Weekly*, 47, 37: 36-42.

Misra, U., 2014. 'Ethnic homelands, traditional power structures, and representative democracy', In Kamal K Misra and NK. Das (Eds): *Dissent Discrimination and Dispossession,* pp. 265-272. Delhi; Manohar Publications.

Riley, AR., 2007. 'Sovereignty and liberalism', *California Law Review*, 95, 3: 799-848.

Siddique, N., 2015. 'Bodoland territorial area district elections 2015', *Economic and Political Weekly*. 50, 31: 5.

Syiemlieh, DR., 1989. *British Administration in Meghalaya: Policy and Pattern.* New Delhi; South Asia Books.

Vijukumar,V., 2013. 'Social exclusion and ethnicity in North East India', *The North Eastern Hill University Journal*, 11, 2:19-35.

## Chapter - 10

# Indebtedness and Credit System among the Rabha of Assam

—*Surajit Kumar Pal*

Discourse on credit or indebtedness means to indicate how nature of relations and interactions between the creditors and the debtors is established and functions in production organisation. In such context, production organisation is meant to stress on the involvement of agricultural communities in the whole production processes of agriculture. Like other communities, the practice of credit transactions and nature of indebtedness prevailed in Rabha society is complex and bears similarity as found in any other Indian agricultural community. In the present context, credit means to deal with agricultural credits only and its intricacy of transactions practised by the Rabha, a plains tribe of the Brahmaputra Valley, Assam.

Agricultural credit is one of the important and essential components in production organisation of any agrarian society. It is universally prevailed in almost all agrarian communities, whether they may be the tribal or the caste or any other community background. Apparently, the farmers in general in one or other way depend on agricultural credit or loan for sustaining their family by cultivating their land. Apart from agriculture, credit is also used to meet other sorts of family expenditures. In the rural belt, the village *Mahajan* (big and solvent land owners), ordinary farmers and the local traders often act as money-lenders and provide a loan to the rural communities. This conventional practice is seen in almost all agrarian societies of rural India.

## Features of Credit and Indebtedness

Credit transaction in production organisation is complex on which a kind of inter-personal relations is established between the credit lending-persons or farmers (creditors) and the credit-taking farmers (debtors). In an agrarian society, credit is primarily utilised in two broad perspectives–consumption and production purposes. It is hardly observed that credit is utilised exclusively for production purposes. However, the commercially motivated peasants utilise it not only for cultivating profit making crops like sugarcane, cotton, oilseeds (namely, soya bean, sunflower, saffola, groundnut, mustard etc) and some high yielding varieties (HIV) of paddy but also for doing other business. Such types of peasants are less in number than the landless, marginal and small categories of farmers. In majority cases these types of peasants (who are economically backwards and impoverished in character) are often indebted to village *Mahajan*, money-lenders and traders.

It is usually found that majority of farmers belonging to marginal, small and landless (also known as the farmers of subsistence agriculture or economy) categories are often compelled to take a loan for cultivation during the agricultural season. Apart from agriculture, such credit is also used to meet other sorts of expenditures such as the purchase of plough, cattle, fertilisers, insecticides and other agricultural inputs. Even it is spent when any exigency arises like children's marriage, treatment of various kinds of ailments etc. The aforesaid farming class prefers to approach the village money-lenders first for credit because the latter is easy access to them (the poor farmers). They provide credit on easy terms and conditions which are more complicated in institutional credit organisations. During distress, the poor peasants have no alternative means than approaching the village money-lenders for help.

In fact, they are often deprived of institutional credits because terms and conditions of the institutional credit firms are complicated and are not well acquainted with them. Moreover, a section of the credit firm staff acts as a coterie who harasses and exploit the loan applicants on different grounds and deprived them of getting the whole loan amount sanctioned in favour of them. Instead, in many cases, it's certain percentage is embezzled by the firm staff on the pretext of service charges and other undefined reasons. In such ground, they try to avoid the institutional credit organisations. Rather, they prefer to approach the village money-lenders or *Mahajan* who help them during their distress period.

Credit can be categorised broadly into two types: (a) institutional credit and (b) non-institutional credit. The institutional credit is available from the financial institutions such as a bank, agricultural credit cooperative societies, and other government agencies, while the non-institutional credit comes from the village *Mahajan* (big and solvent cultivators act as money-lenders) and local money-lenders (petty traders coming from neighbouring towns and business centres). The farmers of landless, marginal and the small category (also involved as share-croppers in many cases) take a loan on easy terms for cultivating their land as well as for meeting other family expenses.

On the contrary, the institutional credit agencies are very much formal in establishing a relationship with the debtors. In other sense, beyond credit transaction, no other informal relationships are established between the creditors and the debtors. In such case no kinship, caste or communities are considered as the primordial criterion for credit disbursement. But credit from non-institutional sources often follows other kinds of relationships. In such case, kinship, caste and community obligations, employment etc. get special importance in establishing a credit-debtor relationship. In other sense, the non-institutional creditors are called the 'indigenous creditors' in rural communities of India. Before the emergence of modern institutional credit organisations, the non-institutional creditors alone used to meet the credit demands of the village communities *vis-à-vis* the peasant communities of rural India. The credit provided by them was used for both consumption and production purposes. It is the fact that the rural communities whether tribal or non-tribal peasants utilise the substantial percentage of a loan of any kind taken from either institutional or non-institutional sources usually for consumption or other purposes like marriage, education and healthcare.

The characteristic features of credit types and its nature discussed before are relevant in the context of the Rabha society. Despite tribal background, they have similar peasant types and also bear the similar characters of interaction level of all the peasant categories. Like the caste societies, they are also indebted to creditors for sustenance. In their society both the sources of loan flow, but major loans come from non-institutional creditors. The institutional credit organisations in the Rabha area are being functioned since recent past. But its popularity is not much among the Rabha farmers because its official formalities are complex and burdensome to them. Instead, they prefer to take a loan from the non-institutional creditors where the loan is provided without any formalities. Rather, informal relations between the creditors and the debtors are considered in such case.

In this context, the money-lending cultivators may be classified into two categories from the nature of credit transactions. The two categories are: (i) ordinary or common agriculturist money-lenders and (ii) the professional agriculturist money-lenders. The first category of money-lenders usually lends credits to the petty agricultural labourers and the landless cultivators on a short-term basis. The landless cultivators and the agricultural labourers often also act as either tenants or agricultural workers employed by the middle level or big farmers. In fact, this type of money-lenders usually provides loan on mutual trust. Sometimes they keep a small security against their loan. In the case of security free loan, the debtors have the obligations to the creditors as and when any exigency arises the former cannot refuse. In that case, the debtors repay the creditors' loan by providing labour or plough during the agricultural or non-agricultural season. When the credit is given with a small security (like brass or bell metal utensils, silver or gold ornaments), the same (security articles) is returned to the debtors after recovery of the entire loan amount. This type of credit transaction takes place only when an informal relationship between the creditors and the debtors is established.

While the professional agriculturist money-lenders or the *Mahajan* on the other hand, normally provide credits on long-term basis against securities like land (cultivable and homestead), gold and silver ornaments. This is a common practice prevailed in Rabha society. The study indicates that normally cash loan is provided against mortgage of land. Even the quantum of loan amount depends on the amount of land given to be mortgaged. This category of money-lenders also maintains informal relations with the debtors. The loan is repaid either in cash or kind depending upon the nature of contract made before providing the loan amount.

Apart from the agriculturist money-lenders, the local traders of neighbouring market centres transact credit business with the Rabha. They visit Rabha villages with various household and other stuff like cloth, *saree*, and utensils etc. for vending. These items are sold in credit or in cash. The items sold usually on credit basis are charged with much higher rate than the market price. And they prefer to realise the cost of their products by agricultural commodities of the purchaser which are more profitable in character. When a Rabha fails to manage loan from his fellow brethren for any purpose he approaches the local traders of nearby market centres for his required loan. The concerned trader (money-lender) prefers to lend money against security. Without security, such type of money-lenders never provides a loan to any debtor. Another kind of traders is found who do money-lending business in Rabha villages. This class of traders provide a loan to the Rabha cultivators against cash crops. This means when their money is recovered by paddy and some other cash crops like oilseeds, jute, and areca-nut collected from the debtors. These crops are abundantly grown in their areas. The traders prefer to take crops against their loan amount which is more profitable than realising cash. Hence, crops are usually collected from the debtors after harvest when the market price of different agricultural produces is low and the debtors have no alternative means to surrender their commodities at a very low price. Such transaction stands on contract done between the creditors and the debtors before lending loan and under no circumstances creditors can snap the contract.

Some traders and *Mahajan's* provide both crop and cash loan to the needy persons as an advance, locally known as *dadan*. And in turn, the loan is repaid by crops with principal and interest after harvesting season only. This type of transaction prevails when they face acute crisis particularly during the lean period when adequate employment is not available to them in their villages. But the interest of such type of loan is exorbitant and burdensome to the debtors.

In fact, the loan is repaid with two-three times more than the principal amount. On the contrary, the interest rate of the village *Mahajan* is comparatively lowered than the rate of local traders living outside the Rabha villages and market centres. However, credit transactions between the creditors and the debtors depend on socio-economic conditions of both the parties. Credit system prevailed among the Rabha is of various kinds operating in different parts of their territory.

## Type and Nature of Credit Operations

*Sudbandhak or sudbandhaki:* It means when the loan is provided in cash or kind (mainly paddy) against mortgage of land. *Sudbandhak* is a very familiar system of credit transaction prevailed not only among the Rabha but also among the neighbouring peasant communities. The land is regarded as the principal security of such type of credit transaction. In such case, the creditor cultivates the mortgaged land for recovering the interest of the principal loan amount only. In fact, cultivation of such land continues years together till the principal amount is repaid by the debtor. In that case, no separate interest is imposed by the creditor; rather crop yields grown in mortgaged land by the creditor are treated as an interest on his principal loan amount.

The amount of land given to be mortgaged depends on the quantum of the loan amount to be provided. During distress, if a person (debtor) takes one *bike* of paddy (equivalent to one quintal) for a full season he has to repay the same along with an additional quantity of 50 to 60 kg of rice as interest. Even the same rate prevails when any debtor takes paddy (rice) in middle of the year. Paying additional quantity of rice also varies from place to place or area to area of their territory. Repayment of rice is made usually after the harvest of the crop. The terms and conditions related to the land mortgage are framed before proving a credit to the debtor. It reveals from data collected from four sample villages that land is considered as the principal economic resource used for credit transactions. The four sample villages are Salpara, Joyramkuchi, Chotomatia and Debitola of which first three are in the district of Goalpara and the last one is in Kokrajhar district. Finding no other major alternative resource than land, the Rabha farmers of subsistence economy prefers to mortgage their land for a loan. The major credit transactions often take place mainly among their own community members. It is found that of the total households 79 (29.48 per cent) households are indebted to the village *Mahajan* and 21.64 percentage of cultivable land were given for mortgage (Table 10.1).

**Table 10.1: Distribution of Indebted Households by Land Mortgage in sample villages**

| *Name of the village* | *Household under mortgage of land* | | *Mortgage free households* | | *Total number of households* | |
|---|---|---|---|---|---|---|
| | *No.* | *Per cent* | *No.* | *Per cent* | *No.* | *Per cent* |
| Salpara | 17 | 32.08 | 36 | 67.92 | 53 | 100.00 |
| Joyramkuchi | 22 | 25.88 | 63 | 74.12 | 85 | 100.00 |
| Chotamatia | 15 | 27.27 | 40 | 72.73 | 55 | 100.00 |
| Debitola | 25 | 33.33 | 50 | 66.67 | 75 | 100.00 |
| **Total** | **79** | **29.48** | **189** | **70.52** | **268** | **100.00** |

The table indicates that the percentage of indebted households in respect of land mortgage in Salpara, Joyramkuchi, Chotamatia and Debitola is 32.08, 25.88, 27.27 and 33.33 respectively. Moreover, of all these indebted households over 80.00 per cent belong to the classes of marginal and small farmers (Table 10.2). Sometimes big farmers also take loans against mortgage of land as noticed in Joyramkuchi village. Under certain circumstances particularly when crop failure takes place due to natural calamities like drought, flood, cyclones, lack of proper care and management, poor soil condition, low productivity, etc., this type of farmers are compelled to take credit for maintaining their livelihood. In some cases, they are also involved as wage earners. Even the mortgage free households belonging to the aforementioned agrarian classes are not always self-sufficient in an economic sense.

The agrarian classes of the creditors, who do money-lending practice, are belonged to the category of marginal, small, medium, big and even landless farmers of which the first three categories are dominant in character (Table 10.3). However, in majority cases, both creditors and debtors belonging to aforementioned agrarian classes are basically the owner-cultivators or self-cultivators. Agrarian categories of debtors and creditors shown in Table 10.2 and 10.3 envisage that they are mutually interdependent as far as their sustenance is concerned. All these peasant categories interact mutually and also simultaneously play the roles of creditors and debtors.

**Table 10.2: Agrarian Class of the Debtors of the Sample Villages in Respect of Land Mortgage**

| *Name of the village* | *Agrarian class of the debtors* | | | | | | | | | | | |
|---|---|---|---|---|---|---|---|---|---|---|---|---|
| | *Marginal* | | *Small* | | *Medium* | | *Big* | | *Landless* | | *Total* | |
| | *No.* | *Per cent* | *No.* | *Per cent* | *No.* | *Per cent* | *No.* | *Per cent* | *No.* | *Per cent* | *No.* | *Per cent* |
| Salpara | 9 | 60.00 | 5 | 33.33 | 1 | 6.67 | - | - | - | - | 15 | 100.00 |
| Joyramkuchi | 8 | 53.33 | 4 | 26.67 | 2 | 13.33 | 1 | 6.67 | - | - | 15 | 100.00 |
| Chotamatia | 2 | 33.33 | 3 | 50.00 | 1 | 16.67 | - | - | - | - | 6 | 100.00 |
| Debitola | 2 | 20.00 | 7 | 70.00 | 1 | 10.00 | - | - | - | - | 10 | 100.00 |
| **Total** | **21** | **45.65** | **19** | **41.31** | **5** | **2.18** | **1** | **2.17** | - | - | **46** | **100.00** |

**Table 10.3: Agrarian Classes of the Creditors of the Villages in respect of Land Mortgage**

| *Name of the village* | *Agrarian class of the creditors* | | | | | | | | | | | |
|---|---|---|---|---|---|---|---|---|---|---|---|---|
| | *Marginal* | | *Small* | | *Medium* | | *Big* | | *Landless* | | *Total* | |
| | *No.* | *Per cent* | *No.* | *Per cent* | *No.* | *Per cent* | *No.* | *Per cent* | *No.* | *Per cent* | *No.* | *Per cent* |
| Salpara | 5 | 45.46 | 3 | 27.27 | 2 | 18.18 | 1 | 9.09 | - | - | 11 | 100.00 |
| Joyramkuchi | 2 | 18.18 | 2 | 18.18 | 5 | 45.46 | 1 | 9.09 | 1 | 9.09 | 11 | 100.00 |
| Chotamatia | 2 | 18.18 | 4 | 36.36 | 4 | 36.37 | - | - | 1 | 9.09 | 11 | 100.00 |
| Debitola | 3 | 25.00 | 4 | 33.33 | 5 | 41.67 | - | - | - | - | 12 | 100.00 |
| **Total** | **12** | **26.67** | **13** | **28.90** | **16** | **35.55** | **2** | **4.44** | **2** | **4.44** | **45** | **100.00** |

When the credit is provided in cash, say ₹ 500.00 the debtor has to repay the principal amount plus a lump sum amount of interest ranging from ₹ 120.00 to ₹ 150.00. The rates fixed by the village *Mahajan's* or the ordinary money-lenders (primarily the farmers of subsistence agriculture) are usually followed by the debtor members. But this type of transactions is not applicable to unscrupulous traders and money-lenders. Rather, their rate of interest is more exorbitant than any other form of interest prevailed in society. In fact, it is more exploitative in character. In reality, the mortgage system is an apparatus of exploitation prevails in almost all village communities of rural India and it is very difficult for the people of a subsistence economy to get free from the clutch of the unscrupulous *Mahajan's* or money-lenders.

And in course of time, the lands which given for mortgage are ultimately grabbed forever by the creditors because in majority cases debtors fail to repay the loan amount. In this context citing, an old case bears certain relevance how one Rabha victim was able to restore his land from the clutch of an unscrupulous *Mahajan*. The case was settled in the Goalpara court.

> 'In 1935 a case on the issue of 'sudbandhaki' was dealt in the Goalpara court between one Halong Rabha (mortgagor or debtor) of Hatimura village and Geldhai Mahajan, a Rajbanshi by caste (mortgagee or creditor) of Dohela village. The mortgage once took a sum of ₹ 100.00 from the mortgagee and the latter enjoyed the interest of his loan by cultivating the debtor's land. After 10-12 years of cultivation, the debtor wanted to get back his land from the said creditor. Because debtor accused the concerned creditor of grabbing the former's land and refused to get back the same to the actual owner. The victim argued that the said money-lender had already recovered his principal amount by cultivating the victim's plot over the years. The crop yields produced during such period were more than enough from the principal capital lent to the victim. After hearing the entire matter the court passed the verdict in favour of the victim debtor. Under court verdict finally, the accused was forced to return back the victim's land'.

In recent time this system of credit business has almost disappeared from the villages of the Rabha Hasong area. Now they are conscious about their rights and privileges and the present generation is educationally and politically empowered to a great extent for which the Rabha Hasong Autonomous Council (RHAC) has come into existence in recent time for governing their society in a democratic way. Now money-lending, land grabbing and other illegal activities, etc are one of the concerned issues of the RHAC authorities.

*Kartani bandhak* : Under this system when land is mortgaged for a particular period of time against cash loan and by cultivating such mortgage land the creditor (mortgagee) recovers principal capital and the interest too. That means, the debtor (mortgagor) is not obligated to repay the creditor's loan again in a fresh manner. The entire crop yields produced during the mortgage period are exclusively owned by the mortgagee. When mortgage period ends, the mortgagor gets back his land from the mortgagee. The practice of *kartani bandhak* system stands usually for a year only. For example, if a person takes a sum of ₹ 10,000.00 he has to mortgage an amount of 3.0 *bighas* to 3.5 *bighas* (equivalent to one acre of land area) of the cultivable land area. However, the amount of land to be mortgaged against the loan depends on the quality of land. The quality of land is considered an important precondition of this system.

In the past, the village *Mahajan* (creditor) were the sole agent to do money-lending business in the Rabha localities situated at the Mechpara and other zamindari estates of the then Goalpara district. The creditor used to cultivate the mortgaged land for realising the interest of his capital amount only. Cultivation of such land continued till the principal amount was repaid by the *dharua* (debtor). But in reality, during his lifetime the debtor was never able to repay the creditor's (mortgagee) principal amount and ultimately his ownership right on such land ceased to exist permanently. In fact, such system of credit bears resemblance with *sudbandhaki*.

*Karali bandhak:* The Rabha are familiar with another form of mortgage, known as *karali bandhak*. This implies when paddy is given for loan to any person against his land. In other sense, the land is given for mortgage against paddy loan. This system is followed when the debtor faces acute crisis to sustain his family. In such case, the creditor recovers his loan by the cultivation of the debtor's land given for mortgage. Here entire crop yields grown in such land are equated with his principal loan amount (i.e. paddy). Although the crop yields produced in such land is much higher than the paddy given for loan. This system of credit transaction takes place usually during distress or lean season when they face difficult to get employment.

The method of realising the paddy loan is similar to the method of *kartani bandhak*. The prevailing rate per *bigha* of land ranges from one *bihi* to one and a half *bihi* of paddy (i.e. equivalent to 1 quintal or more). The present market value per quintal of paddy varies from ₹ 1,000.00 to ₹ 1,200.00. It was a decade back around 150.00 to ₹ 200.00. The average production per *bigha* now is around three to four *bihis* (equivalent to three to four quintals) of paddy depending upon the quality of land. Accordingly, on the basis of average production per *bigha* amount of paddy loan is fixed. The *kartani or karali bandhak* system was not in existence in the past in their society. Its practice came into existence in post-independence era particularly during the 1960s when their area was exposed to the communication network and other infrastructural facilities.

*Murimara/Monimara*: In some areas of Goalpara district particularly in tribal inhabited areas a system of credit transaction is prevailing since recent past. It is reported that *murimara,* also called *monimara* was introduced by the *Kabli* (a native of Kabul, Afghanistan) who used to do money lending business in various market and trade centres of Goalpara district. Under this system, cash used to be given for loan to the debtors against crops like *gua / tamol* (areca nut) and *dhan* (paddy) only. The Rabha and other neighbouring communities used to take cash on credit basis from the *Kabli* who used to stay in local market centres. *Murimara* system is very exploitative in nature and more profitable to the *Kablis*. It can be cited as an example how the poor men were to be deeply indebted to the creditors.

If a man used to take a sum of ₹ 40.00, in turn, he had to provide 40 kg. of paddy which is more profitable than accepting cash. If the terms of contract were made that the loan amount could be realised by delivery of areca-nut or *tamol*, then the debtor had to give a bagful or *basta* of areca-nut. One bagful of areca nut is equivalent to 2.5 *kaon* of ripe areca nut and one *kaon* means twenty *pun* (one *pun* = 80 number of nuts). The market price of areca-nut is very high than any other local crops. Hence instead of cash the *Kablis* (creditor) used to prefer to take cash crops like areca-nut and paddy. Since decades back the *Kablis* are not found to do money-lending business in their area. They have left the Rabha areas particularly after emerging political development of Afghanistan and volatile political situation emerged in the North East India.

Like the *Kablis* the small traders belonging to Bengali refugees and the *Bhatias* (the term implies the Muslim of erstwhile East Pakistan, now Bangladesh who migrated to India and settled permanently) were to be travelled to the tribal villages of Goalpara and Garo Hills and provided certain amount of money as *dadan* (advance) to the owners of the crop-yielding areca nut trees and also for paddy. Money given for *dadan* used to be realised against these crops after harvest. The rate was to be fixed in such a way under no circumstances the owners could sell his crops to any other persons or traders in a higher rate or any alternative price. In a practical sense, *dadan* system was exploitative in character.

Like other agrarian communities, the Rabha are no longer inefficient or backwards in terms of method of credit operations. The features and nature of credit operations discussed before are not different from the manifestation of credit transactions followed by various advanced agricultural communities. Indebtedness leads to land alienation which is one of the major causes of their economic backwardness. In spite of this situation, they prefer to approach their neighbours who act as money-lenders or *Mahajan.* Debtor-creditor relationship is still cordial because they are both interrelated and interdependent by strong kinship bond. Thus, the existence of indebtedness in their society is a social reality that cannot be overlooked at this juncture.

## Observation and Conclusion

The existing system of credit transactions in Rabha society discussed before bears relevance in the context of defining the 'tribe' particularly in the Indian situation. The terms and conditions applied in credit transactions do not differ from the terms and conditions followed during credit operations by the non-tribal peasant communities. The land is considered the principal economic resource to them which gets special importance in almost all economic transactions. The mode of credit operations done by the Rabha bears similarity as the non-tribal peasant communities do. Like the non-tribal peasants, they are not free from the ambit of credit operations. The loan for which they approach the village money-lenders or the *Mahajan's* (solvent farmers) is used for multiple purposes like cultivation, purchase of plough cattle, children's marriage and even for subsistence purpose when they face an acute crisis for maintaining sustenance.

The majority of debtors belong to the farmers of subsistence agriculture. They are mainly the marginal, small and landless farmers and sharecroppers though some big farmers are indebted. Under certain circumstances, big farmers (at least in terms of their landholding position) are forced to mortgage his land for credit which is unusual to our conventional notion. Even they are not always economically self-sufficient. Causes of such situation are crop failure due to natural calamities, lack of proper care and management, low productivity, unfertile soil etc. The existing agrarian categories found in their society are mutually interdependent for survival and also simultaneously play the roles of creditors and debtors. This dual role always prevails in all village communities whether the tribal or the non-tribal segments of Indian peasant society. It is a conventional notion that only the big farmers often act as money-lending *Mahajan*. But this notion is not perfectly true at least in a practical sense. Hence, the present study negates this view.

The characteristic features found in different types of credit systems are very complex that leads to making perpetual indebtedness of different categories of farmers. They bear all peasant characters as found in non-tribal peasant communities. Thus, from these points of characters, it is surmised that they cannot be considered an egalitarian society because existing production relations including the credit relations between the debtors and creditors and other socio-economic characters is complex as found in non-tribal peasant communities. The practice of unequal distribution of economic resources is an emerging development that leads to class formation in their society, though it is in a nascent stage.

It is a common notion that the tribal societies are exploited by the outsiders and exploitation causes mass alienation from their own land and they roam for earning subsistence from place to place as seasonal agricultural labourers and labourers of unorganised sectors found in different parts of the country. It is true that in many cases the tribals are exploited by the immigrant landowners, moneylenders, traders, etc. But the insight of the present study does not confirm this fact. Rather, in many cases, the insiders of the society also exploit their own people. The degree of exploitation depends on nature of relations and exploitation varies from place to place and even person to person of the concerned community. The Rabha farmers are not free from the purview of exploitation resorted to by their own people. Exploitation is a universal phenomenon and it is a social reality. And the people of subsistence economy like the Rabha are no exception to this fact.

Despite exploitation, all categories of Rabha farmers still, maintain cordial relations among themselves as they are mutually obligated to each other for socio-economic reasons. Moreover, they are integrated by strong kinship bond that plays the vital role in maintaining cordial relations among all categories of farmers. As a result unlike other peasant societies any tension and conflict on the issue of indebtedness, land alienation is not remarkably seen to exist in their society. However, in recent past, some political manoeuvres were to be taken by the Krishak Sabha, the peasant wing of the Communist Party of India (CPI) to organise them against landlessness, indebtedness, land encroachment, eviction of the tribal farmers from the forests, etc. But its influences started to be eroded when the Assam Movement (1979-1985) against aliens spread throughout Assam. Of late, Asom Krishak Mukti Sangram Samiti (AKMSS) led by Mr Akhil Gogoi has started to influence the Rabha and other indigenous tribal peasants for their legitimate rights on land and forest and for other allied issues.

Indebtedness and credit operations are interrelated, rather inseparable in character. The Rabha are not properly accustomed to approaching the institutional credit or the government financial organisations like bank, credit cooperative societies for the purpose of agricultural and other kinds of loan because these institutions are very much formal in credit transactions and one has to face various hurdles to get a loan. To avoid hurdles and formalities they prefer to approach the village *Mahajan's* or money-lenders for loan and during distress or any other situation, they are easy to access to them. Thus, the activity of the village *Mahajan* and the money-lenders still gets certain relevance among the Rabha and other neighbouring indigenous tribal peasant groups like Garo, Bodo-Kachari, Mishing, etc though the influences of the aforesaid credit operators are being started to wane.

It is reported that when any loan scheme is launched by the government under the Integrated Tribal Development Programme

(ITDP) the sanctioned amount for the beneficiaries are not properly distributed. Even in many cases, beneficiaries are cheated by the touts and corrupt officials of the credit institutions. Sometimes, a certain portion of the loan amount is deducted unscrupulously from the quota of each beneficiary as 'service charge' or in other sense it may be called as 'bribe'. In fact, a nexus between the touts or the corrupt Panchayat officials and the officials of the credit institutions operates in the system.

Of late, their economic hardship has considerably improved by the cultivation of rubber plantation introduced during the late 1970s and the early 1980s. In fact, right from Baida to Barjhora, Baida to Joyramkuchi and Bardamal to Dariduri areas of the old Mechpara Estate and other parts (Krishnai, Dudhnai, Rongjuli, Dhupdhara and other areas) of Goalpara district are under the rubber plantation for which Rabha are benefited to great extent in improving their socio-economic condition. This *en masse* plantation programme is one of the significant developments in Rabha society and it is blessings to the entire Rabha masses. This has considerably brought down their poverty, indebtedness and other sorts of economic hardships. This has not only improved their living condition but also enhanced their economic solvency to some extent. Meanwhile, the Rabha Hasong Autonomous Council (RHAC) has come into existence recently that has taken certain steps for safeguarding the survival interests of the Rabha and other tribal and non-tribal communities living within its jurisdiction. This development has also ceased the influences of the traditional credit operators (village *Mahajan*, money-lenders and local traders) to great extent.

The findings envisage that their economic interactions in terms of debtor-creditor relations are not confined to their own people only. As they are encysted by tribal and non-tribal communities their economic interactions often take place with neighbouring castes (Koch-Rajbanshi, Kalita, Sutradhar, and the migrant Hindu Bengalis) and tribal groups (Garo, Bodo-Kachari, etc). In the truest sense, they were never outside the periphery of caste mode of production organisation. The study pinpoints that the characteristic features and insights related to credit transactions followed by them are not different from tribal and non-tribal peasant societies. Their interactional pattern in respect of credit transactions is complex in nature as found in other Indian peasant communities. Thus, from this point of view, the notion of 'tribe' requires being redefined at this juncture. And this may be substantiated by other Indian studies.

## Note

The present exercise is an outcome of a study conducted periodically among the Rabha of Goalpara and Kokrajhar districts of lower Assam.

# Chapter - 11

# Traditional Village Institutions of the Karbis of Assam

—*R. P. Athparia*

## Introduction

The Karbis are one of the many tribes in North East India. According to the 2001 Census, there is a total of 419,534 Karbi speakers in India (Census of India, 2011). They were earlier known as the Mikirs. Most Karbis reside in Karbi Anglong district of Assam, besides, other areas in the neighbouring districts and states. Along with the Karbis, there are other tribal communities such as Dimasa, Rengma Naga, Kuki, and Tai-speaking Man, Khasi, Garo, Bodo and Chakma tribes in the district. With a total area of 10,434 sq. km and a density of 93 persons per sq. km, it is the largest and yet one of the less densely populated districts in Assam. As per the 2011 Census, the total population of Karbi Anglong district is 9,65,280. The Scheduled Tribes (ST) communities comprise 56.33 per cent of the total population of which 88.18 per cent population are rural and the rest 11.82 per cent urban. The literacy rate is 73.52 per cent in the district. Sex ratio is 956 per 1000 males. A total number of villages as per 2011 census are 2928. According to the government website of the district, there is a total of 775 revenue villages across four revenue circles, namely, Diphu, Phuloni, Silonijan and Donka in the district (Government of Assam, 2013).

Being predominantly inhabited by tribal communities, traditional village institutions occupy a unique position in the district of Karbi Anglong. The chapter concentrates on the traditional village institution of the Karbis. With the introduction of Sixth Schedule in the district resulting in the constitution of the Autonomous Council in the early 1950s and the devolution of powers and responsibility to village level institutions in the form of Panchayati Raj institutions in other parts of the state and country after the Constitution (Seventy-third Amendment) Act, 1992, an examination of the situation in Karbi Anglong was long overdue. The chapter explores the changes that these traditional institutions have undergone across time and discusses the need to look for new avenues and ideas for them to be relevant and useful for the tribal society in the overall context of developmental activities directed towards them.

## Traditional Village Institutions of the Karbis

The traditional institution of village headman is one of the most important institutions in a Karbi village. The headman is known as *Sarthe* or *Rong-a-Sarthe* in Karbi (*rong* = village, *sar* = elder, *the* = senior). An individual is chosen by the villagers as their *Sarthe* for his personal qualities. According to a noted Karbi writer, an individual who is experienced, wise, resourceful, and is just in his conduct is generally selected as the *Sarthe* (Timung, 2003). In normal conditions, the eldest son of the *Sarthe* inherits the *Sarthe*-ship; and in the absence of a son, his brother, cousin, nephew and other relatives from his clan are then considered for the post.

The *Sarthe* organises and administers all the works related to the village through the village council locally known as *Mei*. He initiates all the community-related ceremonies and festivals in the village, such as the *Rongker*. *Rongker* is a traditional religious festival of the Karbis held once in a year by every village for the prosperity and well-being of all the villagers in the village since indigenous tradition and religion are mostly intertwined in a tribal society, he also performs the religious duties for the village. Moreover, he also assists the community in the time of disaster and personal tragedy. Justice is dispensed by him in cases of disputes and minor crimes. He also acts as a witness to major events in the village like marriages and other social occasions. The villagers in Karbi villages pay house tax known as *Chang Khazana* to the *Bor Gaobura* or *Sarkari Gaonbura*. The *Sarkari Gaonbura* acts as the liaison officer between the village and the district council. The villagers, however, respect the *Sarthe* more than the *Sarkari Gaonbura* and do contribute materially and personally to him in cases of community events or activities. He is the custodian of all the land that belongs to the village. He allocates the land among the villagers for the purpose of building houses and cultivation. The unallocated land remains under his guardianship. He may allocate the unallocated land to villagers from other villages as long as they participate in the village events. Apart from these activities, the *Sarthe* is generally regarded as an expert on the tradition, culture and oral history of the tribe and is approached for his counsel and advice. Besides these traditional roles, his contemporary role also includes as a facilitator between the villagers and the officials from various government departments.

The *Sarthe* is assisted by an assembly comprising of the male heads of all the households of the village. He presides over the meeting of village council or *Mei* and consults with the village functionaries while taking important decisions. Among the noteworthy functionaries of the village, the assembly is the *Pherangke* and the *Risobasa*. The *Pherangke* conveys messages from the *Sarthe* to the rest of the villagers. The *Risobasa* is the head of the youths of the village. He is responsible for gathering the youths whenever they are required for any community purposes.

In the context of the traditional administrative arrangement among the Karbis which is still prevalent in Rongkhang area of Hamren subdivision of Karbi Anglong district, the *Sarthe* is a minor official in comparison to the *Lindokpo* (king), *Pinpos* (king's councillors) and the *Habes* (officials superior to the *Sarthe*). Traditionally, the Karbi chief or Raja knew as *Recho* is the head of the whole Karbi territory. There are three broad Karbi territories in the Karbi land. These are Rongkhang, Chinthong, and Amri. Of the whole, the Karbi *Recho* presides over the Karbi judicial and socio-religious affairs through the *Pinpo Arong*. This village is also known as *Barua Gaon*, located at Hamren subdivision of Karbi Anglong district as mentioned above. However, in an arrangement where powers and duties are clearly delineated, as far as the affairs of the village are concerned, the *Sarthe* is the most powerful and influential person in the village.

In areas other than Rongkhang, such as Nilip and Lumbajong, and other Karbi inhabited areas in North East India where traditional kingship (*Lindok*-ship) did not develop, the *Sarthes* function on their own without any interference from anyone. There are altogether nine *Lindoks* in the traditional Karbi territory. Out of these nine *Lindoks*, the Ronghang *Lindok* provides the Karbi *Recho* on hereditary principle. The reason for the inconsistent development of kingship across the Karbi inhabited areas according to Sri Dharamsing Teron, a prominent Karbi researcher and political activist, can be attributed to the political turmoil that followed the occupation of Assam by the Burmese army and the establishment of British administration in North East India following the Treaty of Yandaboo in 1826 (personal correspondence). He argues that Karbi society was gradually undergoing a transformation from tribalism and was slowly acquiring feudal characteristics under the influence of other cultures such as the Khasis and the Assamese who were their neighbours. The administrative system of Rongkhang which still survives today has an elaborate system which mirrors feudal system to some extent; however, this process was disrupted and could not develop in other areas due to the reasons discussed earlier.

## Traditional Administration of the Karbis

*Habai*: The ancient Karbi kingdom had twelve administrative units locally known as *Longris* and each *Longris* were governed by the *Longri* headman known as *Habai*. But a king can dismiss him anytime if not loyal to the king and to the *Pinpomar,* found physically unfit, married more than one wife, delays some trials and embraces Christianity. Though the *Habai* is the primary authority in the village, he is assisted by the Regional Council called *Longri-a-Mei*. The council consists of different members; such as-*Habai Kethe* (principal *Habai*), *Habai Riso* (assistant *Habai,* must be a younger in age), *Brutemen* (expert in traditional laws), *Mutiar* (organising secretary), *Hemai* (assistant to *Mutiar*), *Basapo* (one who arranges the settings of the *Longri-a-Mei*), *Pheranke* (Messenger) and the *Sarthes* (Headmen of the villages under the *Habai*).The *Habai* settles all the local disputes with the help of the council which is sent for the final decision of the *Lindokpo*. Since he is the protector of the traditional laws and social order, he is supposed to be a wise and responsible person. Under its jurisdiction, *Habai* looks after all the matters civil and judicial and can impose fines or punishment. The post of the *Habai* is hereditarily transferred, but can be changed if he is dismissed by the *Lingdokpo* or dies without a male issue. In such situation, *Lindokpo* can appoint a suitable male member of the clan the deceased *Habai* belonged to (Sarmah, 2011).

## Functions of *Habai*

The *Habai* performs functions related to civil and judicial matters. He is the provincial head of the villages. A *Habai* is appointed by the *Lindokpo* and placed as the head of a *Longri*. A *Longri* comprises of several villages, including the village of the *Habai*. Under his jurisdiction, he exercises various powers and functions. One of such important functions is that he can appoint the *Sarthe* or the *Gaonbura* of the village under him. *Habai* also looks after the law and order situation of his *Longri*. Any dispute in his *Longri* referred by the *Sarthe* is decided by him. His decisions are final in such instance but if fails to provide any decision he can take the help of the *Lindokpo*. Being the head of the *Longri* he can take decisions over the customary laws relating to *Jhum* cultivation and other social practices. It is the responsibility of the *Habai* to look into disputes relating to land and collective cultivation and is also empowered to impose a fine for illegal activity (Sarmah, 2011).

## Village Council (*Mei*)

The Karbi traditional council is a three-tier one. The *Alongri* council stands at the top. The middle is represented by the *Longri* council and *Mei*, and the village council occupies the base. The Karbi state is headed by a chief locally known as *Recho*. In discharging his duties, he depends on three regional centres. Each region is known as *Alongri*. The three *Alongris* are the Ronghang, Chintong, and Amri. The chief had got a council known a *Rechomei*. The representatives of the *Rechomei* are known as *Lindoks* representing the different clans of the community. The chieftainship and *Lindokship* are hereditary (Sengupta, 2011:377).

The second tier *Longri*, the council is headed by the local chief known as *Habai*. In all, there are twelve such *Longris* in the Karbi society. All the *Habais* are appointed by the chiefs. The jurisdiction of the *Habai* extends over a number of villages of a *Longri*. The administration of each village is run by the village council known as *Mei*. Each council is prescribed over by a headman or *Gaonbura* called *Sarthe*. The *Gaonbura* is chosen for his personal character by the householders. On election, he repairs, with beer and spirits, to the head *Gaonbura* or *Mauzadar*, bringing with him two or three other *Gaonburas* (Lyall, 1972: 22). Beside *Sarthe*, the village level functionaries are the *Bruteman* (acts as an advocate), the *Mutiar* (messenger), the *Pheranke* (cashier), *Kurusor* (priest of the village), etc. Nowadays, the District Council appoints the *Sarthe* and the *Sarso* (assistant *Gaonbura*; *ibid)*.

## Functions of *Mei*

In the true sense of the term, the *Sarthe* is the pivotal actor of the whole traditional political system. The democratic vision of the institution can be understood by looking into the powers of the *Sarthe*. It has been observed that a *Sarthe* can never alone make any decision, as it needs prior consent of the members. He can only issue proposals relating to the village affairs in a meeting of the Council for its

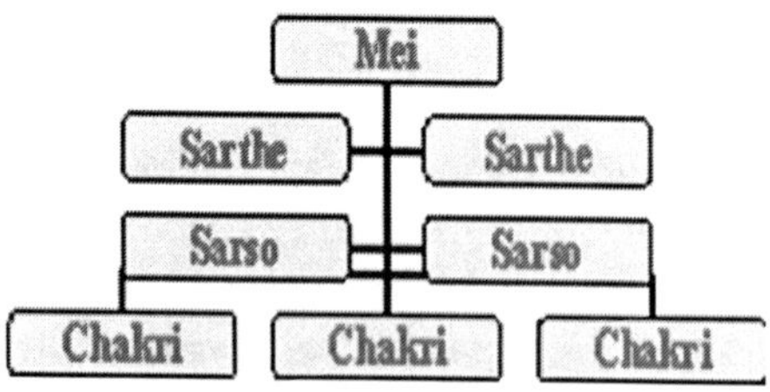


approval. Under the *Sarthe,* there are some assistants to help him, which are locally known as *Sarso*. The order of command, therefore, is as follows:

The Village Councils look into the matters of development of the village as also works as the trial court of the village. Whenever any dispute in relation to ownership of the land, theft, quarrel or adultery, etc., takes place, it is referred to the council which settles it cordially. It can impose a fine on the person found guilty, not exceeding ₹ 50 normally. On the other hand, the unsettled case is sent to the *Habai* or *Lindokpo* or the District Council for final settlement (Sarmah, 2011).

The representation of women in their traditional village council is less in comparison to men in their society.

> Mr Dhoromsing Teron an elderly man straightway said that 'No, there are no woman members in the council because they don't have any authority in the administrative activity'. Ms Kuntila Ronghangpi a female politician by profession also expressed similar comment, she said that 'No, there was no woman as its member in the village council of the Karbi society'. Kasang Derapi, a female teacher said that even though village council is a men's domain but there are women members who are also represented, 'In some place there are one or two women members but women member is very less compared to men members'. Mrs Tado Terangpi opines that 'women can give suggestions but cannot make a decision. Women do have important roles to be performed in our Karbi society apart from political roles. All the important customary practices cannot be completed without any involvement of women. But there are also certain taboos against women, like women are not allowed to certain places like in the holy places, and female do not change their surname, it is our tradition and we cannot change the customs. We have a patriarchal society so it is more male dominated. We have different types of belief, for example, when I die my clan or sub-clan can name the baby after me. When there is a cremation, people cremate the dead in a particular clan's land. Married woman are cremated in their husband's clan land but those unmarried to their natal clan's land'.

From the foregoing discussion, it is clear that women can be the members of the traditional council but the patriarchal mindset is still dominant. The people still consider that women are living in the four walls of the house. Therefore, the figure of women members in Village Council is very minimal.

## Impact of Colonial Rule on the Traditional Village Institutions

With the extension of British administration into the Karbi areas in the early 1830s, the British revenue system was also introduced amongst them. The records show that the British Government collected revenues from Karbi villages as early as the years 1834-1835 (Butler, 1855). To facilitate the collection of revenues, various villages were grouped into a *Mauza* in 1835-36 and the post of the *Mauzadar* as the head of the *Mauza* was created. The collection of revenues in kind was subsequently abandoned and a new settlement was effected in 1837-38 *(ibid)*. Although the British Government did not interfere with the traditional institutions of the Karbis and kept them intact, they also introduced new institutions to facilitate revenue collection.

The traditional *Sarthes* were initially not brought within the ambit of any formal laws or regulations by the British administration. It all changed with the introduction of the Chin Hills Regulation, 1896 in Mikir Hills (present Karbi Anglong district) by the government in 1911. Among many things, Chapter 3 of the Regulation formally delineated the powers of the 'headman' and defined his relations with the government officials of the British Empire. The Regulation stated that the headman within the local limits of his jurisdiction in accordance with the local custom will have a general control over the clan or the village or both. There were provisions that allowed him to collect customary dues from the villagers and impose punishments authorised by local customs as long as they were not 'barbarous, excessive or unusual'. He was also allowed to try any person charged with a punishable offence subject to his general control under the Indian Penal Code as specified in the Regulation.

## Post-Independence Period

The Independence of India in 1947 saw the abolition of the Chin Hills Regulation, 1896. A new framework to administer the tribal areas in the region as now known as North East India was put in place in the form of the Sixth Schedule to the Constitution with the adoption of the Constitution in 1950. The Sixth Schedule provides for the constitution of District Councils that are empowered to make laws with respect to the establishment of village or town committees or councils and their powers; any other matter relating to village and town administration; the appointment of or succession of chiefs and headmen; and social customs; among 10 different subjects enumerated in paragraph 3(1) of the Schedule. Furthermore, with the enactment of the Sixth Schedule to the Constitution (Amendment) Act, 1995 both the District Councils (henceforth known as the Autonomous Councils) of Karbi Anglong and North Cachar Hills (present Dima Hasao) were empowered to make laws on 15 additional subjects.

The Karbi inhabited areas in the form of Mikir Hills Tract of Nowgong and Sibsagar districts and parts of the United Khasi and Jaintia Hills district along with the North Cachar Hills sub-division of Cachar district were constituted as the United Mikir and North Cachar Hills district of Assam in 1951. The North Cachar Hills Autonomous District Council was inaugurated on 19 April 1952 followed by the inauguration of Mikir Hills Autonomous District Council on 23 June 1952 under the provisions of the Sixth Schedule as per Article 244(2). Clause 3 of the Assam United District of Mikir and North Cachar Hills (Administration) Regulation, 1951 provided that the two 'autonomous districts' be united as one 'administrative district' for the administrative purpose (Pakem, 1972: 355; Chaube, [1973] 2010: 105). The two autonomous districts were separated into two separate districts in 1970 as Mikir Hills and North Cachar Hills districts. In 1976, Mikir Hills district was subsequently renamed as Karbi Anglong district.

By the Assam Reorganisation (Meghalaya) Act, 1969 the State of Meghalaya was established comprising of the United Khasi-Jaintia Hills District and the Garo Hills District. The tribal people of Karbi Anglong and North Cachar Hills District were dissatisfied with the quantum of autonomy available to them under the existing provision of Sixth Schedule and there has been a demand of constituting an autonomous State within the State of Assam comprising the said two districts. A memorandum of understanding was signed on 1st April 1995 between the Government of Assam and some of the representative bodies of the two districts in the presence of the Home Minister, Government of India.

As far as Panchayati Raj institutions are concerned, the autonomous districts under the Sixth Schedule including Karbi Anglong do not have any of these institutions. However, these institutions are endowed with tremendous powers and functions in relation to development-related activities. The Constitution (Seventy-third Amendment) Act, 1992 provides for the inclusion of the Eleventh Schedule into the Constitution. The Eleventh Schedule contains 29 items that are under the domain of the Panchayats. Article 243G lays down the prerequisites for the state government to make laws to empower the Panchayats with powers and authority to function as institutions of self-government and for the further devolution of powers and responsibilities to them.

## Traditional Village Institutions and the Autonomous Council

The Sixth Schedule to the Constitution was framed with an understanding that the tribal people of erstwhile Assam, which now comprises the states of North East India, have distinct 'civilisation' and 'culture' compared to the tribal and non-tribal people from other parts of India and so it necessitates a different administrative arrangement for them.

As discussed earlier, the Sixth Schedule envisioned the creation of a separate entity in the form of the District Council which would act as a bridge between the tribal people and the state and the Central Government. Although it is not explicitly mentioned in the Sixth Schedule but it is understood that the district council is not only to work for the development of the tribal people but also to support the traditions, cultures and institutions belonging to them.

The abolition of the Chin Hills Regulation, 1896 led to the withdrawal of the formal recognition of the traditional village institution of headman and the village assembly by the government. Instead, the Autonomous Council is given the power to make law with regards to the establishment of village committee or council and the appointment and the succession of village chief or headman. However, after the constitution of the Autonomous Council in Karbi Anglong in 1952, no legislation has so far been enacted to provide any legal legitimacy to the traditional village institutions.

Besides having the post of the *Mauzadar*, the government has also introduced the post of *Sarkari Gaonburah* (SGB) to supervise over a number of villages who function independently of the *Sarthe*.

## Panchayati Raj Institutions, the Autonomous Council and the State Government

In non-Sixth Schedule areas, Panchayati Raj institutions are developed as institutions for local self-government. As discussed previously, these institutions are given enormous powers in relation to development matters. The Eleventh Schedule lists 29 such items which range from agriculture; small scale industries; roads; rural electrification; poverty alleviation programme; education, including primary and secondary schools; health and sanitation; to public distribution system. Besides, the provision for the creation of a State Finance Commission by the state government ensures that the Panchayats are financially functional.

In contrast to them, the Autonomous Councils under the Sixth Schedule despite having substantial 'autonomous' powers do not have much say regarding the development activities. For instance, the Sixth Schedule does not confer powers to the Autonomous Councils with regard to either rural electrification and distribution or poverty alleviation programme or public distribution system. Moreover, the Sixth Schedule does not make provisions for the formation of State Finance Commission to support the Autonomous Councils as is the case with the Panchayats.

However, both these sets of institutions share a commonality which is their dependence on the State Government despite the presence of constitutional provisions. In fact, the allocation of powers enlisted in both the Sixth Schedule and the Eleventh Schedule depend heavily on the political will of the State Government. Mathur (2013) has discussed at length the lack of uniformity in the allocation of the items listed in the Eleventh Schedule to the Panchayats by various State Governments depending on their political objectives. In a similar fashion, a substantial amount of finances meant for the Autonomous Councils are managed by the State Government. This allows the State Government to always exert considerable influence on the 'autonomous' Councils whenever they decide. Baruah (1997) writes that the budget of the Autonomous Council requires being prepared by the State Government in consultation with the Autonomous Council but in practice, it is solely prepared by the Finance Department of the State Government. He further writes that 'the District Council has no right even to suggest amendments to its own budget' (pp. 144). Both the Panchayati Raj institutions and the Autonomous Councils are, thus, unable to function to their full potential as envisaged by the Constitution.

## Conclusion

Presently numerous institutions exist with different objectives and overlapping activities in the districts. The Autonomous Council is yet to constitute Village Councils or Committees. It is also not known whether such councils or committees will be based on the traditional village institution of the *Sarthe* with them being accorded formal status. Nor is there any sign of the introduction of Panchayati Raj institutions in the district by the Autonomous Councils. It also remains to be seen whether Panchayati Raj institutions will be yet another institution in the plethora of institutions in the district or whether the traditional institutions would be modified into Panchayati Raj institutions.

Apart from these primary questions, it is also uncertain whether the State Government is ready to grant the fullest level of autonomy as envisaged in the Constitution to the Autonomous Councils and the Panchayati Raj institutions. Moreover, it is also unclear whether the Autonomous Council will be prepared to delegate powers to the traditional institutions. The question also remains as to the status of traditional institutions vis-à-vis the Panchayati Raj institutions if the latter is ever introduced in the district.

The Report of the Expert Committee constituted by the Ministry of Panchayati Raj, India, in their recommendation has urged the Autonomous Council to constitute Village Development Boards along with the traditional Village Councils in the manner of those in Nagaland. The non-implementation of Panchayati Raj institutions nor the formalisation of traditional village committees or councils in

Karbi Anglong has meant that developmental work are still carried out by the District Administration and the Autonomous Council despite them being specifically allocated to the village level institutions whether they are known as Panchayats in the rest of the country or as Village Development Boards in Nagaland.

As of now, powers and resources are concentrated with few departments of the government and bureaucrats are the main decision-maker for the various developmental schemes; whereas such decisions should ideally be made by the villagers with their village institutions. The presence of various agencies resulting in overlapping of activities has meant that more bureaucrats and their staff are recruited and maintained. This has created multiple centres of authority and decision-making resulting in the wastage of resources as well as the weakening of democratic traditions in the grassroots level. Most important of all, developmental activities in the district have not produced the results as expected.

The continued relevance of the traditional village institutions such as that of the *Sarthe* will depend on upon their utility and effectiveness. Formalising them by introducing legislation by the Autonomous Council would be the first step. However, modernisation of these institutions will also be required to confirm to the democratic ethos of the country. Representation of women and minority communities would not only pave the way for the democratisation of these institutions but will also prepare them for the future in a fast changing world. In addition, the introduction of Panchayati Raj institutions in the district would mean giving the community a greater say in the development of their future and issues close to them. This will also instil in them the feeling of responsibility towards their village and society. The modernisation of these traditional institutions will require that the traditional system is reconciled with modern requirements while modern elements, such as the Village Development Board as in Nagaland, are introduced. The key will essentially lie in the harmonious balance of the old and the new traditions and the wholehearted support of both the Autonomous Council and the State Government to achieve development for the people and the region.

## References

Baruah, A., 1997. 'State Government-District Council relationship in Karbi Anglong District'. In LS. Gassah (Ed.): *The Autonomous District Councils*. pp. 140-148. New Delhi; Omsons Publications.

Butler, J., 1855. *Travels and Adventures in the Province of Assam, During a Residence of Fourteen Years*. London; Smith Elder and Co.

Census of India. 2011. Statement 8: Growth of Non-Scheduled Languages-1971, 1981, 1991 and 2001. Retrieved 2013 December 15from http://www. Census India. gov. in /Census_Data_2001/Census_Data_Online/Language/ Statement8.aspx.

Chaube, SK. 2010. *Hill Politics in Northeast India*. New Delhi; Orient Black Swan.

Government of Assam. 2013. *Karbi Anglong District Profile*. Retrieved 2013, December 15 from http://karbianglong.nic.in/

Government of India. 2006. *Planning for the Sixth Schedule Areas (and those areas not covered by Parts IX and IX-A of the Constitution):* Report of the Expert Committee. New Delhi; Ministry of Panchayati Raj.

Mathur, K., 2013. *Panchayati Raj: Oxford India Short Introductions*. New Delhi; Oxford University Press.

Pakem, B., 1972. 'The socio-political system of the Jaintia Tribe of Assam: An analysis of continuity and change'. In KS. Singh (Ed.), *Tribal Situation in India,* pp. 352-363. Shimla; Indian Institute of Advanced Studies.

Sarmah, A., 2011. 'Role of traditional institutions in governance-Experience from Karbi Anglong, Assam'. *Dialogue*; October-December: 2:2.

Timung, L., 2003. *Choti-Choter Lapen Sar Kebat* (Formal conversations and the installation of the Headman). Diphu; Karbi Lammei Amei. (Original in Karbi).

# Chapter - 12

# Effects of Certain Socio-economic and Demographic Variables on the Prevalence of Stunting among Adolescent Girls of Assam

—*Nitish Mondal, Jyotismita Sharma and Kh. Narendra Singh*

## Introduction

Undernutrition is considered to be a major public health problem and principal cause of the ill-health condition, premature mortalities and morbidities among children in developing countries (Nandy *et al.,* 2005). The prevalence is found to be very high due to large population size, socio-economic disparities, illiteracy and inadequate access to healthcare facilities in India (Nandy *et al.,* 2005; Parasuraman *et al.,* 2009; Mondal and Sen, 2010; Sen and Mondal, 2012). Recent trends suggested that the prevalence of stunting i.e. low-height-for-age, a chronic undernutrition condition assessed by one's height-for-age (<-2 standard deviation of the reference) affects a large number of children and adolescents globally (Mahgoub *et al.,* 2006; Abudayya *et al.,* 2009; Herrador *et al.,* 2014; Keino *et al.,* 2014; Zelellw *et al.,* 2014) and continues to be a major public health issue in the developing countries such as India (Venkaiah *et al.*, 2002; Deshmukh *et al.*, 2006; Rao *et al.*, 2006; Medhi *et al.,* 2007; Das *et al.*, 2007; Mondal and Sen, 2010 a, b; Banerjee *et al.,* 2011; Sen and Mondal, 2012; Mondal and Terangpi, 2014). Anthropometry is considered as non-invasive, inexpensive and widely used the technique to assess the nutritional status in epidemiological and clinical investigations. Several anthropometric measures of stunting, underweight i.e. low weight-for-age and thinness i.e. low BMI-for-age reflect the distinct biological processes, and have been used widely to assess the undernutrition in children and adolescents (WHO, 1995, 2007; Deshmukh *et al.*, 2006; Medhi *et al.*, 2007; Mondal and Sen, 2010 a, b; Sen and Mondal, 2012). The prevalence of stunting is considered to be irreversible long-term nutritional and as well as social deprivation (WHO, 1995; Medhi *et al.*, 2007; Mondal and Sen, 2010b). The prevalence of stunting is transversely prevalent in different Indian ethnic populations residing in rural and urban regions and general trends suggest that girls are more vulnerable than male counterparts (Rao *et al.*, 2006; Deshmukh *et al.*, 2006; Medhi *et al.*, 2007; Das *et al.*, 2007; Mondal and Sen, 2010; Mondal, 2014).

The World Health Organisation (WHO) has defined 'adolescence' as the transition period between childhoods to adulthood aged 10-19 years and also characterised by an exceptionally rapid physical growth (WHO, 1995). Nutritional status of adolescents needs to be monitored closely as they constitute the next generation of the parenthoods. The nutritional status of the adolescent girls, the future mothers, bears special significance as they contribute significantly to nutritional and health status of the population (Venkaiah *et al.*, 2002; Deshmukh *et al.*, 2006; Medhi *et al.*, 2007; Parasuraman *et al.*, 2009; Sen and Mondal, 2010b). Currently, it is estimated that adolescents (aged 10-19 years) contributes to 1.20 billion of the total world population and belonging to the largest population of an adolescent cohort of 243 million (20.00 per cent) in India (Parasuraman *et al.*, 2009; UNICEF, 2011). Most importantly, a very high proportion of adolescent girls get married at an early age and even before completion of their physical growth (Venkaiah *et al.*, 2002; Moore *et al.*, 2009). Recent national survey report of National Family Health Survey (NFHS-3) has shown that 50.40 per cent adolescents (aged 15-24 years) are married and among them, 39.0 per cent female either have a child or are currently pregnant (Parasuraman *et al.*, 2009). Studies have been reported the associations of socio-economic and socio-demographic variables with the prevalence of stunting among adolescents (Mahgoub *et al.*, 2006; Abudayya *et al.*, 2009; Herrador *et al.*, 2014; Keino *et al.*, 2014; Zelellw *et al.*, 2014).

Therefore, it is becoming imperative and very daunting task for the researchers to identify the major socio-economic and demographic determinants of stunting especially focusing on the population investigation so that preventive measures can be taken to reduce the prevalence of undernutrition. The nutritional status among the adolescents has been found to be very vulnerable and the magnitudes are observed to be greater among the rural population of India. Therefore, the objectives of the present investigation are to assess the prevalence and effects of certain socio-economic and demographic factors on stunting among rural adolescent girls of Diphu, Assam. Furthermore, the foremost objective of the nutritional assessment is to suggest measures for the improvement of the human health condition and nutritional status of the vulnerable segments of India. Thus, the findings of incorporated in the chapter may be helpful for the policy-makers, government and non-government agencies to formulate the appropriate strategies, an intervention programme to improve the existing human health conditions and the efficacy of ongoing intervention programmes in population.

## Materials and Methods

The present cross-sectional investigation was carried out among heterogeneous adolescent girls of Diphu, Karbi Anglong district of Assam in North East India. The district Karbi Anglong (located at 25°33′ N to 26°35′ N latitude and 92°10′ E to 93°50′ E longitude) is the largest district amongst the 27 districts of Assam and covers an area of 10,434 km$^2$ of Assam. According to the Census of India 2011, the district had a population of 9,65,280 individuals (4,93,482 males; 4,71,798 females) with an average literacy rate of 59.52 per cent (56.82 per cent males; 43.18 per cent females).

A total of four higher secondary schools in an around of Diphu town were covered. The total student strength of these schools was almost identical in nature. A total of 1,306 adolescent girls in the age group 10-16 years belonging to heterogeneous ethnic groups were identified and out of which a total of 1,214 adolescent girls were selected and the overall participation rate was 92.96 per cent. The subjects whose ages that were found beyond the age group of 10-16 years or absent on the day of measurement were excluded. The age of the subjects was identified and recorded from the school records and was subsequently verified from their birth certificates and other relevant documents issued by government authority.

The necessary investigation approvals were obtained from the school authorities and local governing bodies prior to the commencement of the investigation. A verbal consent was obtained from the subjects and their parents prior to the collection of the anthropometric, socio-economic and demographic data. The present investigation was conducted following the ethical guidelines of human experiments as laid down in the Helsinki Declaration (Touitou *et al.*, 2004).

The anthropometric measurements were recorded using the standard procedures (Hall *et al.*, 2007). Height was obtained with the help of the anthropometric rod to the nearest 0.1 cm. The body weight of the subject was recorded using a portable weighing scale. The individuals were barefooted and wearing minimum clothing at the time of measurement which was to the nearest 0.10 kg. The anthropometric instruments were checked in regular interval to control the systematic errors during the measurement procedure. The technical error measurement (TEM) was calculated following the standard method to determine the accuracy of the anthropometric measurements (Ulijaszek and Kerr, 1999). The TEM was calculated using the following equation:

TEM= $\sqrt{(\Sigma D^2 / 2N}$ , D=difference between the measurements, N=number of individuals.

The coefficient of reliability (R) was subsequently calculated from TEM using the following equation:

$R=\{1-(TEM)^2/SD^2\}$, SD= standard deviation of the measurements.

Very high TEM values (>0.976) were obtained for the both intra- and inter-observer TEM analysis. The intra-observer TEM were observed to be within the cut-off values of 0.95 as suggested by Ulijaszek and Kerr (1999). Hence, the measurements recorded in the present investigation were considered to be reliable and reproducible.

A structured schedule was used to obtain the necessary information on age, sex, and occupations of parents, family size, and the number of siblings, birth order, house pattern and toilet facility, as well as a number of living rooms. The relevant data of the present study was collected from the school as well as from the household through visits made by the study team. An informed consent was also collected from the parents and subjects prior to the collection of the anthropometric measurements as well as socio-economic and demographic data. The subjects included in the investigation were free from any physical/limb deformities, previous episodes of surgery and not suffering from any form of the disease at the time of data collection. The data were collected during the period of January 2013 to December 2013.

The stunting is a conventional anthropometric index that measures the linear growth retardation primarily reflecting long-term chronic undernutrition. The age-specific Z-scores value was calculated using the LMS-method. This method is based on three important curves known as L (lambda), M (mu), and S (sigma) curves. The M curve is the median or 50th percentile curve, the S-curve is a measure of the coefficient of variation, and the L-curve is the power of the Box-Cox transformation, which measures the changing skewness of the distribution with age.

The Z-score for height-for-age (HAZ) was calculated using following equation: $Z=\{(X/M)^{*L}-1\}/(L*S)$. [Where, X=height, L, M, and S are the age-specific values of the appropriate table corresponding reference populations].

Recently proposed L, M, and S age and sex-specific reference values of World Health Organisation (WHO, 2007) were used to calculate HAZ for the assessment of stunting among children. The HAZ value was found below the '<–2 to–3' and '<–3' was considered to be 'moderate' and 'severe' grades of stunted (WHO, 1995, 2007).

The data were statistically analysed using the Statistical Package for Social Sciences (SPSS, Chicago-II, version 17.0). The anthropometric variables were depicted in descriptive statistics of mean and standard deviation (SD). Homogeneity of variance was tested using Levene's test of equality of variance. For all anthropometric variables, the p-value was observed to be statistically significant

($p<0.01$) thus showing that the variance is the same for both the groups of all the variables. The one-way Analysis of Variance (ANOVA) using the Scheffe procedure was done to assess age and sex differences in the anthropometric variables. Binary Logistic Regression (BLR) analysis was fitted to estimate the Odds Ratios (ORs) and 95 per cent confidence intervals (CIs) associated with stunting. To create dichotomous dependent variables (normal vs. stunting) normal was coded as '0' and the stunting was coded as '1' in BLR models. The predictor variables of age, family size, the number of sibs, birth order, fathers' and mothers' occupation, house pattern, and toilet facilities were entered as a set of dummy variables and results were obtained by comparing with the reference categories. A p-value of less than 0.05 and 0.01 was considered to be statistically significant.

**Results**

Age-specific subject distribution, descriptive statistics (mean and the standard deviation) of weight and height, HAZ and prevalence of stunting (<-2SD) using the WHO reference among indigenous adolescent girls are depicted in Table 12.1. The overall mean weight, height, HAZ were found to be 40.29±7.99 kg, 147.41±7.39 cm and 1.33±0.85, respectively. The age-specific mean weight and height were increased with age with an exception observed in 16 years. The highest mean attainment of height and weight were observed in 15 years, girls. The mean age-specific Z-score values were found to be increased with age in adolescent girls, but the exception was observed in 14 years. The higher age-specific mean values in higher ages (e.g., 15-16 years) indicate poor nutritional status with the advancement of ages in adolescents. The comparison of age-specific mean height with the CDC, 2000 (Kuczmarski *et al.,* 2002) and WHO (2007) showed that adolescents were observed to be below the 50th percentile of reference values in 10-11 years, but the mean values were found to be lower below the 25th percentile in 12-16 years. However, the age-specific mean values were found (Figure 12.1) to below the 5th percentile in 15-16 years girls of CDC, 2000 (Kuczmarski *et al.,* 2002). The greater and lower age-specific mean Z-score values were obtained in 10 years and 16 years girls, respectively. Age-specific mean differences were found to be statistically significant (Table 12.1)

**Table 12.1: Descriptive Statistics and Prevalence of Stunting among Tribal Adolescent Girls of Assam**

| *Age group* | *Subjects* | *Weight (kg)* | *Height (cm)* | *HAZ* | *Prevalence of Stunting (<-2SD) WHO, 2007* | | |
|---|---|---|---|---|---|---|---|
| | | | | | *Moderate (<-2 to -3 SD)* | *Severe (<-3 SD)* | *Overall (<-2 SD)* |
| 10 years | 170 | 31.21±5.54 | 137.77±6.96 | -1.01±1.05 | 37(21.76) | 03(1.76) | 40(23.53) |
| 11 years | 145 | 35.32±7.22 | 143.76±6.99 | -1.02±1.03 | 21(14.48) | 08(5.51) | 29(20.00) |
| 12 years | 210 | 38.23±7.06 | 146.45±5.95 | -1.37±0.86 | 43(20.48) | 07(3.33) | 50(23.80) |
| 13 years | 229 | 42.86±6.26 | 149.30±4.62 | -1.47±0.66 | 50(21.83) | 05(2.18) | 55(24.01) |
| 14 years | 180 | 43.91±5.54 | 151.38±5.16 | -1.34±0.74 | 40(22.22) | 03(1.67) | 43(23.89) |
| 15 years | 150 | 46.58±5.66 | 151.85±4.61 | -1.48±0.68 | 35(23.33) | 03(2.00) | 38(25.33) |
| 16 years | 130 | 44.28±5.98 | 151.74±5.48 | -1.61±0.81 | 50(38.46) | 07(5.38) | 57(43.85) |
| **Total** | **1214** | **40.29±7.99** | **147.41±7.39** | **-1.33±0.85** | **276(22.73)** | **36(2.97)** | **312(25.70)** |

*$p>0.05$; $p<0.05$, values are in parenthesis indicates percentage; HAZ: Height-for-Age Z-Score.

in height (F-value: 130.30; d.f. = 6,1213), weight (F-value: 137.92; d.f. = 6,1213) and HAZ (F-value: 12.07; d.f. = 6,1213) using ANOVA ($p<0.01$).

The overall prevalence of severe (<-3SD) and moderate (<-2SD to -3SD) and overall stunting (<-2SD) was found to be 2.97 per cent, 22.73 per cent, and 25.70 per cent respectively (Table 12.1). The age-specific overall stunting was found to be higher at the age of 16 years (43.85 per cent) and lower prevalence was observed among 11 years (20.00 per cent). The age-specific prevalence of severe stunting was ranged from 11 years (5.51 per cent) to 14 years (1.67 per cent), but the moderate stunting was found to be higher among 11 years (14.48 per cent) to 16 years (38.46 per cent).

The results of the BLR analysis and the associations of socio-economic and demographic variables on the prevalence of stunting among adolescents girls are depicted in Table 12.2. The results also showed that adolescents aged 13-16 years and 1-2 birth order groups were found to have significantly 1.33 times and 1.40 times greater Odds for being stunted ($p<0.05$). The results further show that adolescents belonging to the large family (≥5 member), and ≥3 sibs categories were found to have 1.15 times and 1.26 times greater risks for being stunted ($p>0.05$). Similarly, adolescents belonging to the

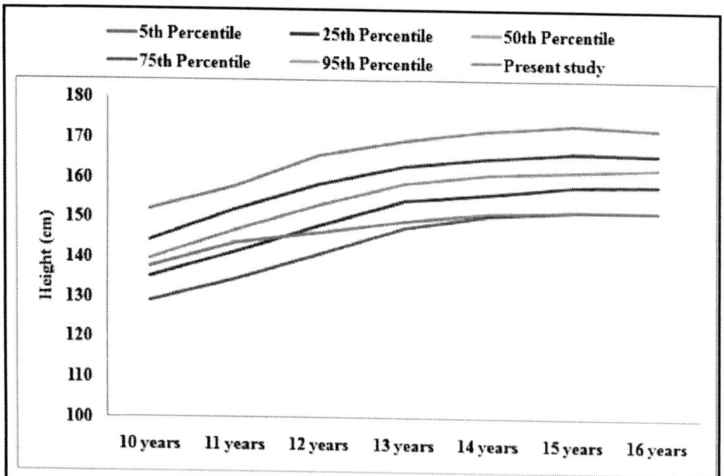


(A) CDC, 2000

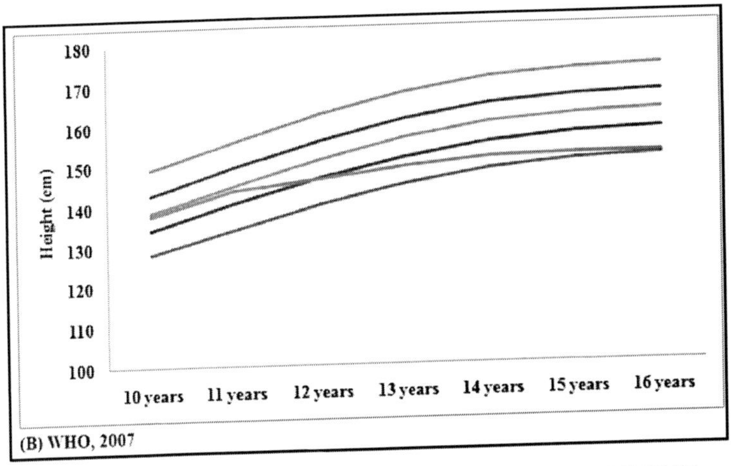


***Figure 12.1: Age-specific Comparison of Mean Height with CDC (2000) and WHO (2007) Growth References among Adolescent Girls.***

**Table 12.2: Effect of Socio-economic and Socio-demographic Variables on the Prevalence of Stunting among Tribal Adolescent Girls of Assam**

| *Variables* | | □ | *Wald* | *Odds* | *95 per cent CI of Odds* | *p* |
|---|---|---|---|---|---|---|
| Age | 10-12 years® | - | - | 1 | - | - |
| | 13-16 years | 0.28 | 4.44 | 1.33 | 1.02-1.72 | 0.035 |
| Family size | ≤4 | - | - | 1 | - | - |
| | ≥5 | 0.14 | 0.67 | 1.15 | 0.82-1.62 | 0.415 |
| Number of sibs | 1-2® | - | - | 1 | - | - |
| | ≥3 | 0.23 | 2.23 | 1.26 | 0.93-1.71 | 0.235 |
| Birth order | 1-2 | 0.34 | 5.89 | 1.40 | 1.07-1.841 | 0.015 |
| | ≥3 | - | - | 1 | - | - |
| Fathers occupation | Cultivator/ Labour | 0.20 | 2.30 | 1.22 | 0.94-1.59 | 0.130 |
| | Non-cultivator® | - | - | 1 | - | - |
| Mothers occupation | Housewife | 0.05 | 0.15 | 1.06 | 0.80-1.39 | 0.702 |
| | Working/service® | - | - | 1 | - | - |
| House pattern | Non-bricked | 0.39 | 7.63 | 1.47 | 1.12-1.93 | 0.006 |
| | Bricked® | - | - | 1 | - | - |
| Toilet facility | Sanitary toilet | - | - | 1 | - | - |
| | Non-sanitary toilet | 0.37 | 7.76 | 1.45 | 1.17-1.88 | 0.005 |

® Reference category

cultivator/ wage labour fathers' occupation (1.22 times) and housewife mothers (1.06 times) groups found to have slightly greater Odds for being stunted than their reference counterparts, respectively ($p>0.05$). The risk associations of stunting prevalence were also found to be significantly 1.47 times and 1.45 times greater among adolescents belonging to the non-bricked house pattern and non-sanitary toilet facility groups families respectively ($p<0.01$).3.

## Discussion

The prevalence of stunting is an important anthropometric failure reflects various physiological consequences, physical growth retardation, maturation and developmental delay, impaired immune function, reduced cognitive function and elevated risk of metabolic disorders into adulthood (Prendergast and Humphrey, 2014). Poor socio-economic status, ignorance and lack of health promotional facilities in the developing countries, such as India lead to the long-term nutritional deprivation resulting in linear growth retardation among children and adolescents (Venkaiah *et al.*, 2002; Medhi *et al.*, 2007; Mondal and Sen, 2010; Sen and Mondal, 2012). The present investigation highlights the importance of identifying prevalence ranges to assess the magnitude of stunting in adolescents girls residing in rural areas to provide the indication about public health situation and to establish appropriate intervention. It is generally evident that the adverse living conditions and environmental variables are greatly influenced the physical growth patterns which manifested as various retardations in growth variables as compared to the reference populations (Deshmukh *et al.*, 2006; Medhi *et al.*, 2007; Mondal, 2014). Moreover, the physical growth retardation in height manifested as stunting among the adolescents probably due to long-term chronic undernutrition during the childhood (WHO, 1995; Medhi *et al.*, 2007; Mondal and Sen, 2010a). It is an indicator of undernutrition that resultant of prolonged health and nutritional deprivation and/or disease or illness, and is considered to be the legacy of nutritional deprivation during the childhood in Indian adolescents (Deshmukh *et al.*, 2006; Medhi *et al.*, 2007; Sen and Mondal, 2010b). This index reflects distinct biological processes and is associated with socio-economic, demographic and environmental factors, thus their use is necessary for determining appropriate interventions. The relationship between the socio-economic status and undernutrition is well-established fact where the prevalence of stunting is regarded as measures of overall social deprivations in population (WHO, 1995; Deshmukh *et al.*, 2006; Medhi *et al.*, 2007; Mondal and Sen, 2010 a, b).

The result of the present investigation showed a moderate prevalence (25.70 per cent) of stunting among adolescent girls of Karbi Anglong, Assam. In a recent investigation among adolescents, Medhi *et al.* (2007) reported that 43.1 per cent of girls from Assam suffered from stunting. A high prevalence of stunting (52.5 per cent) has also been documented from West Bengal (Das *et al.*, 2007). Deshmukh *et al.* (2006) also reported a high prevalence of stunting (69.8 per cent) from rural Wardha, Maharashtra. Utilising the data from the National Nutrition Monitoring Bureau (NNMB), Venkaiah *et al.* (2002) reported about 39.0 per cent of the rural adolescents was stunted. A similar finding (41.0 per cent) also reported by Anand *et al.* (1999) from North India. Mondal and Sen (2010) reported a higher prevalence of stunting (50.3 per cent) among rural adolescent girls of Darjeeling, West Bengal. Several studies have reported serious situation and very high prevalence of stunting among Indian adolescents (Figure 12.2) residing in rural habitats with prevalence of $\geq$40.0 per cent (e.g., Das *et al.*, 2007; Medhi *et al.*, 2007; Mondal and Sen, 2010; Sen *et al.*, 2011). The adverse socio-economic conditions have significant influences along with the inadequate dietary consumption delaying the physical developmental to meet their optimal physical growth potential in Indian adolescents (Rao *et al.*, 2006; Medhi *et al.*, 2007). Studies have already advocated that the extent of stunting was greater among the lowest as compared to the higher socio-economic group in Indian adolescents in India (Deshmukh *et al.*, 2006; Medhi *et al.*, 2007; Mondal and Sen, 2010; Mondal, 2014). Recently, the WHO published growth standards for attaining weight and height to replace the previously recommended National Centre of Health Statistics-World Health Organisation reference (WHO, 2007). These new standards were based on breastfed infants and appropriately fed children and adolescents of different ethnic origins, raised in optimal conditions and measured in a standardised manner. These reference data were proposed so as to identify the individual at risk, assessment response to intervention and facilitate international comparisons. The existing literature suggested that the adolescents suffering from stunting during early ages (e.g., childhood and/or adolescence) are more likely to develop into overweight and obesity in adulthood (Keino *et al.*, 2014). Several studies have confirmed that under-nutrition and poor height attainment (e.g., stunting) among women of childbearing age is a risk factor for adverse pregnancy outcomes or poor intrauterine growth retardation (Victora *et al.*, 2008; Sen *et al.*, 2010). Furthermore, prevalence of stunting is generally considered as a cyclical process because women who were themselves stunted in childhood tend to have stunted offspring, creating an inter-generational cycle of poverty, several short-term and long-term health issues and reduced human capital that is difficult to reduce (Martorell and Zongrone, 2012; Prendergast and Humphrey, 2014).

It is evident from the above discussion, that the problem of stunting is persistent transversely among different Indian populations with variable proportions especially among adolescents residing in rural India (Figure 12.2). The under-nutrition during childhood and adolescence has not only delays growth but affects all the linear mechanism of growth processes and slow attainment of maturation of sexual characteristics (WHO, 1995; de Onis *et al.*, 2001). The results of BLR showed that adolescents aged 13-16 years exhibited significant 1.33 times greater Odds for being stunted ($p<0.05$). The risks of being stunted with the advancement of ages were also reported among children and adolescents (Medhi *et al.*, 2007; Mondal and Sen, 2010b; Herrador *et al.*, 2014). Zelellw *et al.* (2014) reported that adolescents in the age group of 13-15 years were having 2.70 times greater the risk of stunting as compared to the younger age groups (7-8 years). The results of the present study showed that the Odds for the 1-2 birth orders were found to be significantly greater for stunting among adolescents girls ($<0.05$). A similar study has also reported that the children higher birth order ($\geq$3rd) had significantly 2.50 folds higher risk of stunting ($p<0.05$) than those born with lower birth orders (Biswas and Bose, 2010).

Adolescent girls belonging to the families of cultivator fathers and housewife mothers found to have insignificantly 1.10 times and

1.06 times greater Odds for being stunted (p>0.05). Studies have advocated that the outdoor economic engagement of the parents could lead to giving less attention to the child and protecting the latter from undernutrition (Mahgoub *et al.,* 2006; Tigga *et al.,* 2015). Similar studies have also reported that the adolescents belonging to parents' who are in service or employed categories found to have significantly lower Odds of being undernourished (Abudayya *et al.,* 2009; Zelellw *et al.,* 2014). Researchers have pointed out that the nutrition levels are not merely dependent on access to nutritious foods and several other supporting factors include clean drinking water, a proper sanitary environment, and appropriate caring practices, particularly in case of children, are equally important and play major roles in the nutritional status (Ramachandran, 2014; Tigga *et al.,* 2015). The results of the BLR analysis showed that adolescents belonging to non-bricked house and non-sanitary toilet facilities categories were found to have significantly 1.47 times and 1.45 times greater risk factor for being stunted than the adolescents from bricked house (p<0.01). Studies have already reported the significant association of environment, sanitation and household pattern with a prevalence of undernutrition

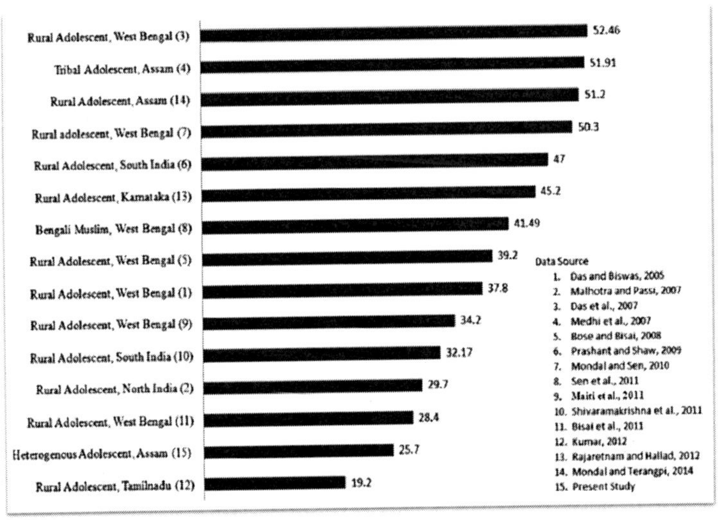


***Figure 12.2: Prevalence of Stunting among Indian Adolescents.***

among children and adolescents (Herrador *et al.*, 2014; Keino *et al.*, 2014; Tigga *et al.*, 2015). In the present investigation, family size and a number of sibs in the family had statistically not significant association with the prevalence of stunted among adolescents ($p < 0.01$). It has already been reported that the family size and the number of sibs found to have strongly explanatory powers for the stunting variation among children and adolescents (Sinnaeve *et al.*, 2006; Mondal and Sen, 2010; Sen and Mondal, 2012).

## Conclusion

Nutritional status is considered to be an integral component of the overall health of an individual or a population group. As the quality of future human resources depends on the present day child and adolescent population, therefore, improvement of the nutritional status should be given top priority. With the advancement of age towards puberty, the height falls below the normal standards among adolescents gradually. This is in all probability due to the lack of proper nutrition and healthcare facilities during childhood and adolescence period. The effect of socio-economic and demographic determinant factors (such as age, birth order, house pattern, and toilet facilities) leading to the prevalence of stunting among adolescent girls in India have been analysed. It reflects longstanding processes, which adversely affect the linear growth attainment among adolescents. Since the ultimate goal of such nutritional studies is to improve health, nutritional intervention becomes a priority for these children. The appropriate nutritional intervention programmes among the target population to ameliorate the undernutrition problem is necessary. The existing schemes on various healthcare programmes need to be strengthened and special focus should be made to provide adequate nutrient supplements, including healthcare facilities. Nutrition and health education programmes for adolescent and reproductive mothers are to be encouraged. Further, the Government of India and public health agencies should employ effective health programmes, especially for the adolescent groups in order to ameliorate such undernutrition among adolescent girls especially living in the rural areas.

## Salutation

The authors gratefully acknowledged the School authorities and local governing authorities, participants and their parents for their help and co-operation during the investigation. The extended help of Department of Anthropology, Assam University: Diphu Campus is also acknowledged.

## References

Abudayya, AH., H. Stigum, Z. Shi, Y. Abed and G. Holmboe-Ottesen. 2009. 'Socio-demographic correlates of food habits among school adolescents (12-15 year) in North Gaza Strip'. *BMC. Public. Health,* 9:185.

Anand, K., S. Kant and SK. Kapoor. 1999. 'Nutritional status of adolescent school children in rural North India'. *Indian Pediatr.,* 36:810-5.

Banerjee, S., A. Dias, R. Shinkre and V Patel. 2011. 'Under-nutrition among adolescents: A survey in five secondary schools in rural Goa'. *Natl. Med. J. India,* 24:8-11.

Biswas, S and K. Bose. 2010. 'Sex differences in the effect of birth order and parents' educational status on stunting: A study on Bengalee preschool children from eastern India'. *Homo.,* 61:271-6.

Bose, K and S Bisai. 2008. 'Prevalence of underweight and stunting among school children in West Bengal'. *Indian J. Pediatr.,* 75:1272.

Cole, TJ and PJ. Green. 1992. 'Smoothing reference centile curves: The LMS method and penalised likelihood'. *Stat. Med.,* 11:1305-19.

Cole, TJ., JV. Freeman and MA Preece. 1998. 'British 1990 growth reference centiles for weight, height, body mass index and head circumference fitted by maximum penalised likelihood'. *Stat. Med.,* 17:407-29.

Das, DK and R. Biswas. 2005. 'Nutritional status of adolescent girls in a rural area of North 24 Parganas district, West Bengal'. *Indian J. Public Health,* 49:18-21.

Das, P., SK. Ray, GK. Joardar and S. Dasgupta. 2007. 'Nutritional profiles of adolescents in a rural community of Hooghly district in West Bengal'. *Indian J. Public Health,* 51:120-1.

De Onis, M and JP. Habicht. 1996. 'Anthropometric reference data for international use: Recommendations from a World Health Organisation Expert Committee'. *Am. J. Clin. Nutr.,* 64: 650-8.

De Onis, M., P. Dasgupta, S. Saha, D. Sengupta and M Blossner. 2001. 'The National Centre for Health Statistics reference and the growth of Indian adolescent boys'. *Am. J. Clin. Nutr.,* 74:248-53.

Deshmukh, PR., SS. Gupta, MS. Bharambe, AR. Dongre, C. Maliye, S. Kaur and BS. Garg. 2006. 'Nutritional status of adolescents in rural Wardha'. *Indian J. Pediatr.,* 73:139-41.

Hall, JG., JE. Allanson, KW. Gripp and AM. Slavotinek. 2007. *Handbook of Physical Measurements.* New York; Oxford University Press.

Herrador, Z., L. Sordo, E. Gadisa, J. Moreno, J. Nieto, A. Benito, A. Aseffa, C. Canavate and E. Custodio. 2014. 'Cross-sectional study of malnutrition and associated factors among school aged children in rural and urban settings of Fogera and Libo Kemkem Districts, Ethiopia'. *PLoS ONE.*, 9: e105880.

Keino, S., G. Plasqui, G. Ettyang and B van den Borne. 2014. 'Determinants of stunting and overweight among young children and adolescents in sub-Saharan Africa'. *Food. Nutr. Bull.,* 35:167-78.

Kuczmarski, RJ., CL. Ogden and SS. Guo. 2000. 'CDC growth charts for the United States: Methods and development'. National Centre for Health Statistics. *Vital Health Stat.,* 2002: 1-190.

Kumar, AT., 2012. 'Nutritional status of Adolescent girls in rural Tamilnadu'. *Nat. J. Res. Com. Med.,* 1:48-51.

Mahgoub, SEO., M. Nnyepi and T. Bandeke. 2006. 'Factors affecting prevalence of malnutrition among children under three years of age in Botswana'. *Afr J Food Agric Nutr Dev.,* 6:1.

Maiti, S., D. De, K. Chatterjee, K. Jana, D. Ghosh and S. Paul. 2011. 'Prevalence of stunting and thinness among early adolescent school girls of Paschim Medinipur district, West Bengal'. *Int. J. Biol. Med. Res.,* 2:781-83.

Maiti, S., D. Ghosh and S. Paul. 2012. 'Determinants of nutritional status among tribal adolescent in girls Paschim Medinipur District of West Bengal'. *Int. J. Prev. Med.,* 3: 298-99.

Malhotra, A and SJ. Passi. 2007. 'Diet quality and nutritional status of rural adolescent girl beneficiaries of ICDS in North India'. *Asia. Pac. J. Clin. Nutr.,* 16:S8-16.

Martorell, R and A. Zongrone. 2012. 'Intergenerational influences on child growth and under nutrition'. *Paediatr. Perinat. Epidemiol.,* 26:S302-14.

Medhi, GK., NC. Hazarika and J. Mahanta. 2007. 'Nutritional status of adolescents among tea garden workers'. *Indian J. Pediatr.,* 74:343-7.

Mondal, N., 2014. 'Thinness is major underlying problem among rural adolescents of Northeast India'. *J. Nepal Paediatr. Soc.,* 34:39-47.

Mondal, N and J. Sen. 2010a. 'Prevalence of under nutrition among children (5–12 years) belonging to three communities residing in a similar habitat in North Bengal, India'. *Ann. Hum. Biol.*, 37:198-216.

Mondal, N and J. Sen. 2010b. 'Assessment of nutritional status among rural adolescents of Darjeeling district, West Bengal, India using anthropometry'. *Italian J. Pub. Health,* 7:54-61.

Mondal, N and M. Terangpi. 2014. 'Prevalence of under nutrition among tribal adolescents of Karbi Anglong district of Assam, North East India'. *Sri Lanka J. Child Health,* 43:154-7.

Moore, AM., S. Singh, U. Ram, L. Remez and S. Audam. 2009. *Adolescent Marriage and Childbearing in India: Current Situation and Recent Trends.* New York; Gutimacher Institute.

Nandy, S., M. Irving, D. Gordon, SV. Subramanian and GD. Smith. 2005. 'Poverty, child under nutrition and morbidity: New evidence from India'. *Bull. World Health. Organ.,* 83:210-6.

Parasuraman, S., S. Kishor, SK. Singh and Y. Vaidehi. 2009. *A Profile of Youth in India. National Family Health Survey (NFHS-3), India, 2005-06.* Mumbai: International Institute for Population Sciences; Calverton, Maryland, USA; ICF Macro.

Prashant, K and C. Shaw. 2009. 'Nutritional status of adolescent girls from an urban slum area in South India'. *Indian J. Pediatr.,* 76:501-4.

Prendergast, AJ and JH. Humphrey. 2014. 'The stunting syndrome in developing countries'. *Paediatr. Int. Child Health,* 34:250-65.

Rajaretnam, T and JS. Hallad. 2012. 'Nutritional status of adolescents in northern Karnataka, India'. *J. Family Welfare,* 58:55-67.

Ramachandran, N., 2014. *Persisting Under Nutrition in India: Causes, Consequences and Possible Solutions.* New Delhi; Springer.

Rao, KM., A. Laxmaiah, K. Venkaiah and GN. Brahmam. 2006. 'Diet and nutritional status of adolescent tribal population in nine states of India'. *Asia Pac. J. Clin. Nutr.,* 15:64-71.

Sen, J., A. Roy and N. Mondal. 2010. 'Association of maternal nutritional status, body composition and socioeconomic variables with low birth weight in India'. *J. Trop. Pedtr.,* 56:254-9.

Sen, J and N. Mondal. 2012. 'Socio-economic and demographic factors affecting the composite index of anthropometric failure (CIAF)'. *Ann. Hum. Biol.,* 39:129-36.

Sen, J., N. Mondal and S. Dey. 2011. 'Assessment of the nutritional status of children aged 5-12 years using upper arm composition'. *Ann. Hum. Biol.* 38:752-9.

Sharma, J and N. Mondal. 2014. 'Prevalence of double nutrition burden among adolescent girls of Assam, North East India'. *J. Nepal Paediatr. Soc.,* 34: 132-7.

Shivaramakrishna, HR., AV. Deepa and M. Saritha Reddy. 2011. 'Nutritional status of adolescent girls in rural area of Kolar District - A cross-sectional study'. *Al. Amer. J. Med. Sci.,* 4: 243-6.

Sinnaeve, O., J. Testa, E. Ablefonlin and B. Ayivi. 2006. 'Epidemiologic aspects of infant–Juvenile malnutrition in Cotonou, Benin'. *Med. Trop. (Mars),* 66:177-81.

Tigga, PL., J. Sen and N. Mondal. 2015. 'Association of some socioeconomic and socio-demographic variables on wasting among pre-school children of North Bengal, India'. *Ethiop J. Health Sci.,* 25:63-72.

Touitou, Y., F. Portaluppi, MH. Smolensky and L. Rensing. 2004. 'Ethical principles and standards for the conduct of human and animal biological rhythm research'. *Chronobiol. Int.,* 21:161-70.

Ulijaszek, SJ and DA. Kerr. 1999. 'Anthropometric measurement error and the assessment of nutritional status'. *Br. J. Nutr.,* 82:165-77.

United Nations Children's Fund (UNICEF). 2011. *The State of the World's Children 2011; Adolescence, an Age of Opportunity*. New York; UNICEF.

Venkaiah, K., K. Damayanti, MU. Nayak and K. Vijayaraghavan. 2002. 'Diet and nutritional status of rural adolescents in India'. *Eur. J. Clin. Nutr.,* 56:1119-25.

Victoria, CG., L. Adair, C. Fall and PC. Hallal. 2008. 'Child under nutrition study: Maternal and child under nutrition: Consequences for adult health and human capital'. *Lancet,* 371: 340-57.

World Health Organisation (WHO). *WHO Child Growth Standards: Head Circumference-for-Age, Arm Circumference-for Age, Triceps Skin Fold-for-Age and Sub-scapular Skin Fold- for- Age: Methods and Development*. Geneva; World Health Organisation,2007,available:http://www.who.int/childgrowth/standards/second_set/technical_report_2/en/.

World Health Organisation. 1995. *Physical Status: The Use and Interpretation of Anthropometry.* Technical Report Series No. 854. Geneva; World Health Organisation.

Zelellw, DA., BG. Gebreigziabher, KA. Alene, BA. Negatie and TA. Kasahune. 2014. 'Prevalence and associated factors of stunting among school children, in Debre Markos Town and Gozamen Woreda, East Gojjam Zone, Amhara Regional State, Ethiopia, 2013'. *J. Nutr. Food. Sci.,* S8: 007.

# Chapter - 13

# Nutritional Status and Food Consumption among Karbi Adolescent Girls of Kamrup District of Assam

—*Ritu Geu Goswami and*
*Mini Bhattacharyya Thakur*

## Introduction

The period of adolescence requires utmost care and attention as this is a transition period from childhood to adulthood and involves human growth and development. Adolescence period is also considered as vulnerable from the point of view of health, food habits, nutritional care, and hygiene which extends from the age of eleven years to eighteen years. Rapid growth in height, weight, muscle mass and fat mass during the peak of adolescent growth spurt calls for the need of a balanced diet. Apart from physical changes, with the onset of puberty, there are social and psychological changes that take place among all adolescent and needs to be taken care of so that the adolescent feels free to adjust to the changes. To live one must eat and to live healthy one should have a balanced diet with adequate nutrients. Knowledge of what to eat and in what quantities is a prerequisite to the healthy and happy life. The average nutritional requirements of groups of people are fixed and depend on such measurable characteristics such as age, sex, height, weight, and degree of activity and rate of growth. Every food item whether solid or liquid from plant or animal origin has a chemical composition, which enables the food to provide energy to the individual. Good nutrition requires a satisfactory diet, which is capable of supporting the individual consuming it, in a state of good health by providing the desired nutrients in required amounts. It must provide the right amount of fuel to execute the normal physical activity. If the total amount of nutrients provided in the diet is insufficient, a state of undernutrition will develop. During adolescent period, with the rapid growth, there is an increased demand for nutrients like proteins, energy, vitamins and minerals. Proper dietary habits are reflected in the nutritional status of any given population. Census (2011) estimated 6.5 million (21.3 per cent) adolescents are staying in the state of Assam which is 243 million as a whole in India. With the above in view, this chapter reveals the food habits and dietary intake among adolescent Karbi tribal girls in the age group of fifteen to eighteen years of Kamrup district of Assam.

## Methodology

This is a cross-sectional descriptive type of study conducted in two blocks of Kamrup district namely, Chandrapur and Dimoria which were densely populated by Karbi population. Chandrapur which is a semi-urban area is located approximately fifteen km from Dispur, the capital of Kamrup district. Due to its hilly terrain, Karbis are found densely populated along with other non-tribes. Although Chandrapur area is easily accessible to the market but yet the food habits of the population were not influenced by the modern junk foods. The traditional Karbi food habit was seen intact among the population of Chandrapur area. Dimoria is in the outskirt of Guwahati city and has several communities including Karbi, Tiwa, Boro, Rabha, Garo, Tea Tribes and some others living together. Dimoria was a rural area whereas Chandrapur is a semi-urban area but yet there seems no difference between the food habits and traditions among the respondents of the areas. From the two blocks, fifteen numbers of villages were selected. The subject of this study is the adolescent girls from the age group of fifteen to eighteen years. A total of 100 adolescent girls were selected by using purposive random sampling method. The adolescent girls selected were all unmarried. The primary data was collected from individual adolescent girls by interviewing them. An interview schedule was prepared to elicit information from the adolescent girls regarding socio-economic background, food consumption and nutritional status. Anthropometric measurements were recorded using stadiometer and weighing machine following standard techniques (Lohman *et al.*, 1988) and Body Mass Index (BMI) was computed following Cole (2007).

## Results

The study reveals that among 100 adolescent girls, 20 per cent were matriculated, 39 per cent were under-matric and 38 per cent studied up to class V. The percentage of illiteracy was 2.00 and one per cent was just literate. All Karbi adolescent girls were Hindu. Maximum (52.00 per cent) have *kutcha* house followed by 39.00 per cent whose houses were *pucca* and nine per cent have semi-*pucca* houses. Almost similar percentage (41.00 per cent and 46.00 per cent) of adolescent girl's families' occupation was daily wage earner and service. Only three percent and 10.00 per cent family's occupations were agriculture and business respectively. Maximum (66.00 per cent) families income were up to ₹ 5,000 followed by 28.00 per cent whose monthly income ranged from ₹ 5,000 to ₹ 10,000 and only 6 per cent family had a monthly income above ₹ 10,000. Among the adolescents', 77.00 per cent belonged to nuclear families followed by 23.00 per cent having joint families.

## Consumption of Food

The staple food of North East Indian people is rice. The Karbi populations in the studied area were rice eaters. In all the three meals as breakfast, lunch, and dinner they prefer to take rice. Some of the respondents mentioned that if they avoid lunch they prefer taking other rice products like puffed rice *laddu* prepared with jaggery and black tea without sugar. Due to urban influence, the girls below 18 years prefer to take *chappati* but the mothers were not willing to prepare it as they feel it is tedious. Cereals are one of the most important sources of energy, which provides carbohydrates and protein. So cereals which formed the bulk of their dietary were taken every day. A study conducted by Marak (2007) reported that staple food of Garos, a tribe of Meghalaya is also rice.

Regarding consumption of pulses, it was found that 54.00 per cent of the subjects in the age of below eighteen years have pulses six to seven times per week, 17.00 per cent three to five days and 29.00 per cent one to two days. Quamra (2007) also found Bhil tribe of Madhya Pradesh consume pulses like *moong* and *urad* frequently. Cooked *dal* was found to be much diluted with water, with a lot of red and green chillies. This was in contrary to what was observed among Karbis. The *dal* which is prepared is semi-thick. The Karbis prefer to have the *dal* prepared without oil or they prepared with alkali (*khar*). In the half boil *dal*, the Karbi women put vegetables like papaya, white gourd, plantain flower, drumstick leaves, pumpkin leaves, etc. along with *Khar*. *Khar* is prepared by burning the peel of banana or banana stem and dipping the burnt part in water. The strained water is kept in a bottle or jar which can be kept for many months. The strained water is called *Kolakhar* in Assamese. The variety of banana used for preparing *Khar* is known as *Athia kol* (a heavily seeded variety of banana).

All the Karbi women, as well as the girls under the age of 18 years under study, were non-vegetarians. They prefer eating non-vegetarian items like fish, mutton, chicken, pork, egg, dry fish, and meat. Most of the tribals of India are non-vegetarians (Mittal and Srivastava, 2006; Saikia, 2012). The study found that 69.00 per cent of the subjects reported to include eggs one to two days per week followed by 18.00 per cent who include three to five times per week. Very few (13.00 per cent) consume egg six to seven days per week. There was no special cuisine for the preparation of egg among the Karbis. Alam *et al*., (2010) found in a study among adolescent girls of Bangladesh that consumption of non-staple food items, such as meat, eggs, *dals* (lentils), fruits and vegetables were not frequent in rural areas which are in contrary to the present study regarding consumption of non-vegetarian foods.

Karbis are fond of fresh as well as dry fish. They prepare fish with bamboo shoot and green leafy vegetables (*mesta tenga pat*). Dry fish is prepared with chillies, onion, garlic and tomato. Another delicacy mentioned was dry fish prepared with alkali (*Khar*). The Karbi prepare dry fish by putting it in boil water with a white gourd, garlic, and ginger and adding *Khar* to it. They don't use turmeric while preparing delicacies with *Khar*. All alkaline preparations are known as *kang-moi*. A delicious cuisine of dry fish is prepared by roasting the dry fish and making it into a paste with red chillies, ginger, and garlic. This dry fish *chutney* is very hot and it is liked by one and all. Among the girls, 78.00 per cent mentioned to include fish six to seven days per week followed by 22.00 per cent who included three to five days per week. Fish ranked highest among the other two non-vegetarian foods viz. meat and egg. This is so because of easy availability of fish in nearby ponds and flooded paddy fields.

Frequency of consumption of meat among the girls below the age of 18 years is 65.00 per cent (6-7 days/week), 15.00 per cent (3-5 days/week) and 20.00 per cent (1-2 days/week). Meat especially mutton and pork is prepared by marinating the meat with ginger-garlic paste and adding to boil water. They prefer boil meat with green leafy vegetables. It is cooked till the meat is tender and before serving lot of chilli is added to give a hot taste. In this regard it may be mentioned here that all tribal population are non-vegetarians but information with regard to the frequency of consumption of non-vegetarian foods (Quamra, 2007; Mittal and Srivastava, 2006) is not available.

The Karbi women have no liking for milk. Even if they have a domesticated cow in their family they prefer to sell the milk in the market. But as of today because of education and awareness gave by Anganwadi workers, ASHA, ANM and media like television and newspaper, they are consuming milk to some extent. Due to awareness about health and nutrition they make it a point to give milk to small children and adolescent girls. No traditional delicacies were prepared from milk among the Karbis. Milk and curd are sometimes taken with flaked rice or puffed rice. Milk is given to elderly persons in the family and also to pregnant and lactating mothers. The frequency of consuming milk/week was 53.00 per cent (1-2 days/week), 35.00 per cent (3-5 days/week) and very few (12.00 per cent) consume it 6-7 days/week. The approximate amount of milk consumed per children per day is one cup i.e. 200 ml. The milk products other than card such as paneer, *khoya, channa*, etc were never found in the dietary of studied Karbi population. Mittal and Srivastava (2006) also found milk and milk products almost missing in the diet of all age groups of Oraon tribes of West Bengal. Another study conducted by Quamra (2007) found among Bhil tribe hardly any respondent consumed milk despite they domesticate buffaloes and cows. They denied giving milk even to infants and small children.

All types of underground vegetables such as potatoes, onions, colocasia bulbs, carrots, radish, beetroot, etc., are rich sources of energy, carbohydrate, vitamins, and minerals. Among the below 18 year aged girls, 64.00 per cent consume such item six to seven days per week, 32.00 per cent includes these items in their menu three to five days per week and a very negligible percentage (4.00 per cent) includes roots and tubers in their diet one to two days per week. The vegetable groups also included green leafy vegetables which are rich sources of pro-vitamin A as well as iron and calcium. The leafy vegetable category includes dark green vegetables as amaranths, spinach, fenugreek, colocasia leaves, etc. and light green vegetables such as cabbage, spring onions, lettuce leaves, etc. Some green leafy vegetable which Karbis include were drumstick leaves, spinach, curry leaves, *mayong sak, mesta tenga, kasidoria, semerang tenga,* etc. which grows wild in the hills or forest area. Among the adolescent girls, 31.00 per cent included green leafy vegetables three to five days per week and 69.00 per cent included six to seven days per week. The other vegetables which were covered in this category were ash gourd, bottle gourd, and pumpkin; French beans, cucumber, cauliflower, brinjal, etc. These vegetables are also good sources of minerals, vitamins, and fibre. The stem of some varieties of banana which is called *posola* in Assamese and rich in fibre is taken by Karbi women. They cook the banana stem without oil with *dals* or putting alkali and grams. It was observed that the percentage of other vegetables included by Karbis for six to seven days was 25.00 per cent, three to five days was 65.00 per cent and 10.00 per cent was once to twice per week.

Fruits are categorised under one category but their sources of nutrients differ. The yellow fruits like oranges, mango, ripe papaya, watermelon, wood apple, etc. are very good sources of pro-vitamin A. The vitamin C-rich fruits include *amla* (Indian gooseberry), carambola, guavas, lime, berries, pears, etc. The other fruits are bananas, musk melon, grapes, apple and pomegranate, etc. are good sources of other minerals, vitamins, and fibre. The Karbis consume the locally available fruits such as wood apple (*bael*), pineapple, ambarella (*omora*), olive (*jalphai*), Carissa carandas (*korja*), mango, litchi, etc. The inclusion of fruits was seen very less among Karbis than vegetables and other food groups. Most of the Karbi women included fruits for once or twice per week. Consumption of fruits and vegetables except green leafy vegetables were found to be low among Karbi women population. Low consumption of fruits and vegetables was reported by Planning Commission also. In a report of Planning Commission, Venkatasubramanian (2000) mentioned that although specific efforts have been made in production and access to vegetables at an affordable cost both in rural and urban areas yet consumption of vegetables and fruit continue to remain low.

## Nutritional Status

Nutritional status is the condition of the body which can be determined by the intake of balanced diet and the capacity of our bodies to digest, absorb and use those nutrients properly. One-fourth Karbi girls were underweight which may be stated as very less as compared to other tribal groups of Assam and India. Another fact may be mentioned here that none of the girls falls into moderately and severely underweight category. Their Body Mass Index (BMI) is just below of 18.5 kg/m$^2$. In Assam, a study conducted by Medhi *et al.* (2007) reported that 41.3 per cent of adolescent tribal girls of tea garden of Dibrugarh were thin. Deshmukh *et al.* (2006) reported that majority (53.8 per cent) of adolescent girls of Wardha were thin and only 2.2 per cent were overweight and 44.00 per cent were normal. The present study found that very few (7.00 per cent) were overweight and the majority (67.00 per cent) were normal which reveals that the dietary intake of Karbi girls was good. This may be due to the inclusion of cereals, pulses and fresh foods and green leafy vegetables which were found to be good among below 18 years Karbi girls. Patil *et al.* (2009) in a study amongst adolescent girls of rural Ratnagiri district of Maharashtra reported 69.3 per cent girls were underweight and 2.4 per cent were overweight as per WHO guidelines. Shahid *et al.* (2009) studied nutritional status of adolescent college girls of Rawalpindi and the findings were similar to the present study where 20.00 per cent of girls were having BMI<18.5, 77.00 per cent were above 18.5 and 3.00 per cent were obese. Good nutritional status may be attributed to the reasons that all Karbi girls were non-vegetarians especially fish and green leafy vegetables included every day which is collected either from homestead garden or from hilly terrain.

## Discussion

The adolescent Karbi girls under the study found to be non-vegetarian. The consumption of cereal, non-vegetarian foods, and green leafy vegetables was found to be good which may be the reason for good nutritional status. The study revealed that the food consumption habits among Karbi adolescent girls were proper but needs little nutrition education regarding consumption of milk and fruits.

## References


Alam, A., SW. Roy, T. Ahmed and AMS. Ahmed, 2010. 'Nutritional status, dietary intake and relevant knowledge of adolescent girls in rural Bangladesh'. *Journal of Health, Population and Nutrition*, 28, 1: 86-94.

Cole, TJ., 2007. 'Body mass index cut offs to define thinness in children and adolescents: international survey'. *British Medical Journal*, 335, 7612: 194.

Deshmukh, P., S. Gupta, M. Bharambe, AR. Dongre, C. Maliye and S. Kaur, 2006. 'Nutritional status of adolescents in rural Wardha'. *The Indian Journal of Pediatrics*, 73, 2:139-41. DOI: 10.1007/BF02820204.

Lohman, TG, AF. Roche and R. Martorell, 1988. *Anthropometric Standardisation Reference Manual*. Chicago ; Human Kinetics Books.

Marak, NR., 2007. 'Food habits of the Garo tribe of Meghalaya'. *Tribal Health Bulletin*, 13,1-2: 42-49.

Medhi, GK., NC. Hazarika and J. Mahanta, J. 2007. 'Nutritional status of adolescents among Tea Garden Workers'. *Indian Journal of Pediatrics*, 74, 4: 343-347.

Mittal, PC and S. Srivastava, 2006. 'Diet, nutritional status and food related traditions of Oraon tribes of New Mal (West Bengal), India'. *Rural and Remote Health*, 6,1: 385.

Patil, SN., V. Wasnik and R. Wadke, 2009. 'Health problems amongst adolescent girls in rural areas of Ratnagiri district of Maharashtra India'. *Journal of Clinical and Diagnostic Research*, 3: 1784-1790.

Quamra, SR., J. Roy and DK. Mishra, 2007. Food consumption pattern and associated habits of the Bhil tribe of Dhar District of Madhya Pradesh'. *Proceeding of National Symposium on Tribal Health*, pp. 211-220.

Saikia, S., 2012. 'Food pattern of Tea Tribes of two selected tea garden, Dibrugarh, IJCAES'. *Special Issue on Basic, Applied and Social Sciences*, II: 302.

Shahid, A., FR. Siddiquif, MA. Bhtti and MK. Ahamed, 2009. Assessment of nutritional status of adolescent college girls at Rawalpindi. HOD Community

Venkatasubramanian, K., 2000. 'Planning Commission Report on key factor in development'. *The Hindu*, Tuesday May 16.

# Chapter - 14

# Ethnomedicinal Practices among the Dibongiya Deoris of Assam

*—Juri Borah and S. Sengupta*

## Introduction

Ethnomedicine represents the traditional medicinal practices that are confined to a particular group of people. It represents a community's culture or way of living, perceptions regarding various diseases, etc. It shows the knowledge of the people to use the available natural product for curing various diseases and also to some extent economic status of the people too. Although nowadays modern medical science has attracted people a lot, still different communities prefer traditional remedies for curing their ailments as it is relatively less costly affairs and maybe people are not aware of the available facilities.

Each and every society, in general, has different perceptions with regards to various diseases they have experienced in their lifetime. Accordingly, their mode of treatment also varies noticeably. People have identified diverse locally available plant species and animal products for getting relief from diseases, knowledge of that is also passed on from one generation to the next orally.

The study of the traditional medicine scientifically is therefore of utmost importance since people are upholding this traditional medical practices for that they must have got benefit out of it. A good number of research works have been published in this regard by the scholars from different parts of the world. In India, especially in North East India mention may be made of the works. The works of Jain and

Borthakur, 1980; Guha, 1986; Medhi, 1995; Dutta and Nath, 1999; Sharma Thakur, 1999; Choudhury, 2000; Medhi and Paul, 2004; Bhardwaj *et al.* 2005; Bhasin, 2005; Das *et al.* 2008; Sonowal and Baruah, 2011, etc may be mentioned in this regard. But scientific documentation of the same is not yet done satisfactorily.

The present chapter attempts to textualise the existing plant and animal product based ethnomedicinal wisdom among the Dibongiya Deori of Lakhimpur district, Assam.

## Materials and Methods

The villages selected for the present study were Borchapori and Kinapather, both exclusively inhabited by the Dibongiya Deori in Lakhimpur district of Assam. Both the villages are in a far-flung area with inconvenience in communication and therefore the villagers are dependent on the locally available natural resources. Information collected from a number of the traditional ethnomedicinal practitioner (*Kuchi liya mochi*) and some elderly knowledgeable persons of both sexes from the village. Observation, interview and case study method were taken into consideration for the purpose of data collection.

The Dibongiya (*Jimochayan*) represents one of the important territorial groups/sub-tribe of Deori, others being the Borgonya, Tengaponiya, and Patorgonya. The last territorial group, at present, could not be traced in any places of Assam. Some believe that the Patorgonya section has been assimilated with Tiwa tribe of middle Assam at the time of their migration from Sadiya, while some other believes their presence in Kachin tract near Yangon in Myanmar. At present Lakhimpur, Sibsagar, Jorhat, Dibrugarh, Lakhimpur, Shonitpur, Dhemaji and Tinsukia besides Lohit and Changlang district of Arunachal Pradesh are the major habitation of the tribe. They have firm faith in god and are known for their religiosity. Only the Dibongiya can speak their mother tongue. They belong to Tibeto-Mongoloid racial group.

## Results and Discussion

Plants play a very important role among Dibongiya, both for their nutrition and medicinal properties. However, their method of preparation and the administration of the medicines differ from other neighbouring communities. The medicines prepared from the plants were generally prepared by collecting their sap/extract, or preparing a decoction, or applying the paste after grinding.

The Dibongiya Deori people are the followers of traditional remedies and use home remedies for curing a variety of diseases. Occasionally, an assortment of varied plant species also consumed by them to enrich their health status. They prefer propitiation of various malevolent spirits for getting relief from different ailments. They have a firm belief in supernatural forces and strongly believe that any violations of taboo will enraged/annoy them and cause harm to the individual or his/her family. Therefore, they observed some restrictions in high esteem. Some of the traditional medicines used in commonly occurred diseases are:

**Table 14.1 List of Ethnomedicinal Plants used to Cure Various Diseases**

| *Ethnomedicine* | | | | *Disease* |
|---|---|---|---|---|
| ***Local name*** | ***English name*** | ***Scientific name*** | ***Part used*** | |
| *Hiju* | Indian spurge tree | *Euphorbia ligularia* | Leaves | Discharge from ear/ Otorrhoea |
| *Satiyana* | Indian devil tree | *Alstonia scholaris* | Juice | Boil/abscess |
| | | | Bark | Malaria |
| *Kimaru* | Camphor tree | *Eupatorium cannabinum* | Leaves | Eye problem |
| *Laijabori* | Heartleaf drymary | *Drymaria cordata* | Leaves | |
| | | | Leaves | Eczema |
| *Nache bashi mushe* | Common lantana/ Red sage | *Eupatorium odoratum* | Leaves | Injury |
| *Shatamuli* | Garden asparagus | *Asaparagus recemosus* | Root | Dysentery |
| *Mikaci* | Duggal fiber tree | *Debregeasia wallichiana* | Leaves | |
| *Letaguti* | Gray nicker | *Caesalpinia bonduc* | Seeds | Pneumonia |
| *Jaluk* | Black pepper | *Piper nigrum* | Seeds | |
| *Dubori bon* | Indian dog grass | *Cynodon dactylon* | Leaves | Jaundice |
| *Cirota* | Mugwort/ Wormwood | *Swertia chirayita/ Andrographis paniculata* | Leaves/ bark | Malaria |

*(Contd...)*

| *Raghumola* | Crepe ginger | *Costus specious* | Leaves | Tuberculosis |
|---|---|---|---|---|
| *Mohanim* | Margosa leaves | *Azadirachta indica* | Leaves | Worm |
| *Nilokontha* | Blue justicia | *Ecbolium linneanum* | Root | |
| *Cubi citi* | Hog plum | *Spondias mombin, Spondias purpurea* | Seeds | Tape worm (*fitapelu*) |
| *Tiyah* | Cucumber | *Cucumis sativus* | Seeds | |
| *Aamar koli* | Mango seed | *Mangifera indica* | Seeds | Piles |
| *Thiriyo thari* | Plantain/ Banana plant | Musa balbisiana colla | Bark | Fungal infection |
| *Cabun titi* | Chinese soapberry | *Sapindus mukorossii* | Seeds | Tonsillitis |
| *Aatiya thidiyo thadi* | Heavily seeded variety of banana plant | *Musa balbisiana colla* | Bark | Tooth pain |
| *Pudina* | Peppermint | *Menthe piperita* | Juice | Vomiting |
| *Tezmoi* | Prickly ash | *Xanthozylum nitidum* | Leaves | Chest pain/ Angina |

Table 14.1 show the list of various plants uses to cure different diseases. For the preparation of some ethnomedicines, they have used either the leaf of a plant or the seed or the bark of the plant. Sometimes, they use these medicinal plants as vegetables in their daily menu. They also use ashes collected from few medicinal plants after burning and smeared in their body before rituals.

**Table 14.2: List of Ethnomedicines based on Animals to Cure Various Diseases**

| ***Ethnomedicine*** | | | | |
|---|---|---|---|---|
| ***Local name*** | ***English name*** | ***Scientific Equivalent*** | ***Part used*** | ***Disease*** |
| *Mepu* | Indian monitor lizard | *Varanus bengalensis* | Skin | Itching in ear |
| *Chifu vuu* | Porcupine | *Erethion dorstum* | Dried material | Malaria |
| *Valuk Pichu* | Bear | *Ursus americanus* | Skin | Severe fever/ Ague |
| *Garh pichu* | Rhinoceros | *Rhinoceros unicornis* | Skin | |
| *Mechuru pichu* | Fox | *Vulpes vulpes* | Meat | Tuberculosis |
| *Goroichiya* | Snakehead fish | *Channa punctatus* | Whole body | |
| *Ajagarh* | Indian python | *Python molurus* | Fat | Body pain |
| *Xihu* | River dolphin | *Gangetic dolphin* | Fat | Rickets |
| *Churiyo aadiring* | Mud collected from the body of pig | - | Mud | |

Table 14.2 shows the list of ethnomedicines based on the animal to cure various diseases. Some of the animal products collected fresh for medicinal purpose and otherwise it has been preserved from a prolonged period of time depending upon the availability of the same.

Apart from using the plants and animals for ethnomedicines separately, they are also prepared medicines by using both plant and animal products. Here are the descriptions of some of the medicines used commonly:

1. Discharge from the ear/otorrhoea (*aakuha fuhora caba*): One leaf of Indian spurge tree (*Hiju;* Sc. Name *Euphorbia lingularia*; Assamese term *siju*) which has grown in the southern direction of the homestead is kept near the fire. After boiling it is dried in sunlight for at least one hour and one drop extracted from it is used in that affected ear.
2. Itching in the ear (*akuha ghari caba*): When a child is suffering from itching in his or her ear and having scalded skin lesion, the skin of Indian monitor lizard (*mepu;* Assamese term *Gui sap*) is roasted in the fire and the ashes collected. It is mixed with oil and smeared in the affected area. They believe that if the hide of that lizard is collected on Saturday or Tuesday, it will have more effect.
3. Boil/abscess (*gangothi diyaduba*): When a child has been suffering from boil or any type of abscess, he/she is taken to an Indian devil tree (*Satiyana;* Sc. Name *Alstonia scholaris*; Assamese term *Satiyana*) to offer prayer with betel nut. A little amount of white sap is extracted from the tree by cutting it. It is kept in a bowl and used time to time in that affected area at least for two to three times in a day.
4. Eye problem: When an individual is suffering from eye problem like itching, three leaves of camphor tree (*kimaru;* Sc. Name *Eupatorium canabium;* Assamese term. *tongloti)* and *heart-leaf drymary* (*laijabori;* Sc. Name *Drymaria cordata;* Assamese term *laijabori*) is ground to make paste together and three drops extracted out of it is put in the eye twice a day, preferably in morning and in evening. The eye

should be cleaned thoroughly with water before application. Spicy and sour foods are avoided during medication.

5. Injury (*youngbem*): Grinding the leaf of a plant called *jarmani bon* (*Nache bashi mushe;* Sc. Name *Eupatorium odoratum*) and is used in that injured area.
6. Dysentery (*otosang na chitamoh cijori jaba*): The root of garden asparagus (*shatmuli*; Sc. Name *Asparagus recemosus*), three pieces of Duggal fibre tree (*mikaci;* Sc. Name *Debregeasia wallichiana*; Assamese term *mecaki*) is kept for some time in a pot of homemade rice beer (*suje*) and taken in empty stomach to get relief.
7. Pneumonia (*ducuruba*): When a child is suffering from pneumonia one tablet (*bori*) is prepared by grinding 1/3 piece of a seed of gray nicker (*letaguti*; Sc. name *Caesalpinia crista* L; Assamese term *letaguti*) and three number of black pepper. It is recommended to take thrice in a day after having food. In the case of an adult individual, half of the seed of gray nicker and 21 numbers of black pepper is required for preparing the tablet.
8. Jaundice: Three leaves of Indian dog grass (*dubori bon*; Sc. Name *Cynodon dactylon)* and heart-leaf drymary ground together to extract about half glass juice and is given to take in empty stomach for three consecutive days. Spicy and sour food item are forbidden when one is suffering from jaundice.
9. Malaria: The dried intestine of porcupine (*chifu vuu*; Sc. Name. *Erethion dorstum*), bark of the Indian devil tree (*Satiyana tree*) that has grown in southern direction of a homestead and the leaf or bark of creat/green chirayta (*chirota;* Sc. Name *Andrographis paniculata*) boiled together and the juice is advised to take in empty stomach.
10. Severe fever with shivering: (*mugang na cha nimi*): To get rid of severe fever, the meat of bear (*Valuk pichu;* Sc. name *Ursus americanus;* Assamese term *Valukar mangkho*) or rhinoceros (*Garh pichu;* Sc. Name *Rhinoceros unicornis*; Assamese term *Garhorir mangkho*) is put in water and the

same water is given to the patient. Nowadays, both these items are not readily available.

11. Tuberculosis: The meat of fox (*mechuru pichu*; Sc. Name *Vulpes vulpes*; Assamese term *Siyalor mangkho*) is prescribed for getting relief. The curry prepared from snakehead fish (*goroichiya*; Sc. Name *Channa punctatus*; Assamese term *Goroi mash*) with crepe ginger (*raghumola;* Sc. Name *Costus specious*; Assamese term *Raghumola*) and *titaful* (*Phlogocanthus thyrsiflorus*) and is given to the patient.

12. Tape Worm (*fitapelu*): The leaf or bark of mugwort / wormwood (*Cirota;* Sc. Name. *Artemisia vulgaris*), margosa leaves (*Nim*; Sc. Name. *Azadirachta indica*; Assamese term. *Mohanim*), and root of blue justicia (*Nil-kot*; Sc. Name. *Ajuga bracteosa;* Assamese term. *Nilokontho*) is ground and one glass of its extract is taken in empty stomach for three days. The medicine is also recommended to the patients suffering from piles also.

13. *Worm* (*pelu)*: They are taking either hog plum (*cubi citi;* Assamese term. *Amara;* Sc. Name *Spondias pinnata*) or cucumber (*tiyanh;* Sc. Name *Cucumis sativus*) without removing its bark in empty stomach for expelling roundworm, particularly pin worm infection among children.

14. Piles (*kechumuria*): The three years old seed of mango to take out the mesocarp within that mango seed (*aamor koli*). The same is ground and mixed with one or half glass of milk and given to the sufferer for three to four days.

15. Eczema (*madhubaci*): The paste of *heart-leaf drymary* is used in the affected area for getting relief.

16. Fungal infection (*aakaji haba*): The ashes from the kitchen (*garoni*; in Assamese. *elandhu*) is mixed with oil and applied to the affected area. The bark of banana plant (*thiriyo thari;* Assamese term. *Kolor thari*) is roasted in the fire and applied to the affected area. If one side of the bark of bitter rattan palm tree (*coka*; Sc. Name. *Calamus viminalis*; Assamese term. *Bet gasor thari*) is roasted in the fire, the

smokes (*dhuwa*) comes out from the other side. The smoke and ash are applied in the affected area.

17. Tonsillitis (*ditoya bikh*): About half of the seed of Chinese soapberry (*cabun titi;* Assamese term. *Monisal*), 21 numbers of black pepper is ground together and boiled in three to four glass of water with the little amount of salt and is recommended to rinse/wash one's mouth and throat by gargling. In the case of a child, the prescribed amount is three to nine numbers of black pepper and a small amount of the seed of *Sapindus mukorossii.*

18. Toothache (*hatiyo bikh caba*): The tender bark of the banana plant, *Musa balbisiana colla* (*aatiya thidiyo thadi*) is roasted in the fire. Then it is chewed in morning before washing the mouth. In the case of carious tooth also same medicine is prescribed.

19. Vomiting (*gibaba*): In the case of vomiting, the juice of spearmint or garden mint (*pudina*; Sc. Name. *Menthe viridis*; Assamese term *Podina*) is given.

20. High Pressure: One garland (*mala*) with six faces *rudraksha* (*fokiciti;* Sc. Name *Elaeocarpus ganutrus;* Assamese term. *Rudakhya;*) is tied in the left hand to lower down the level of high pressure.

21. Angina pectoris (*ceh bikh cari*): Patients suffering from pain at chest or itching, three leaves of camphor tree (*kimaru;* Sc. Name. *Eupatorium cannabinum;* Assamese term. *tongloti*), three pieces of prickly ash, a kind of creeper (*tezmoi;* Sc. Name *Xanthozylum nitidum*) is pasted together and roasted in the fire. It is prescribed to consume in empty stomach for three consecutive days.

22. Body ache (*cah bikh cari*): The fat extracted from any snake (*dubuiatu*) is massaged into the body. They have a strong belief that if the fat extracted from a cobra or Indian python (Sc. Name. *Python molurus*), its efficacy is more.

23. Rickets (*poya loga*): The fat from river dolphin (*Xihu*; Sc. Name. *Gangetic dolphin*; Assamese term *sihu*) is used as

massage oil in rickets. They also collect the mud from the body of the pig (*churiyo aadiring)* and use it at the time of massage of a patient suffering from rickets.

## Conclusion

The present study documented some aspects of the indigenous knowledge among Dibongiya Deori population with regards to curing various diseases they have experienced. It also records their way of living that is orally transmitted from generation to generation. The chapter demonstrates that wild plant resources and its utilisation are still indispensable for the Dibongiya people. It is worthwhile to be mentioned here that several plants having medicinal values are incorporated into their routine diet, which provided health benefits and in terms of immunity. Obviously, now a day governmental health care centres have been opened up close to their villages but economic conditions of the villagers and easily accessible medicines at a cheaper cost are the most notable thing in this regard. The ethno-medicinal practitioner should be given patronage as custodian of their traditional knowledge. The present trend of acculturation may dilute their indigenous knowledge on ethnomedicines.

## Salutation

The authors are thankful to all the villagers as well as the traditional ethnomedicinal practitioner of the village Bor Chapori and Kinapather Deori Gaon for sharing their knowledge and experiences regarding the treatment of various diseases they have been suffering at a time to time.

## References

Bhardwaj, S and SK. Gakhar. 2005. 'Ethno medicinal plants used by the tribals of Mizoram to cure cuts and wounds'. *Indian Journal of Traditional Knowledge*, 4, 1:75.

Bhasin, V., 2005. 'Tribals of Ladakh: Ecology and health'. *Studies of Tribes and Tribals*, 3:1-13.

Choudhury, S., 2000. 'Indigenous belief and practices of herbal medicine among the few Arunachalis'. *Resarun*, 26: 72-81.

Das, FA., I. Barua and DD. Das. 2008. 'Ethno medicinal practices: A case study among the Sonowal Kacharis of Dibrugarh, Assam'. *Ethno-Medical*, 2, 1: 33-37.

Dutta, M and SC. Nath. 1999. 'Ethno-medico botany of the Tai-Ahoms of Assam, India'. *Journal of Economics and Taxonomic Botany,* 23, 2: 591-598.

Guha, A., 1986. 'Folk medicines of the Bodo-Kacharis - A plain tribe of Assam'. In B. Choudhury (Ed.): *Tribal Health* , pp. 191-199. New Delhi; Inter India Publications.

Jain, SK and SK. Borthakur. 1980. 'Ethno botany of Mikirs of India'. *Journal of Economics and Taxonomic Botany*, 34: 264-272.

Medhi, BK., 1995. 'Ethno medicine: A Study among the Mishings in a rural context', *Bulletin of the Department of Anthropology, Gauhati University*, 9: 61-68.

Medhi, BK and B. Paul. 2004. 'Health and hygiene of the Nahs of Arunachal Pradesh. *Studies of Tribes and Tribals,* 2, 1: 23-27.

Sharma Thakur, GC., 1999. 'Indigenous health practices and system of cure among the tribes of Assam plains'. In S. Sengupta (Ed.): *Health, Healers and Healing: Studies in Medical Anthropology,* pp. 239-249. Dibrugarh; N. L. Publications.

Sonowal, R and I. Baruah. 2011. 'Ethno medical practices among the Tai Khamyangs of Assam, India'. *Ethno Medicine*, 5, 1: 41-50.

# Chapter - 15

# Body Image and Reproductive Health of Married Adolescent Women in Manipuri Muslim Community

*—M C Arunkumar and Irengbam Bijeta*

The body is not only biological but also a social construct. Several scholars have provided different perspectives on the study of the 'body' and the importance of perceptions thereof to our understanding of experiences of health and illness (Chernin, 1985; Willis *et al.*, 2001). Equally, the concept of body image is necessary for understanding different issues of health. Body image is what how one thinks about and feels towards one's own body (Cash and Smolak, 2011). It can be broken down into an effective component or how people feel about their own bodies–and a cognitive component-what people think their body should be or look like (Gendenbein and Smith, 1992).

Body image is an important element in sexuality, the way in which we experience and express ourselves as sexual beings (Rathus *et al.*, 1993). Understanding the linkage between body image, sexuality, and reproductive health is of utmost importance. Dixon-Mueller (1993) opines that understanding the linkages is necessary. In the linkage, body image plays a vital role in the sexuality and sexual activities; hence in the reproduction. Positive or negative body image directly affects the sexual desires and subsequent sexual activities. He further expresses that the understanding will be useful to family planning providers, policy makers, and researchers in a variety of ways.

For the present study, the researcher did field work, in between 2010 and 2013, in three Muslim villages in Manipur: Golapati (Imphal

East District), Kwakta (Bishnupur District) and Tarahei (Thoubal District). In-depth interview was employed as a tool for data collection. About 75 married adolescent girls were interviewed.

In their narration, their Islamic society perceives woman's body as a source of sexual corruption and sin. They have to cover their '*awra*' as soon as they attain menarche. *Awra* is the Islamic vocabulary for the part of a woman's body that arouses a man sexually. Every part of a woman's body including her face is considered as '*awra*' in their society. Their society usually makes them feel that a woman's *mapan thongi fajaba/sak fajaba* (physical beauty) is more important than her *magun* (inner qualities). One finds the same sense of prudence in the *hadith*, narratives about the Prophet's life, which is jealously guarded by the Muslims. Women, in the *hadith,* are considered as 'evil temptresses, the greatest *fitna* (temptation) for men', 'unclean over and above menstruation', 'morally and religiously defective', 'the larger part of the inhabitants of Hell, because of their unfaithfulness and ingratitude towards their husbands', and as having 'weaker intellectual powers' than men (Stowasser, 1994). However, the married adolescent girls, in the field site, feel that a woman's body, howsoever physically and sexually alluring, also has the ability to work for hours to meet the domestic needs of their families. Moreover, their bodies have the ability to bear and nourish a child. Early age at marriage and their poor socio-economic condition also force them to develop inner qualities like *thouna faba* (courage), *akhang kanba* (perseverance) and *hotnaba kanba* (hardworking). With these qualities, they and their families struggle to survive in the society. They feel that married adolescent girls like themselves should possess these qualities to enable them in facing domestic hardships of an early marriage and of the low economic condition. They also feel that a woman can be beautiful only when she has the mental strength to nurture good thoughts and uphold her morality and integrity amidst all the adversities of an early marriage. Therefore, they do not perceive their body solely in terms of physical appearance or sexuality; they evaluate their bodies in terms of its *wakhan* (mind), *litchat sajat* (character) and *magun* (inner qualities) which can enhance a woman's beauty.

They expressed that their *magun* prevents them from having a negative body image even when they are not *sak fajadaba* (physically beautiful). This is because their *magun* enable them to appreciate and enhance the value of their body. Therefore, they expressed that their society should not overlook their *magun* while evaluating them solely on the basis of their looks or sexuality. One 19 years old Rahena from Golapati expresses her personal opinion on this matter. She narrates that her alcoholic husband often taunts her for being unattractive and useless. She says:

> 'My husband often yells at me with demeaning words. He often told me that I do not contribute anything to the family other than sleeping with him. He does not want to acknowledge the fact that I spend my whole day doing household chores and in raising our son. Besides, I run the family by selling wool while he spends his meagre earning on alcohol and phone call to his girlfriends. He acts as if his responsibility towards our son got over after impregnating me. A woman needs unwavering courage and determination to handle such a stressful life. It is easy to break down with such marital strife....but I am still going strong! My husband often told me that I am not pretty. But I feel that abilities and qualities would better define a woman's beauty rather than physical appearance. I know I am not pretty....but physical beauty will not feed me or my son. So, I am happy with what I am and how I look like'.

Rahena's narrative provides an insight into the social reality of these girls. They are socialised with the belief that there is more to their body than its physical appearance and sexual function. They wish to receive appreciation, admiration, and acknowledgment for intrinsic qualities and abilities of their body. However, they have left lamenting when their spouse or society overlooks their qualities and abilities. Their contributions, other than sexual and reproductive, receive less appreciation in their families and society. Their perception about their body is often contradictory to that of their society and spouse. Regardless of their spousal and societal perception, what is also evident is the appreciation they have about their own body. Rahena accepts that she is not physically attractive, but denies of her a negative body image. She has the pride on her inner qualities and abilities. She believes that she can take care of her family amidst adversities.

Her inner qualities and abilities gave her a positive feeling about her own body.

Having said this, the practice of early marriage is influenced to a great extent by the adolescent girls' desire to prove their physical beauty after menarche and their societal support for it. Many of the adolescent girls enter into early wedlock with the intention to prove that they are not only beautiful and attractive but also able to face all the challenges. The parents, however, have a notion of measuring the attractiveness of a girl by demand in the marriage sector right after menarche. To probe deeper into this issue, a Focus Group Discussion (FGD) was held with eight women from Kwakta village that were actively involved in social work and played an active role in women-centric issues of the village. The group consisted of women health workers and Anganwadi teachers. The FGD reveals that:

> 'In Kwakta, many of the parents compete amongst themselves to marry off their young daughters. They have a notion that beautiful girls are desired immensely by men, so girls are encourage eloping or get married earlier. In olden days, people in Kwakta village were just following the Islamic tradition of marrying off the girl right after menarche. But nowadays, early marriage is mainly due to the competition of being more attractive and desirable. People of Kwakta usually ridicule the tribal girls of the neighbouring villages for getting married after 25 years of age in spite of being beautiful. Their marriage at that age is considered as a late marriage. They feel that there is something wrong with tribal girls even though they are beautiful'. (FGD 1, Kwakta).

It is learnt from the FGD 1 that there is a conflict in their thought and attitude among the married adolescent girls. On one hand, they are unhappy with the emphasis on physical appearance and the sexual ability of a woman's body by overlooking their inner qualities and abilities. On the other hand, they willingly elope or enter into early marriage in order to portray themselves as physically and sexually attractive. They obey the society. They engage in such behaviour in order to have a positive body image, defined by the society. They seldom think that such behaviour can increase their reproductive health risk. Studies (Miller and Lester, 2003; Santhya, 2009; UNICEF, 2001 and others) have indicated that early marriage typically coincides with early childbearing and young, first-time mothers face an increased risk of maternal and infant mortality. Emerging evidence also suggests that early marriage may place young women at heightened risk of STIs, including HIV (Bruce and Clark, 2004; Santhya and Jejeeboy, 2007).

Unaware of the risk involved, the married adolescent girls aspire for early pregnancy and childbirth after marriage. Their young age does not deter them from delayed pregnancy and childbirth. Fertility, they believe, is one of the most important factors that shape their body image after marriage. It is expressed in their day-to-day conversation and in their narratives using phrases like *chabokpa ngamba/ macha pokpa ngamba* (ability to bear children). They consider *chabokpa* (reproduction) as the most important contributions of a female's body. A *chabok fabi nupi* (a woman who can bear many children without any complications) is highly regarded by them. They consider a physically unattractive yet fertile woman is more beautiful than a *macha poktabi/akhungbi/chaboktabi nupi* (an infertile woman) attractive woman. An infertile woman's body is considered as *soinaiba / asoiba* (disabled/ defective) and *meeoi sudabi* (imperfect person) no matter how so beautiful she is. Thus, they are motivated to become a *chabok fabi nupi* as it would give them a positive feeling about their own body. Fisher and Cleveland (1958), consider body image as 'a psychological experience and individual's feelings and attitudes towards his or her body' and for the married adolescent girls, fertility plays an important role in shaping their feelings and attitudes towards their body. This is reflected in the narrative of 18 years old Mumtaz from Golapati who is newly married. She says:

> 'I am still young and can bear many children to my husband. What's the use of my beautiful body and face if I could not make my husband happy and bear many fruits? My husband often tells me that he likes to have many kids who are beautiful like me. I am quite confident about fulfilling his wish'.

Married adolescent girls like Mumtaz who are yet to have reproductive experience of their body and are new to the domestic affairs of married life usually have a positive body image.

Their youthfulness, physical beauty and glossiness of a newly married life give them a positive body image. Their positive body image gives them the confidence of fulfilling the sexual and reproductive desires of their husband and society. It makes them lead an active sex life and aspire for unlimited childbearing. Childbearing can enhance their positive body image. If they could not bear a child, their positive body image shaped by their youthfulness and physical beauty will disappear leading to a negative body image.

Societal perception of a perfect woman body is important because it influences one's perception of one's own body. Mr Abdur Nur, a social worker from Golapati, explains the importance of fertility in the society:

> '*Macha poktaba* (infertility) and *nupa poktaba* (inability to bear a male child) are one of the main reasons for *talaq* (divorce) in Golapati. There is a beautiful Muslim girl in our neighbour who is just 14 years old but whose body appears matured, like that of a woman of 20s. Due to her physical beauty, she eloped quite early and got married to her lover. However, she separated from her husband after a year and has to come back to her natal place as she could not conceive soon after marriage'.

The statement of the social worker reveals the inner meaning of woman's ability in the society. Physical attractiveness of a woman is of no value in their society if she could not perform the duty of giving births(s). Sooner the pregnancy a young married woman earns more value in the family and society. What is important is the reproductive ability of her body. The physical maturity and attractiveness of a young girl might be appealing to many men. The attractiveness of a body vanishes into the heat of lust unless it gives yields.

Another dimension of the issue of body image comes up in the following interview with 18-year-old Majida from Tarahei village. She expresses that:

> 'My husband is well endowed. He is admired by many ladies. Even today, many girls from my village desire to be his wife even though he is married to me. He had many girlfriends before marriage. From them, he had chosen me for marriage. Maybe, by

considering my beautiful face and good looking body! I had a mental pressure to bear a child soon after marriage. It was to prove myself worthy of him. Besides, he is the only son of his parents. I did....not just one but two kids, one after another. I am having another one soon. It makes me feel like I am quite a match for him'.

Their bodies become important in order to keep a constant relationship with their spouse. The subjective evaluation of spouse's idea of a particular body image also plays a major role in shaping the body image of these girls in a positive or negative manner. Majida's statement shows that before marriage, men are attracted to the physical beauty and sexual attractiveness of a woman's body. After marriage, the reproductive ability is added above the physical and sexual attractiveness to their expectations from a woman. The married adolescent girls, thus, subject themselves to unlimited childbearing and try to maintain their physical body. It is very difficult on their parts to meet the reproductive expectation as well as to maintain their body image. They usually undermine their own health and wellbeing in balancing their body and spouse's expectation.

It can be assumed here that the married adolescent girls have a more negative feeling about themselves after undergoing childbearing. Most of them expressed that the physical changes in their body after pregnancy and childbirth like loss of complexion, changes in body shape and health problems make them unhappy and insecure. In an interview, one 18 years old Rashida from Kwakta who have been married for five years expressed her frustration on losing her physical beauty. She is also planning to make use of her reproductive capacity to win over her husband's affection even though she has lost all her 'physical charm'. She says:

'My once beautiful body got wasted with the hardships of early marriage. A woman's beauty ends with childbirth. After becoming a mother of two, my abdomen has become most prominent part of my body. It even looks larger than my sagging breast which makes me appear quite old and unappealing. But men like 'beautiful' women. And here I am living like an old lady with all the domestic burdens! My husbands go nowadays to one beautiful

Muslim widow having kids. However, I still have the ability to give him more kids and bind him to his responsibilities. I am considered as a *chabok phabi nupi* (a woman who can bear many children easily) in our locality. There is more with my body than the outer physical form'.

To them, *chabok phabi*, the ability of fertility is one of the essential qualities of a positive body image. The fertile body is a good body. After a series of early childbearing, however, other aspects of their 'beautiful' body degenerate. They wish for keeping their physical beauty as well as for a good performance in reproduction. They could not achieve both. They have to compromise with their physical appearance over childbirth. This is mainly because of the deterioration of their health and well-being after childbirth. Various socio-economic factors like inability to take proper prenatal and postnatal care also contribute to this situation.

Their domestic burden is further increased with early childrearing. They do not get much emotional or financial support from their husbands. Though working hard for earning their bread, the husbands in poor families lost their sexual appetite of their wives' bodies. Moreover, they become infidel to their wives who are having 'negative' body image. On the other hand, for the wives, the perceived fertility performance of their own body serves as the last straw to overcome the frustration due to this negative body image. It is the only hope to build up their body image once again and rekindle their spousal affection. It often leads to more childbearing.

Thus, positive or negative body image is inseparable from the reproductive health study. A positive body image makes the young wives confident in performing the sexual and reproductive activities. It is the motivating factor for their active sexual life which they do so by entering into early marriage and early childbearing. Again, after childbearing, their physical body becomes 'deformed'. Pertinent to this issue is their perception of an "ideal body" which they aspire to conform in order to achieve a positive body image.

Past researchers have shown how western standards of beauty (Hesse-Biber *et al.,* 2006; Holmstrom, 2004), ethnicity (Caradas *et al.,* 2001; Sussman *et al.*, 2007), religion (Smith *et al.,* 2003, Cline and Ferraro, 2006), and age (Thompson and Smolak, 2001) affect body image and body dissatisfaction. Studies have also indicated that in contrast to the wider society, religious individuals may place less emphasis on the physical body and use their relationship with a higher power and/or the ability to meet moral/religious obligations to evaluate self-worth (Kim, 2007).

The present study finds, in a broader sense, that religion plays an important factor in shaping perception of an ideal body of a woman. The study is on the adolescent married girls whose religion is Islam. This religion ascribes values of woman's body with physical appearance, ability to provide sexual satisfaction and reproductive ability. They internalise such religious values and incorporate it in their ideal body.

Another important factor is the influence of modernity. Modern standard of beauty usually pertains to the western standard of beauty. The western concepts are incorporated in their mind as they are exposed to various media including cable TVs, internet. The western idea of beauty is operates while defining an ideal body image in this Muslim community in Manipur. Most of the studies on western standard of beauty, among different non-European communities, have focused on thin ideal stereotype (Stice, 2001; Dunken *et al.,* 2008). Islamic standard of beauty and western standard of beauty do not suffice all their attributes of their ideal body. This is because they are also influenced by other factors besides Islam and modernity like age and socio-economic condition.

The ideal body type for the married adolescent girls encompasses various attributes ranging from physical form to qualitative and functional aspects of a woman's body. Physical beauty and the body's ability to maintain its beauty even amidst marital adversities and childbearing, sexual charisma and the ability to win spousal affection even amidst other competing females are some of their physical attributes of an ideal body. Their inner qualities of an ideal body includes *aphaba wakhan* (a good mind), *aphaba litchat sajat* (a good character) and *magun* (inner qualities) like *thouna phaba* (courage), *akhang kanba* (perseverance) and *hotnaba kanba* (hardworking) which are necessary for facing the domestic affairs of an early marriage.

None of the above attributes are significant when a woman is *macha poktabi/akhungbi/chaboktabi* (infertile) as she will be considered as *soinaibi/asoibi* (disabled/defective) and *meeoi sudabi* (inadequate sexual organs). Therefore, the most important attribute of an ideal body for a woman is *chabok phaba* (ability to produce many children easily or ability to deliver more children) for the married adolescent girls. They perceive the reproductive capacity of a female's body as the most important beautiful and important aspect of a woman's body.

Anthropological study of the child rearing in Lombok, a Muslim village in Indonesia, has also acknowledged the immense value accorded to children within the family (Bennett, 2005). This is entirely consistent with the value accorded to women as mothers in the Qur'an and the *hadith,* which instructs all Muslims to hold women in high esteem for the critical role they play as mothers. Thereafter, the ability of the body to meet social and family role by giving her is one of the most important factors in shaping the body image for the married adolescent girls. Angela (2008) finds the similar conclusion of her study amongst Black Muslim women, the ability to meet social and family roles shapes their perception of body image.

So, being a *chabok phabi* is what that gives them the most positive body image. Their perception of their body as a *chabok phaba* prevents them from having a negative body image even when they are deprived off all the other attributes of their ideal body. Therefore, when they have lost their physical beauty and spousal affection, they intend for more pregnancies and childbearing in order to build up their body image once again.

Even though the married adolescent girls emphasise on the non-sexual and non-reproductive attributes of their body, they give more importance to their societal values in their body ideal. That is the reason why *chabok phaba* which is a direct result of their sexual and reproductive behaviour is considered as the most important attribute of their body ideal. Bordo (2003) opined that the body embodies societal beliefs and values regarding identity, gender roles, and cultural acceptability and serves as a means of social control. And Islam laid much emphasis on the importance of family and child-rearing for a woman (Abdul-Rauf, 1995). In a similar fashion, the married adolescent girls of the present study also show the embodiment of their societal beliefs and values in their body ideal. They try to conform by undergoing early marriage and childbearing which can have huge implications on their reproductive health.

It is difficult for the married adolescent girls to achieve all the attributes of their body ideal amidst their socio-economic circumstances. For instance, conforming to their most important attribute of body ideal like childbearing makes them compromise with other attributes of their ideal body like physical appearance and well-being. It is mainly due to their young age, economic hardships and their inability to take proper antenatal and postpartum care. It leads to degeneration of body affecting their body image.

Scholars like Steinberg (2007) opine that changes in social status such as marriage and pregnancy cause changes in 'self'. The fact that pregnancy occurs before the adolescent adapts to the bodily changes makes the new situation she tries to adapt herself more confusing. Thus, pregnancy may decrease the self-confidence of the pregnant adolescent and it may create problems on self-esteem (Uyanik and Dogan, 1998). Birthing is a powerful experience that illustrates clearly the utility and ability of the female body; thus, it could generate greater respect and appreciation for women for what their bodies can do. However, pregnancy, birthing, and breastfeeding change the appearance of women's bodies in ways that move them farther away from the idealised, objectified images that many women have internalised as beauty standards; thus, reproductive processes could lead women to have more negative feelings about, and perhaps less respect for, their bodies after they become mothers (Chrisler *et al.,* 2014). After experiencing body dissatisfaction and body shape due to reproductive process or spousal infidelity, the married adolescent girls again resort to uncontrolled childbearing in order to build up their degenerated body image once again.

In order to improve the reproductive health of the married adolescent girls, there is a need for change in their construction of 'ideal' woman which is mainly influenced by their societal and religious values. Representations are relevant to such a discussion because a society's constructions of 'ideal' women also shape its treatment of 'real' ones. That is why 'our understanding of the problems of 'real' women cannot lie outside the 'imagined' constructs in and through which 'women' emerge as subjects' (Sunder Rajan, 1993). The adolescent girls should be discouraged from shaping their body image on the basis of a body ideal that often encourage them into early marriage and uncontrolled childbearing.

According to Baser (2000), preventing the youth from getting married at an early age may be provided by cultural structure changes in the society. In doing so, there is a need for change in societal values which normalises elopement, early marriage, and childbearing so that the girls would be discouraged from constructing and conforming to such societal ideals at a young age. Having said this, even if it is difficult to change their societal and religious values, the changes can be initiated from the married adolescent girls and their spouse. Their narratives on sexuality reveal that many of them are quite receptive to change and embrace modernity even though they are ardent followers of Islam.

On this issue, Bennett (2005) also examines how other factors besides Islam simultaneously influence the ways in which young women approach courtship, sexuality and reproductive health in an era of dynamic social change. Her study demonstrates that Islam is neither alone in trying to control female sexuality, nor entirely successful in doing so. The married adolescent girls and their spouse embrace modernity and are receptive to changes but they suffer from lack of awareness and information.

Therefore, there is a need to increase their awareness and provide their unmet need for information on various aspects of sexuality and reproductive health. This will improve the conditions relating to the formation of their perception of an ideal body image and maintaining the image. They should be provided information and services relating to their sexual and reproductive health needs. The real task is the strengthening Sexual and Reproductive Health (SRH) Service. It should be able to cater to their unmet need for information, provide counselling and look into their sexual and reproductive health needs.

The SRH service should be adolescent friendly and sensitive to their socio-economic background. It can make them aware of the effects of uncontrolled early childbearing which they do so in order to achieve their body ideal. It should provide them with proper prenatal and postnatal maternal care so that they can maintain a good health and physical appearance even after childbirth. Moreover, it should help the adolescent girls in delaying sexual initiation and first birth. Besides, community outreach programme is also needed (Dixon-Mueller, 1993). The outreach programme should be incorporated with various health service missions.

## Salutation

We would like to acknowledge and express our gratitude to the Indian Council of Medical Research (ICMR), New Delhi for funding this research work.

## References

Abdul-Rauf, M., 1995. *The Islamic View of Women and the Family*. 3rd Edition. Alexandria, VA; Al-Saadawi Publications.

Akan, GE and CM. Grilo, 1995. 'Socio-cultural influences on eating attitudes and behaviours, body image and psychological functioning: A comparison of African- American, Asian-American and Caucasian college women'. *International Journal of Eating Disorders*, 18: 181-187.

Alan Guttmacher Institute. 1996. *Risks and Realities of Early Childbearing Worldwide* [Issues in brief]. New York; The Institute.

Angela Odoms, Young, 2008. 'Factors that influence body image representations of Black Muslim women'. *Social Science and Medicine*, (1982) 66, 12: 2573-2584.

Bennett, Linda Rae, 2005. *Women, Islam and Modernity Single Women, Sexuality and Reproductive Health in Contemporary Indonesia*. New York; Routledge Curzon.

Bordo, S., 2003. *Unbearable Weight: Feminism, Western Culture, and the Body*. Berkley; University of California Press.

Bruce, J and S. Clark. 2004. *The Implications of Early Marriage for HIV/AIDS Policy*. New York; Population Council.

Caradas, E., V. Lambert and KE. Charlton. 2001. 'An ethnic comparison of eating attitudes and associated body image concerns in adolescent South African schoolgirls'. *Journal of Human Nutrition and Dietetics*, 14, 2: 111-120.

Cash, TF and L. Smolak, 2011. 'Understanding body images: Historical and contemporary perspectives'. In TF Cash and L. Smolak (Eds.): *Body Image: A Handbook of Science, Practice, and Prevention,* pp. 3-11. New York; Guilford Press.

Chernin, 1985. *The Hungry Self: Women, Eating and Identity.* New York; Times.

Chrisler, Joan, ML. Marvan, JG. Rose and M. Rossini, 2014. 'Body appreciation and attitudes towards menstruation'. *Body Image.* 12C, 1:78-81.

Cline, KMC and KF. Ferraro. 2006. 'Does religion increase the prevalence of incidence of obesity in adulthood?'. *Journal for the Scientific Study of Religion*, 45, 2: 269-281.

Dixon-Mueller, Ruth, 1993. 'The sexuality connection in reproductive health'. *Studies in Family Planning*, 24, 5: 269-282.

Dunkel, TM., D. Davidson and S. Qurashi. 2010. 'Body satisfaction and pressure to be thin in younger and older Muslim and non-Muslim women: The role of western and non-western dress preferences'. *Body Image,* 7: 56-65.

Fisher, S and SE. Cleveland. 1958. *Body Image and Personality.* Princeton; D. Van Nostrand Co. Inc.

Gendebien, ML and MO. Smith, 1992. 'Field dependence and perceptual, cognitive and affective measures of body image in asymptomatic college students personality and individual'. *Differences*, 13: 937-943.

Hesse-Biber, Sharlene, Pareicia Leavy, Quinn, E. Courtney and Julia Zoino. 2006. 'The mass marketing of disordered eating and Eating Disorders: The social psychology of women, thinness and culture'. *Women's Studies International Forum*, 29, 2: 208-224.

Holmstrom, Amanda, 2004. 'The effects of media on body image: A Meta analyses'. *Journal of Broadcasting and Electronics Media*, 48: 1.

Kim, KH., 2007. 'Religion, weight perception, and weight control behaviour'. *Eating Behaviours*, 8: 121-131.

Meken, J., 1972. 'The health and social consequences of teenage pregnancy'. *Family Planning Perspectives*, 4, 3:45-53.

Miller, S and F. Lester. 2003. *Married Young First Time Mothers: Meeting their Special Needs, Presented at WHO/UNFPA/ Population Council Technical Consultation on Married Adolescents*, Geneva.

Noble Cover, J and M. Yanagishita, 1996. *The World's Youth.* Washington DC; Population Reference Bureau.

Ogden, J and C. Elder, 1998. 'The role of family status and ethnic group on body image and eating behaviour'. *International Journal of Eating Disorders*, 23: 309-315.

Phan, T and TL. Tylka, 2006. 'Exploring a model of moderators of disordered eating with Asian American college women'. *Journal of Counselling Psychology*, 53: 36-47.

Rathus, AR., JS. Nevid and L. Fichner-Rathus, 1993. *Human Sexuality: In a World of Diversity*. Boston; Allyn and Bacon.

Reece, D., 1996. 'Covering and communication: The symbolism of dress among Muslim women'. *Howard Journal of Communication*, 7: 35-52.

Santhya, KG and SJ. Jejeebhoy. 2003. 'Sexual and reproductive health needs of married adolescent girls'. *Economic and Political Weekly*, 4370-4377.

Santhya, KG and SJ Jejeebhoy. 2007. 'Early marriage and HIV/AIDS: Risk factors among young women'. *Economic and Political Weekly*, 42, 14: 1291-1297.

Santhya, KG., 2009. *Understanding Pregnancy-Related Morbidity and Mortality among Young Women in Rajasthan*. New Delhi; Population Council.

Smith, FT., RK. Hardman, PS. Richards and L. Fisher. 2003. 'Intrinsic religiousness and spiritual wellbeing as predictors of treatment outcome among women with eating disorders'. *Eating Disorder*, 11,1: 15-26.

Steinberg, L., 2007. 'Risk taking in adolescence: New perspectives from brain and behavioural science'. *Current Directions in Psychological Science*, 16, 2:55-59.

Stice, E., 2001. Risk factors for eating pathology: Recent advances and future directions. In RH. Streigel-Moore and L. Smolak (Eds.): *Eating Disorders: Innovative Directions in Research and Practice*, pp. 51-73. Washington DC; American Psychological Association.

Stowasser, BF., 1994. *Women in the Qur'an, Traditions, and Interpretation*. USA; Oxford University Publication.

Sunder Rajan, R., 1993. *Real and Imagined Women: Gender, Culture and Post Colonialism*. London; Routledge.

Sussman, NM., N Truong and J. Lim, 2007. 'Who experiences 'America the beautiful?: Ethnicity moderating the effect of acculturation on body image and risks for eating disorders among immigrant women'. *International Journal of Intercultural Relations*, 31, 1: 29-49.

Thompson, JK and L. Smolak, 2001. 'Body image, eating disorders, and obesity in childhood and adolescence-the future is now'. In JK Thompson and L Smolak (Eds): *Body Image, Eating Disorders and Obesity in Youth: Assessment, Prevention, and Treatment*, pp. 1-18, Washington DC; American Psychological Association.

Uyanik, D and S. Dogan. 1998. 'Early marriages for girls'. *Research Symposium Proceedings* 98 Proceedings Book, 23-25, pp. 1-9, November, Ankara.

Willis, E., R. Miller and J. Wyn, 2001. 'Gendered embodiment and survival for young people with cystic fibrosis'. *Soc Sci Med*, 53, 9:1163-1174.

Yinger, N., A. de Sherbinin, LH. Ochoa, L. Morris and Y. J. Hirsh, 1992. *Adolescence Sexual Activity and Childbearing in Latin America and the Caribbean: Risks and Consequences*. Washington DC; Population Reference Bureau.

# Chapter - 16

# Return of the Nepalese Migrants Working in the Coal Mines of Jaintia Hills, Meghalaya

***—Rashmi Upadhyay and Geetika Ranjan***

*Rita, a migrant's wife, aged 45 years, knocks at the camp*[1] *door, smiles and says in a loud voice 'ma ta pheri aaye hai yaha' (I have come here again). She adds, 'ke garnu Meghalaya bhulnu sakyena, ma ta aaye pheri; sapana ma Meghalaya tara bipana ma Nepal' (what to do! I could not forget Meghalaya, so I came here again; I dreamt of Meghalaya in my sleep but in reality, I was in Nepal). She along with her family worked in the coal mines for the 13 years. She ran a rice hotel and her husband was a coal mine labourer. With the income earned, they migrated to the plains of Nepal and educated their children. The family returned to Nepal to settle in the plains of Binge Bazaar, Sunsari district in Eastern Nepal three years ago. However, the couple decided to return again to the coal mines. Her husband is not keeping well but she plans to run a rice hotel and open a small shop along with her husband.*

## Introduction

International migration has a long-standing history in Nepal with India being its main destination. Migrants from Nepal reside and work in almost every part of India. Migration from Nepal to India has both historical and cultural connections. The Nepalese reputation as brave, sincere, and honest Gurkhas made it easier for them to find jobs in different sectors like security guards, seasonal agricultural labourers, coolies or even a government employ, etc. Moreover, the treaty of peace and friendship containing ten articles signed between the two countries of India and Nepal on 31st July 1950 after mutual consultations and agreement provide a broad framework for the pursuance of mutually beneficial bilateral relations between the two countries (Upreti, 2009). Therefore, a great advantage of migration from Nepal to India is the open border policy as there is no need for expensive air travel, passports, visas, and there is no restriction on access to official employment (Seddon *et al.,* 1998).

Meghalaya state located in the north-eastern part of India is endowed with a large reserve of mineral resources in which coal deposit is widely available. The present study is conducted in the coal mines of Jaintia Hills of Meghalaya. In Jaintia Hills, the method used for coal extraction is commonly known as 'rat-hole' mining[2]. Because of the abundance of coal production and labour requirement, Jaintia Hills has become a ground for migrant workers. It has attracted migrants not only from different parts of India but from across the border as well, like Bangladesh and Nepal.

The objective of the chapter is to understand the return of the Nepalese migrants and it argues that, for the majority of the Nepalese migrant workers, working in the coal mines is not temporary; rather an experience of circular migration. Return here is used as an analytical concept which can be seen both as imagined and actual return migration of the Nepalese migrant workers. The meaning of home and belonging for Nepalese migrant workers changes over time. On the one hand, the Nepalese migrant workers continuously complain about the grueling condition of the coal mines and repeatedly insist that they would leave this 'foreign land' and return to Nepal permanently but, those who already left for Nepal or found jobs outside often return to the coal mines within a few months. This chapter gives a detailed description about those who return to Nepal; those who stay back in the coal mines and also for those who experience circular migration.

## Methods

Fieldwork was carried out in different coal mining sites in Jaintia Hills, Meghalaya, India and Bhojpur and Sunsari district of Eastern Nepal. Data was collected through participant observation, interviews, census schedules, case studies and life histories. In addition to these, audio-visual aids like camera and voice recorder were utilised for documentation and secondary sources like the books, articles, journals were referred to support the data. To evaluate the data, the recorded interviews were transcribed into English and analysed in software Nvivo used for qualitative data analysis. Analysis of data began by the organisation of data, coding and finally interpretation of data. Secondary sources such as books, journals, articles, and reports catering to coal mining in Meghalaya were also consulted. Since the data collected were wide-ranging and the informants for specific data were not the same, the number of informants was many and varied from subject to subject. Thus, multi-sited fieldwork was carried out among a population of Nepalese coal mine workers who move between Sutnga coal mines in Meghalaya and their home in Eastern Nepal. Data was collected from the region of both hilly and plain districts of Nepal - village Patlepani in Bhojpur and plains of Bange Bazaar in Sunsari district of the Koshi zone of Eastern Nepal.

## Studies on Return Migration

From the past decades, several scholars (Cerase, 1967; King, 1977, 1978, 1986; Rhoadas, 1978; Brettell, 1979; Gmelch, 1980, 1983; Long and Oxfeld, 2004; Brettell and Hollifield, 2014) have studied the return migration extensively in different parts of the world. Gmelch (1980, 1983) defines return migration as a movement of migrants back to their homelands to resettle. Returns may make further migration possible since the returnees provide knowledge of and networks in the host country (Massey, 1987; cited in Oxfeld and Long, 2004). In the work of Oxfeld and Long (2004) return includes the processes leading to returns. As such, return encompasses but is broader than return migration, which does not always include temporary visits or the preparations for return. Nepalese workers migrate to the coal mines with an intention to return to their home country. However, once they reach the workplace, not all return to Nepal, some continue staying permanently and for most, it is an experience of continual return. To King and Christou (2011), return can represent a variety of shades of emotions and outcomes because return can be journeys of hope but also of despair (Ghosh, 2000), it can also be an unsettling path (Markowitz and Stefansson, 2004) and the returnees may be strangers in their own homeland (Tsuda, 2003).

## Types of Return Migration

Cerese (1974) identifies four different types of return migrants based on experiences, aspirations, expectations and needs. He termed it as the return of failure; return of conservatism, the return of retirement and the return of innovation (see also King, 1978 and Cassarino, 2004). Cerase (1967) in his another study provides a time period for his various types of return migrants each related to the length of the stay. According to his findings, the first return is about 6-10 years in which the migrant is unable to achieve their economic perspective in the host country, and in the second case of return after 30 years or more, the migrants consider their return as peaceful and complete retire. Similarly, King (1978) suggested two or more types of return migration. Gmelch (1980) distinguishes between the migrants who intend their return to be temporary and permanent. He writes that the temporary return migrants usually returned to their country of origin after accomplishing a specific objective they had set out to achieve, most often to accumulate a sum of money and maintain the strong family ties. According to the work of King and Strachan (1980) majority of the return, migrants regarded their return as permanent due to the strong family ties. The Nepalese migration to the coal mines is basically temporary in nature. The findings from the study also reveal that most of the Nepalese migrant workers return either on a temporary basis, a few on a permanent basis and most of them experience the continual return to the host country. Similarly, in the case of the returned Nepalese migrant workers some of the first generation returnee migrants returned to villages after accumulating certain some of remittances while some of them returned immediately or after few years for different reasons including poor health condition, inability to adjust to the environment, risk at work, fear of violence, accidents, family pressure, and also due to the age factor.

According to Gmelch (1980), permanent migrants are either forced to return or they choose to return due to some external factors or failure to adjust in the host country. However, in the case of the Nepalese migrant workers sometimes it just works in the reverse order. Most of the temporary migrants experience a continual return to the coal mines and some stay behind permanently due to employment opportunities and a carefree everyday life in the host country. The most prominent example could be cited from the ongoing ban of the coal mines by NGT (National Green Tribunals)[3] where most of the Nepalese migrant workers stayed back with the hope of the mines reopening in the coming days. The experience of the continual return of the Nepalese migrant workers to the coal mines gives them some kind of hope and sense of security in their lives. As such, even the coal mines are now temporarily banned; these workers have been coming to the coal mines or eagerly waiting for the mines to reopen to start their work again as the coal mines were their only option for survival including the *Sardars* (labour supervisor)[4]. Thus, even in the recent ban on coal mines, many *Sardars,* and the workers stayed back with the hope that it may open one day, and they can resume their business peacefully.

## Return-Success and Failure

Two categories of Nepalese migrant workers are found working in the coal mines of Jaintia Hills, Meghalaya. These are the *bara maine* (those working for 12 months) and *cha maine* (those working for six months). The former are those who are either married to the natives i.e. Jaintia or to the migrants of other ethnic groups such as Boro, Tripuri, Mizo etc. and have settled in the Jaintia Hills with their families. There are also other Nepalese migrant workers who seldom go back to Nepal. They do not earn sufficient amount of money and therefore wait for the longer period to accumulate enough money to take back home. The *cha maine* or seasonal workers are the migrant workers. They work for six months, i.e. during the main mining season, from November to April and then return to their respective villages in Nepal where they stay for the next six months and work in their agricultural fields.

Two reasons for return migration seem to be predominating i.e. because they either fail or because they succeed (Guzzetta, 2004). Cerase (1974) writes that the migrants face problems of adaptation, suffering and fear in the destination country which makes them return home after a year or two which he termed as 'return of failure'. To Bovenkerk (1974), a successful migrant worker returns to the home country with savings and skills. The findings from this study suggest that the returnees belonged to both types-some claimed to be failures and some claimed to be highly successful. The main reason given by the Nepalese migrant workers, who returned to Nepal within short period of time that is within some months or a year of their migration is because of their failure to adjust to the host country, fear to live and work in the grueling conditions of the coal mines, health problems and inability to earn. The respondents who have been living in the coal mine areas permanently also consider themselves failures to return. They comprise of those who stayed behind in compulsion, not having enough savings to return home, or lost their way while travelling and for fear of travelling via the same route, ashamed of returning home without sending money, those who had inter-ethnic marriage, and those who got addicted to a life of alcoholism and gambling.

The most successful Nepalese migrant workers are circular migrants or those who experience a continual return to the coal mines. They have been travelling to work and are able to remit to their home country within a short period of time. The continual return to the coal mines enables them a shared sense of economic security when needed and allows them with an opportunity to hope for better future. For some, the reason for their continual return is that they no more feel comfortable at home as they consider themselves strangers or not a part of their home society.

## Imagined Return to Nepal

The migrant workers who plan to return to Nepal are the ones who are permanently settled in the coal mines. They imagine (Oxfeld and Long, 2004) their return to Nepal though it is unlikely for them to return. These are the workers who have been living and working in the coal mines from the past 20-30 years and have been imagining returning to Nepal or planning to go home. Though they have been living in the coal mines, but they remember their past years spend in Nepal by using the photographs of the family, of their original village, of Nepali calendar, keeping *khukuri* (knife) or Nepali cap or other objects as souvenirs, and sometimes narrating the stories of their village. They celebrate festivals like *Dasai* (Dussehra), *Tihar* (Diwali) or *Magesanrati* (Makarsangranti) with the village friends in the coal mines. They spend most of their lives imagining their return to Nepal but most of them are never able to return. As Slyomovice (1998) points out in her study of the Palestinian Arab's past as it is imagined, recounted, written, and drawn from memories that involve images and descriptions of specific places and actual settings. The Nepalese coal mine migrant workers relate and compare to their countries of origin and settlement while continuing to stay in the coal mines. There are many migrant workers who came and never went back to Nepal. They have stayed back in the camps their entire life after arriving and some have died and were cremated here without any information to their families back home.

## Reasons for not Returning to Nepal

Most of the permanent migrants imagine returning to Nepal. These workers choose to reside permanently in the camps for various reasons. Some have remained with compulsion and some voluntarily. They stay back with compulsion as they are not able to earn well and remit back home, some are married with the other migrant communities and sometimes with the Jaintias, and their children are born in the coal mines are grown up and studying. Hence they are unable to decide whether to continue living in the mine sites or to return, whereas for some, coal mine is the only place to earn and make a living. Some do not return as they are now addicted to drinking and gambling in the coal mines. Some are ashamed to return to Nepal as they migrated to the coal mines at an early stage of their life or immediately after leaving school. Unable to earn or save money, they are ashamed to face their families and villagers. These migrants decide to make their living in the coal mines and plan to return only after they can save and take back a certain amount of money to their family.

## Inter-Ethnic Marriages

Suro (1996) identified some factors that seemed to influence the likelihood and rate of return migration. He found that single migrants who married locals and started families were less likely to return to their home countries, while migrants who married partners from the home country were more likely to return. In the coal mines, some migrant workers have stayed back as they have married Jaintias or other migrant ethnic communities and settled either in the villages and towns of Jaintia Hills or in the camp itself. These contacts like friendship and marital relationship may lead to the establishment of a new social group for the migrants or sometime it may form the process of assimilation (Gordon, 1961; Qian and Lichter, 2001, 2007; Pagnini and Morgan, 1990; McCaa, 1993) or what Bovenkerk (1974) observes as a certain amount of integration in the receiving country is a necessary condition for success and as integration proceeds, the chance of return diminishes. Most of the Nepalese migrant workers and the ethnic group have married without any legal marriage documents yet have been accepted by the host society. Many Nepalese migrant workers have married Jaintia and settled in the villages of Jaintia Hills. There are many such examples of Nepalese workers who act as *Malik* or mine owner after marrying Jaintia and have settled in the coal mine areas. These migrants are now in the process of assimilation with the host countries.

## Coal Mines has become Home

Some of the Nepalese migrant workers who have been living for over 30 years consider coal mines as their homes. They imagine Nepal as their homeland in their talks and keep souvenirs from Nepal but at the same time, they have spent most of their lives working and living in the coal mines. These migrant workers are very familiar with the surrounding areas, can speak in Pnar or other local language, dress like them, and have a good relationship with the Jaintias and other migrant communities. They feel no difference living in the coal mines or in Nepal as they are frequently in contact with their friends, neighbours or villagers during the mining seasons. Some of the others say that they feel happier in the coal mines because apart from earning money they can spend their time in the market and with friends.

## Example from the Field-Permanent Migrant Worker

'Coal mine has become my home', says 68 years old (retired) coal mine worker, Lama, living in the camp of Sutnga in Jaintia Hills. He left Nepal at the age of 17 years to work in Bhutan in road construction work. The road contractor brought him to Meghalaya for the same work as in Bhutan. When he saw some of the Nepalese workings in the coal mines he too started to work in the mines, digging out coal. He got married and both his wife and he started running a rice hotel. His wife eloped with another worker leaving their six-year-old son with him. His son was born in the mines and is now 22 years old. Lama has not returned to Nepal since then but desires to do so. He says, 'I remember my family in Nepal. They must be still there. My younger sisters were so small when I left home. Most of my elder sisters must have died already. There is a younger brother. But now it is all cut-off'. He thought of going home several times but could never make it. He has been thinking of going home 'next year', it has been 40 years now and he is still here. He says, 'coal mine is my home' as he has spent more than half his life living in the camps, taking care of his son and working in the coal quarries. He has built a sturdier camp as his house and maintains a kitchen garden surrounding it. Inside the camp, he hangs a *khukuri* and old Nepali calendar as souvenirs.

## Coal Mine as a Hiding Place

There are many migrant workers who have chosen to live in the coal mines and not return to Nepal. These workers have either committed crimes in the past or are continuing to commit crimes in the camp areas. The coal mine is a shelter for all wanting to live and work here. Most of the times, these workers hide their original name and their place of origin as well. There are many Nepalese migrant workers living and working in the coal mines who in the past were involved with the Maoist group during the insurgency time (1996-2006) which they faced a few years ago. It is to be mentioned here that the uneducated and unemployed youth of the villages of Nepal formed the biggest target of the Maoist at that time who forcibly tried to recruit them into their group. Thus, to liberate themselves from the fear of recruitment, a number of youths migrated to work in the coal mines. Due to fear of the Maoist and later of the police, these youths have been living in the camps of the coal mines. Some of them who returned to Nepal after the insurgency time were threatened by the Maoist group and were asked for ransom. To escape from the Maoist groups, many Maoist youths are now hiding in the coal mines of Jaintia Hills. According to the migrant workers, there are not only

Nepalese insurgent groups but also others who choose the coal mines as their shelter after committing their crimes.

## Circular Return Migrants

The circular migrants are the most successful when they experience the continual return to the coal mines. They have been frequently travelling to work in the mines and are able to remit to their home country within a short period of time. The continual return to the coal mines enables them to have a sense of economic security and allows them with an opportunity to hope for better future. Most of the circular migrant workers are provisional returnee (Oxfeld and Long, 2004). They return to Nepal provisionally, during the lean season, or during festivals like *dasai* and *tihar;* to attend the marriage and religious ceremonies; for political participation, etc.

During the election time in Nepal, these migrant workers actively participated in campaigning and electing their members for the new constitution contributing towards political remittances (Piper, 2009). While returning to Nepal, they carry gifts and cash for their families and friends in Nepal. In this short visit, some of them buy livestock and some invest in building a new house while others purchase land in the plains. According to the 'progressed' returned migrant workers, these provincial returnees are the most successful ones in terms of their earnings from the coal mines.

Most of the workers stated that they experience the continual return to the coal mines because for many, coal mine is a constant, one of the most stable sources of income in their lives. Whenever the villagers are in debt or having a shortage of money, they immediately return to the coal mines where they can earn within a week's time. Some of the migrants also stated that the coal mines provide them a sense of economic security in their lives and when needed. This is the reason why many villagers depend on the income from the coal mines. Without the coal mines, they would not have been able to think about their better future and their children's good education.

## Abroad Returnee

The villagers of Patlepani Bhojpur and Bange Bazaar in Sunsari district in Nepal stated that apart from working in the coal mines, many youths apply for a visa to work abroad. However, being unable to work in the foreign country these villagers return and work in the coal mines. In fact, there are migrants who have returned to the coal mines after working a few years in Malaysia, Qatar, and other Gulf countries. They say earning is better in the coal mines than in other countries. The villagers initially earn from the coal mines and from that earning they plan to go aboard with the savings of the coal mines. But due to various problems like visa problems, accidents, health insurance and mostly fake documents produced by the agents, they return to work in the coal mines. Some of the workers reported that even after paying a handsome amount to the agents they are returned from the airport due to lacunae in their travel documents. They spend all their savings in paperwork with the hope that they can work abroad but they are sent back immediately from the airport itself. Thus, they return to the coal mines so that they can regain what they have lost.

In the coal mines and also in Nepal, some of the migrant workers are the second generation migrants working in the coal mines. Most of the return migrants stated, they first went to other states of North East India for wood cutting and some served in Indian Army. Unable to make a satisfactory income there, most of them with the help of their village networks started to work in the coal mines. That time, not many Nepalese worked in the coal mines and only a few stayed back there permanently. They worked during the mining seasons and then returned to Nepal for agricultural works. This continued for several years till their children were young. At present, the children of return migrant's are involved in the same work. Most of the young men have followed the footsteps of their parents and relatives and have been working in the coal mines.

## Stranger at Home

Migrants became sentimental while explaining about their return from the coal mines. When the migrant workers return home after staying for several years in the coal mines, they are treated as strangers and they feel detached from their own home and society as well. Though they return to their homeland they feel completely out of place. In the village Patlepani, there are many migrant workers who report such sentiments. These migrants leave their home at a very early age. Unable to earn, they plan to return only after they have accumulated a certain sum of money. Some are ashamed to return home empty handed and they prolong their stay in the mines. Some say that they do not like to stay in their home village anymore as the villagers treat them as strangers.

## Women and Return

Not only the migrant male workers but even the wives of the migrant workers make a continual return to the coal mines. The wives of the migrants in the coal mines expressed their willingness to work in the coal mines until they can earn well. They expressed that in the coal mines they can earn money and spend as they wish to. They do not have to think much about every little thing like that in Nepal. While in Nepal even though they worked hard from morning till evening, they could not make any money. Some expressed they feel more independent in the coal mines as they are free from their household chores neither they have to follow the strict rules and traditions of home and society. In the mines, they are free to dress according to their choices and consume any food without any restrictions. In this regard, migrant worker's wife Kanta, 35 years old in Sutnga coal mining sites of Jaintia Hills says while she is in Nepal, she waits for the mining season to come so that she can return to the mining area. She has been accompanying her husband since the last 10 years and has been running a rice hotel there. She is more independent here than in Nepal as she need not follow the strict rules and regulations here like working day and night without a break. In the coal mines, she can wear clothes according to her wish; there is no restriction in food and can go around the market freely. She says she is much relaxed here than in Nepal.

Most of the returned Nepalese migrant workers in the studied villages of Nepal can be grouped both under a return to failure and return to success. Some have returned to Nepal due to accidents and some because of their poor health conditions or are too old to work in the mines and some took retirement after fulfilling their desire to earn. Some of these returned migrants were circular migrants, had been successful in buying land in the plains of Nepal and are now settled there. While some prefer to live in their village, investing their income in buying cattle and in constructing more rooms in their houses. Most of the permanently returned migrants have successfully migrated to the coal mines during or after the 1970s from Patlepani village of Bhojpur. They say those days coal mines were known as *koilakhat* and now it has become *koilakhate*. *Koilakhat* means the pile of coal (*koila*-coal; *khat*- pile) and *koila khate* is used by the villagers to refer to those coal mine workers who do not earn money or do not return to Nepal. The meaning of the word itself has changed over time. The coal mines have now become the residences of those who do not return 'home' and merely send remittance to the country of origin. The returned migrants consider the present generation migrants are more into spending money on alcohol or entertainment in the mines rather than saving for their future. They are also in the process of assimilation after marrying with the locals. These groups of migrants hardly return to progress to their home village which may be the sign of downward mobility.

## Memories from the Returned Migrant Workers

The returned migrants to Nepal live on memories of time spent in the coal mines. Whenever they gather for evening tea or gossip, they talk about their different experiences of the coal mines. They have different stories to tell every day. They share both pleasant and unpleasant memories. Some recall their past and compare it with the present working and living conditions. They talk about their relationship with the locals and other migrant communities. They say during the 1970s and 1980's there were very few Nepalese working in the coal mines. The villagers in Nepal considered these migrant workers as 'foreign employed' (*bidesh ma kaam garne*) who prolonged their stay and returned home only after fulfilling their desired income. These workers while living in the coal mines waited to receive letters from their family and friends. Returned worker named Karki 72 years from Bhojpur Nepal, says 'if we see six months workers; it was great happiness for us... letter from home was the means of communication that time... People use to bring a bundle of letters and call us to receive the letter in the *bazaar*... it was a great happiness for us... it was unique to go abroad (*bidesh*) that time from here... Now it is very common'.

Even many months after returning to Nepal, they missed the coal mining place and the environment there especially when they could not earn money in Nepal. They remember how lavishly they spent money on food and in buying other necessary items in the coal mines. They eagerly waited to return home with the saved money and purchased gifts for their families and friends. These returned migrants remember how they spent their time hanging out with their friends after their work. They used to go to the coal mines without their families initially and live with friends there. Those days they worked by lighting candle, unlike today when the workers use torchlight. Even though they worked in candle light, they did not fear accidents, as they were very careful about their work and life. Finishing their work, they unrolled their long pants and full sleeve shirt, combed their hair, and went hanging around with their friends in the market, playing *teer*, dice or eating *puri* with *chai*, and sometimes drinking alcohol or soft drink in a Jaintia hotel. They compare their villages with the coal mines in terms of their social life. They shared that their life in Nepal was 'boring' because they hardly can enjoy or have free time for the social life after the day long hard work in the agricultural field. Moreover, in the coal mines, they can both earn money and have a social life if they can cope up with the strenuous work.

They use to forget all the troubles of undertaking the long journey to Nepal once they received their wage from the first week of work and saved it to return home as soon as possible. However, nowadays it is not like that as the villagers hardly return to their home. Some are unable to earn, some spend their money only in drinking, some are enjoying in gambling while others are married and settled permanently in the camps. It is in this context these returned migrants lament, the pile of coal (*koilakhat*) is now full of a pile of unwanted people (*koilakhate*) as the latter neither return home nor send any remittances to their home village.

## Adjustment Problem

Some of the returned migrant workers failed to live and work in the coal mines and returned to their origin village after a few months or a year. One of the reasons these returned migrants gave was that they were unable to adjust or adapt to the living and working condition of the coal mines. These migrant workers without having the slightest hint come to work in such conditions. Reaching the coal mines they realise they could neither adjust to the environment nor can work in such a place. For some food was the problem while for others work or to adjust in the camp. One such example is of returned migrant worker Bhakta, aged 72 years of Bhojpur, Nepal who worked in the coal mines for only three months. He migrated to the coal mines at the age of 47 years and lived there for only three months. He says, 'Work is enjoyable only if you can adjust to the environment'. He could not work inside the rat hole like others. Other workers could work continuously for six to seven hours but he was not so strong to work. As a result of which he could not make his own expenses for survival. Moreover, he did not like the surrounding around the camps and could not adjust to the food habits in the coal mines since he does not drink alcohol or consume meat. He was also not comfortable when *Dalit* served or cooked food for him as he belongs to a Brahmin caste. As a result, he stopped eating rice in the rice hotel and became sick. He went to earn money like his village friends and pay all his debt but unhygienic living and the working environment pushed him to return home.

### Returned with Ill Health

Some of the migrant workers returned due to their poor health or accidents while working in the coal mines. They reported many health issues as a result of which some of them returned permanently. Most of the returned migrants interviewed, stated that the common ailments in the mining area are malaria and jaundice and some suffered from tuberculosis as well. Unable to get proper treatment, these migrants have returned permanently to their villages. According to health workers, here they become sick as they live in the jungle site which is replete with insects and mosquitoes. Moreover, the water in the mining area is polluted as it is filled with chemicals.

### Family Went to the Coal Mines to Bring their Lost Ones

There are many migrants who have been living in the coal mines and have never returned to Nepal. Some of these workers come to work in the coal mines immediately after their marriage or leaving their pregnant wife. Some come to work leaving their infants and never return home. However, there are also a few returned migrants, whose family made the effort to bring them back to their native village. These families could trace the location of the work through village networks and some are still in search of the near and dear ones. In most of the cases, the networks help in finding or tracking the 'lost' family member.

## Old to Earn

These types of migrants have returned to retire. According to Cerase (1974), return to retirement refers to retired migrants who decide to return to their home countries and to acquire a piece of land and a home where they will spend their old age. Both in the village and the plains of Nepal, the migrants who returned home permanently returned because of their advancing age. These types of returnees look upon their life as fully satisfied, as they were able to survive and work in the risky conditions of the coal mines. They have been able to spend more than half of their lives in the coal mines and bring the remittances. Most of the retired returned migrants are now migrated to the plains of Nepal with their family and some continue to live in the village looking for their agricultural work.

## Work after Return

The successfully returned migrants learn the skills and techniques that they take back home. In the case of the Nepalese migrant workers, they say they have acquired knowledge about the work related to the coal. Some of them have brought with them the knowledge of making the camps by themselves; learned to do electrical repairs, drive an automobile and most importantly work hard to save money. Bringing back this knowledge, these migrants have tried to put them to use in their home country.

From the village Patlepani, Bhojpur, most of the successfully returned migrants have migrated to the plains of Bange Bazaar of Sunsari district and a few remained in the same village especially those who could not earn much preferred to stay back as they could not invest in the plains. The returnees who stayed back in the village continued looking after their cattle and paddy fields. A few looked after their added land with the remittances earned and others are engaged in domestic farming and some work as a carpenter and shamans (*dhami*). Some of the successful migrants who live in the village have opened the grocery shop and a few working as a school teacher in the village.

Those who migrated to the plains of Nepal are engaged in extending their houses or engaged in plantation work and in their kitchen garden. Some of the others still visit the origin village and look after their cultivated lands. They have also opened a petty shop while others have been sitting ideal at home taking care of their grandchildren. However, they say they miss the work and social life in the coal mines.

In the village Patlepani, Bhojpur some of the returned migrants have been actively participating in political affairs. During the election time took a keen interest in campaigning and mobilising the villagers to vote for some political parties. They eagerly followed the debates on the framing of the Constitution. Some of the returnee migrants are now working as acting Ward Presidents and as VDC (Village Development Committee) secretary. They are responsible for all the activities taking place in the ward and the village. For example, returned migrant worker, Karna aged 60 years is now working as a Ward President. Giving an example of his work, he says, his duty is similar to that of the *Gaon Burha* (village head) in Meghalaya. He is responsible for all the activities that take place in the village. The election at the VDC level took place before ten years and since then they are holding the same post. Another returned migrant worker Krishna, aged 53 years is a VDC Secretary. Apart from having his own grocery shop, he looks after the VDC activities including nine wards. He says 'the village requires an urgent election for the local bodies as it is without any representatives for a long time'. Both these returned migrant workers have given their active political participation to their village. They find it difficult to look after the whole village, as there are no active working members in the villages. Moreover, government supplies a limited amount of manures, rice or even seeds which are difficult to distribute among the villagers. The village is surviving only because many youths migrate to work in the coal mines during the mining season otherwise the food cultivated at home and the government supply is not sufficient for the survival of the family.

## Conclusion

This chapter begins with the argument stating that for the majority of the Nepalese migrant workers, working in the coal mines is not temporary; rather an experience of circular return. From the various examples and case studies cited above it can be concluded that for the Nepalese coal mine migrant workers their actual return is a return to the coal mines. The various examples of returns- imagined, circular and permanent show return can take place at any time and through spaces. It should not necessarily mean a physical return to the origin village but can also be through images and memories. Though the Nepalese migrant workers returned permanently to their original village in Nepal, they continued to return to the coal mines through their memories and talk on an everyday basis. For those who live permanently in the coal mines, most of them though imagine a return to their original homeland they consider coal mines as their homes. They have been spending their whole lives in the coal mines and their children are now assimilated with the host country and feel comfortable living there. For those who experience continual or provincial return, coal mines provide them a shared sense of economic as well as mental support. They speak of how coal mines have changed their lives and how they can now think of better future prospects. Return to Nepal can take place anywhere; over space and time as the Nepalese migrants reconstruct their homelands both symbolically and in practice.

## Notes

1. Nepalese migrant miners and their families reside in fragile camps built near the mines. They construct these shelters out of tarpaulin or plastic sheets. These houses are makeshift arrangements for a temporary habitation. Workers do not stay in these for long as they move from one quarry to the next on learning about better payment there or when the coal reserve is exhausted in one quarry.
2. In Jaintia Hills, Meghalaya, the method used for coal extraction is commonly known as 'rat-hole' mining. The hole dug in the ground has a very small

opening on the surface (of barely one meter in diameter). The miners crawl and go deep inside this hole to extract coal. These burrows or holes are only big enough to accommodate one person at a time that crawls in with tools and a basket to carry the extracted coal back to the surface. This is known, as 'rat hole mining' also because the hole dug in the ground looks likes burrows made by rats.

3. On the 17th of April 2014, National Green Tribunals (NGT) ordered a blanket ban on the rat hole mining including the transportation of the trucks. It was banned on the petition filed by the Dimasa Students Union and Dima Hasao District Committee from Assam stating that acidic discharge from rat-hole mining in Jaintia Hills of Meghalaya was polluting the Kopili River and making it acidic which was the only source of livelihood for many people.
4. The coal mine owners have promoted some Nepalese coal mine workers to the position of the *Sardar*. In Meghalaya, no outsider can be the owner of a mine. However, some Nepalese migrants, by sheer dint of their hard work and dynamism have risen to the position of the *Sardar*. The *Sardar* supervises all the work related to mining. From bringing the labourers to the mines, to teaching them different mining operations, he is the manager, who manages man, material, machine and money modalities related to the mines. While the mine owner is a leader in absentia, who seldom visits the quarry; it is the *Sardar* who is the de facto leader of the mining endeavor.

## References

Bovenkerk, F., 1974. *The Sociology of Return Migration: A Bibliographic Essay.* The Hague; Martinus Nijhoff.

Brettell, CB., 1979. 'Emigrar para vooltar: A Portuguese ideology of return migration'. *Papers in Anthropology*, 20, 1: 1-20.

Brettell, CB and JF. Hollifield. 2014. *Migration Theory: Talking Across Disciplines*. New York; Routledge.

Cassarino, J., 2004. 'Theorizing return migration: The conceptual approach to return migrants revisited'. *International Journal on Multicultural Societies,* 6, 2: 253-279.

Cerase, FP., 1967. 'A study of Italian migrants returning from the USA'. *International Migration Review,* 1, 3: 67-74.

Cerase, FP., 1974. 'Expectations and reality: A case study of return migration from the United States to Southern Italy'. *International Migration Review,* 8, 2: 245-262.

Ghosh, B., 2000. *Return Migration: Journey of Hope or Despair?* Geneva; International Organisation for Migration.

Gmelch, G., 1980. 'Return migration'. *Annual Review of Anthropology*, 9: 135-159.

Gmelch, G., 1983. 'Who returns and why? : Return migration behaviour in two North Atlantic societies'. *Human Organisation,* 42, 1: 46-54.

Gordon, MM., 1961. 'Assimilation in America: Theory and reality'. *Ethnic Groups in American Life*, 90, 2: 263-285.

Guzzetta, C., 2004. 'Return migration: An overview'. *Journal of Immigrant and Refugee Services,* 2, 1-2: 109-117.

King, R., 1978. 'Return migration: A neglected aspect of population geography'. *The Royal Geographical Society*. 10, 3: 175-182.

King, R., 1986. 'Return migration and regional economic development'. New York: Routledge.

King, R and A. Christou. 2011. 'Of counter-diasporas and reverse trans-nationalism: Return mobilities to and from the ancestral homeland'. *Mobilities*, 6,4: 451-466.

King, R and A. Strachan. 1980. 'The effects of return migration on a Gozitan village'. *Human Organisation*. 39, 2: 175-179.

King, RL., 1977. 'Problems of return migration: A case study of Italians returning from Britain'. *Tijdschrift Voor Economische En Sociale Geografie,* 68, 4: 241-246.

Long, LD and E. Oxfeld. 2004. *Coming Home? Refugees, Migrants and Those Who Stayed Behind*: Philadelphia; University of Pennsylvania Press.

Markowitz, F and AH. Stefansson. 2004. *Homecomings: Unsettling Paths of Return*, New York; Lexington Books.

Massey, DS., 1987. 'Understanding Mexican migration to the United States'. *American Journal of Sociology*, 92, 6:1372-1403.

McCaa, R., 1993. 'Ethnic intermarriage and gender in New York City'. *Journal of Interdisciplinary History*. 24: 207-231.

Oxfeld, E and LD. Long. 2004. 'An ethnography of return'. In LD Long and E Oxfeld. (Eds.): *Coming Home? Refugees, Migrants and Those Who Stayed Behind*, pp. 1-18, Philadelphia; University of Pennsylvania Press.

Pagnini, DL and SP. Morgan. 1990. 'Intermarriage and social distance among U.S. immigrants at the turn of the century'. *American Journal of Sociology*, 96: 405-432.

Piper, N., 2009. 'Temporary migration and political remittances: The role of organisational networks in the trans-nationalisation of human rights'. *European Journal of East Asian Studies*, 8, 2: 2I5-243.

Qian, Z and DT. Lichter. 2001. 'Measuring martial assimilation: Intermarriage among natives and immigrants'. *Social Science Research*, 30: 289-312.

Qian, Z and DT. Lichter. 2007. 'Social boundaries and marital assimilation: Interpreting trends in racial and ethnic intermarriage'. *American Sociological Review*, 72: 68-94.

Rhoades, RH., 1978. 'Intra-European return migration and rural development: Lessons from the Spanish case'. *Human Organisation*, 37, 2: 136–147.

Seddon, D., G. Gurung and J. Adhikari. 1998. 'Foreign labour migration and the remittance economy of Nepal'. *Himalayan Research Bulletin*, 17, 2: 3-10.

Slyomovics, S., 1998. *The Object of Memory: Arab and Jew Narrate the Palestinian Village.* Philadelphia; University of Pennsylvania Press.

Suro, R., 1996. *Watching America's Door.* New York; Twentieth Century Fund Press.

Tsuda, T., 2003. *Strangers in the Ethnic Homeland: Japanese Brazilian Return Migration in Transnational Perspective.* New York; Columbia University Press.

Upreti, BC., 2009. 'India-Nepal treaty of peace and friendship: Nature, problems and question of identity of Indian Nepalis'. pp 339-350. In TB. Subba, AC. Sinha, GS. Nepal and DR. Nepal (Eds.): *Indian Nepalis: Issues and Perspectives*. New Delhi; Concept Publishing Company.

# Chapter - 17

# Eruption of Permanent Teeth among the Khasi of Shillong, Meghalaya

*—D. K. Limbu and S. Saikia*

## Introduction

Dental anthropology is defined as a study of people from the evidence provided by teeth (Hillson, 2002). It includes a study of the development of teeth in relation to age, their appearance in the mouth, and the processes of wear and other changes that occur once they are in place. Teeth being the hardest and most durable material for all parts of the body, due to the presence of enamel and dentine in them, preserve well and hence account for a large proportion of the human and pre-human fossil remains available for study. Dental eruption is the time when any part of the crown has emerged through the gingival surface. The process by which the crown of the developing tooth passes through its surroundings and is maintained in normal occlusion within the oral cavity is known as dental eruption (Rami Reddy, 1986).Variables like age, sex, heredity, socio-economic level and intrauterine environments influence the sequence and timing of tooth emergence. The chronology of tooth emergence has often been used in the estimation of age.

## Materials and Methods

The present study was based on a cross-sectional sample of 2,517 Khasi children of Shillong, Meghalaya, aged between 5.85±0.18 and 12.3±0.25 years of which 1,254 were boys and 1,263 were girls. Information regarding the eruption of permanent teeth was obtained by orally examining these children who were apparently healthy. Tooth eruption of the subjects was examined with the help of a dental mirror and a spatula in a sufficient daylight. Some missing teeth were counted as erupted when the subject could recall their emergence and/or extraction. Standard techniques of data collection on dental eruption as given by Weiner and Lourie (1981) were followed. Special care was taken to determine the actual ages of the subjects. All the subjects were Christians and thus, were requested to show their baptismal certificate and immunisation card for the birth date record. The subjects who could not show their baptismal certificate or those whose parents failed to give correct information on age were not included in the sample. The sample comprises of only those subjects who's both the parents were Khasi. Age of the individuals was calculated according to the decimal age calendar given by Weiner and Lourie (1969) from his/her birthday to the date of examination. The coding of the teeth is as follows: I, C, P, and M stand for incisor, canine, premolar and molar. The position of the numerals on lower and the upper end of the letter signifies mandibular or maxillary tooth respectively. The median age of eruption for each tooth is calculated using Probit Transformation of Fisher and Yates (1957).

## Results and Discussion

Table 17.1 shows the percentages of permanent teeth eruption among the Khasi boys and girls of Shillong. In the present population, the permanent teeth have emerged first at six years of age where the highest percentage of the eruption was observed in the mandible of girls (17.97 per cent) followed by the boys (9.45 per cent). At this age, the eruption has taken place little later in the lower jaw i.e., 5.30 per cent and 6.45 per cent teeth among the boys and girls respectively. In all the age groups of boys, permanent teeth have erupted earlier in the lower jaw. The same trend was also observed in the girls up to 10 years of age. However, 11 years onward, eruption becomes faster in the maxilla of the girls. At 13 years, eruption completes in the maxilla of the girls and the mandible of boys. By 14 years of age, eruption completes in the remaining jaws i.e., the maxilla and the mandible of boys and girls respectively. Fig.17.1 depicts the jaw and sex-wise percentages of the permanent teeth eruption (M3 is not included) in the Khasi children.

**Table 17.1: Numbers and Percentages of Permanent Teeth among the Khasi Children (jaw-wise)**

| *Age (Yrs)* | *Maxilla ($M^3$ not included)* | | | | *Mandible ($M_3$ not included)* | | | |
|---|---|---|---|---|---|---|---|---|
| | *Boys* | | *Girls* | | *Boys* | | *Girls* | |
| | *No. of teeth* | *Per-centages* | *No. of teeth* | *Per-centages* | *No. of teeth* | *Per-centages* | *No. of teeth* | *Per-centages* |
| 6 | 23 | 5.30 | 28 | 6.45 | 41 | 9.45 | 78 | 17.97 |
| 7 | 80 | 17.86 | 131 | 24.62 | 96 | 21.43 | 187 | 35.15 |
| 8 | 109 | 31.14 | 158 | 38.92 | 136 | 38.86 | 176 | 43.35 |
| 9 | 174 | 38.84 | 206 | 44.59 | 196 | 43.75 | 235 | 50.87 |
| 10 | 205 | 47.23 | 203 | 53.70 | 246 | 56.68 | 215 | 56.88 |
| 11 | 389 | 67.77 | 406 | 76.32 | 428 | 74.56 | 359 | 67.48 |
| 12 | 336 | 85.71 | 379 | 93.35 | 339 | 86.48 | 358 | 88.18 |
| 13 | 487 | 96.63 | 476 | 100.00 | 504 | 100.00 | 472 | 99.16 |
| 14 | 476 | 100.00 | 392 | 100.00 | 476 | 100.00 | 392 | 100.00 |

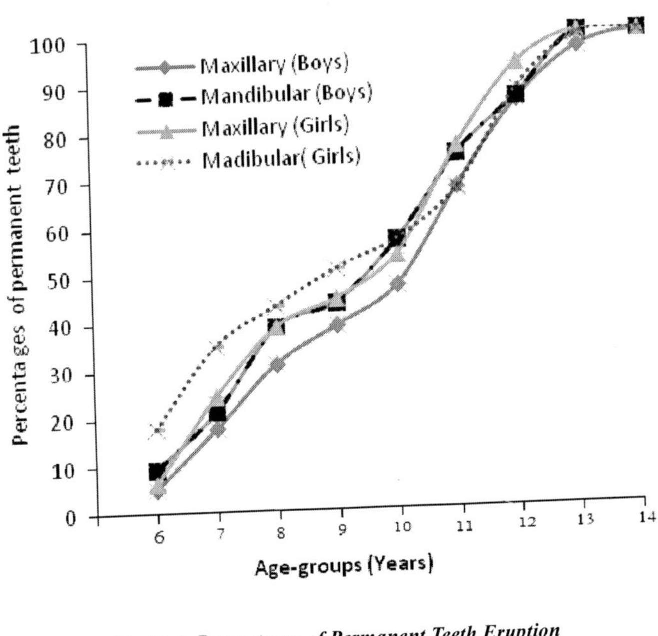


*Fig.17.1: Percentages of Permanent Teeth Eruption among the Khasi Boys and Girls.*

Table 17.2 shows the numbers and percentages of permanent teeth eruption among the Khasi boys of Shillong. The eruption of permanent teeth is observed first at six years of age and it gradually increases with the increase of age. By 10 years, more than 50.00 per cent teeth complete eruption. In the age-groups 11, 12 and 13 years, 817 (71.17 per cent), 675 (86.10 per cent) and 991 (98.31 per cent) teeth are found erupted. By 14 years, all the permanent teeth (excluding M3) complete their eruption in the boys.

**Table 17.2: Numbers and Percentages of Permanent Teeth among the Khasi Boys (both the jaws combined)**

| *Age (Yrs)* | *No. of teeth (M3 not included)* | *Percentages* |
|---|---|---|
| 6 | 64 | 7.37 |
| 7 | 176 | 19.64 |
| 8 | 245 | 35.00 |
| 9 | 370 | 41.29 |
| 10 | 451 | 51.96 |
| 11 | 817 | 71.17 |
| 12 | 675 | 86.10 |
| 13 | 991 | 98.31 |
| 14 | 952 | 100.00 |

The numbers and percentages of permanent teeth eruption in the Khasi girls are shown in Table 17.3. At the ages of 6, 7 and 8 years, 106 (12.21 per cent), 318 (29.89 per cent) and 415 (41.31 per cent) teeth erupt respectively. Thereafter, the eruption process slows down till they reach 10 years, after which it again becomes faster. At 11, 12 and 13 years, the percentages of teeth eruption are recorded to be 765 (71.90 per cent), 737 (90.76 per cent) and 948 (99.58 per cent) respectively. The eruption of all the permanent teeth (excluding M3) complete by 14 years of age. Fig.17.1 depicts the percentages of permanent teeth eruption among the Khasi children of Shillong.

Table 17.4 shows the median age (± S.D) of tooth eruption in the Khasi children of Shillong. It is observed that among the boys, all the teeth in the lower jaw erupt earlier than the upper jaw except the second premolar ($P_2$). In the girls, all the teeth erupt earlier in the mandible except the first and second premolars ($P_1$ and $P_2$). With respect to the sex dimorphism, girls show earlier eruption timing of

**Table 17.3: Numbers and Percentages of Erupted Permanent Teeth among the Khasi Females (both the jaws combined)**

| *Age (Yrs)* | *No of teeth (M3 not included)* | *Percentages* |
|---|---|---|
| 6 | 106 | 12.21 |
| 7 | 318 | 29.89 |
| 8 | 334 | 41.31 |
| 9 | 441 | 47.73 |
| 10 | 418 | 55.29 |
| 11 | 765 | 71.90 |
| 12 | 737 | 90.76 |
| 13 | 948 | 99.58 |
| 14 | 784 | 100.00 |

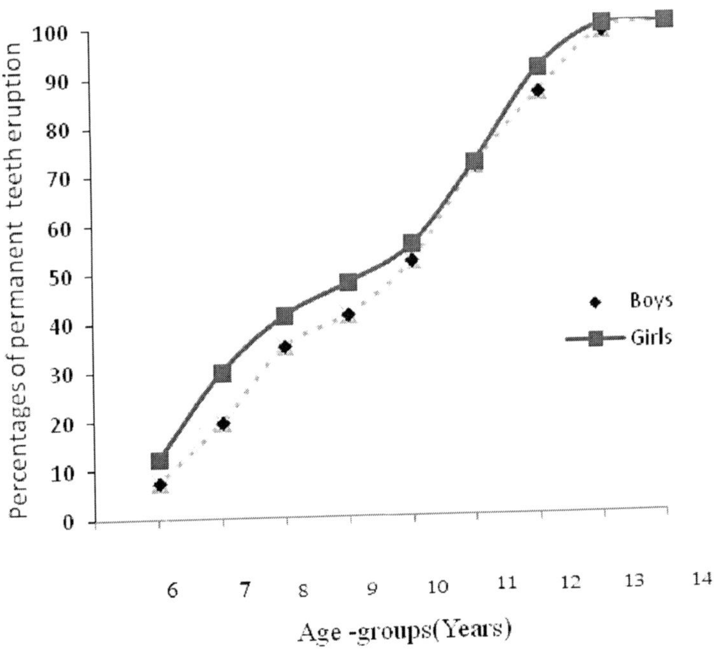


***Fig. 17.2: Percentages of Permanent Teeth Eruption among the Khasi Boys and Girls.***

all maxillary and the mandibular teeth except the second mandibular premolar ($P_2$). In the present population, the permanent teeth erupt first in the mandibular first molar ($M_1$) followed by the second mandibular molar ($M_1$).This is followed by the second incisors ($I_2$). Second molar ($M_2$) erupts very late. All the permanent teeth (less third molars) erupt between the median ages 5.85±0.18 and 12.2±0.6 years in girls and 6.55±0.0.35 and 12.3±0.25 years in the boys.

**Table 17.4: Median Age of Permanent Teeth Eruption in the Khasi Children**

| *Jaw* | *Sex* | $I^1$ | $I^2$ | $C^0$ | $P^1$ | $P^2$ | $M^1$ | $M^2$ |
|---|---|---|---|---|---|---|---|---|
| Maxilla | Boys | 7.45 ±0.35 | 8.35 ±0.35 | 11.05 ±0.23 | 11.3 ±0.38 | 11.25 ±0.30 | 6.8 ±0.38 | 12.3 ±0.25 |
| | Girls | 7.15 ±0.33 | 7.75 ±0.28 | 10.05 ±0.33 | 10.1 ±0.05 | 10.65 ±0.33 | 6.2 ±0.31 | 12.2 ±0.60 |
| *Jaw* | *Sex* | $I^1$ | $I^2$ | $C^0$ | $P^1$ | $P^2$ | $M^1$ | $M^2$ |
| Mandible | Boys | 7.15 ±0.33 | 7.75 ±0.35 | 10.3 ±0.40 | 10.9 ±0.35 | 11.4 ±0.25 | 6.55 ±0.35 | 11.65 ±0.20 |
| | Girls | 6.45 ±0.25 | 6.95 ±0.30 | 9.7 ±0.50 | 10.5 ±0.35 | 11.4 ±0.23 | 5.85 ±0.18 | 11.0 ±0.38 |

The sequence of permanent teeth eruption among the Khasi by jaw and sex is as follows:

Maxilla:

Male : $M^1 > I^1 > I^2 > C^0 > P^2 > P^1 > M^2$

Female : $M^1 > I^1 > I^2 > C^0 > P^1 > P^2 > M^2$

Mandible:

Male : $M_1 > I_1 > I_2 > C_0 > P_1 > P_2 > M_2$

Female : $M_1 > I_1 > I_2 > C_0 > P_1 > M_2 > P_2$

Both the jaws combined:

Male : $M_1 > M^1 > I_1 > I^1 > I_2 > I^2 > C_0 > P_1 > C^0 > P^2 > P^1 > P_2 > M_2 > M^2$

Female : $M_1 > M^1 > I_1 > I_2 > I^1 > I^2 > C_0 > C^0 > P^1 > P_1 > P^2 > M_2 > P_2 > M^2$

In the maxilla, both the sexes show the similar sequence of eruption of permanent teeth excepting the premolars. Among the males, the second premolar ($P^2$) erupts earlier to the first premolar ($P^1$) and in the female it shows a reverse in sequence. Like maxilla, in mandible also, all the teeth show a similar trend of eruption excepting the second premolar ($P_2$) and the second molar ($M_2$).

The second premolar ($P_2$) erupts earlier in the male and in the female the second molar ($M_2$) erupts earlier to the second premolar ($P_2$).

When both the jaws are combined, all teeth show the similar sequence of eruption except the canine (C0) and the premolars (P1 and P2) in the present population.

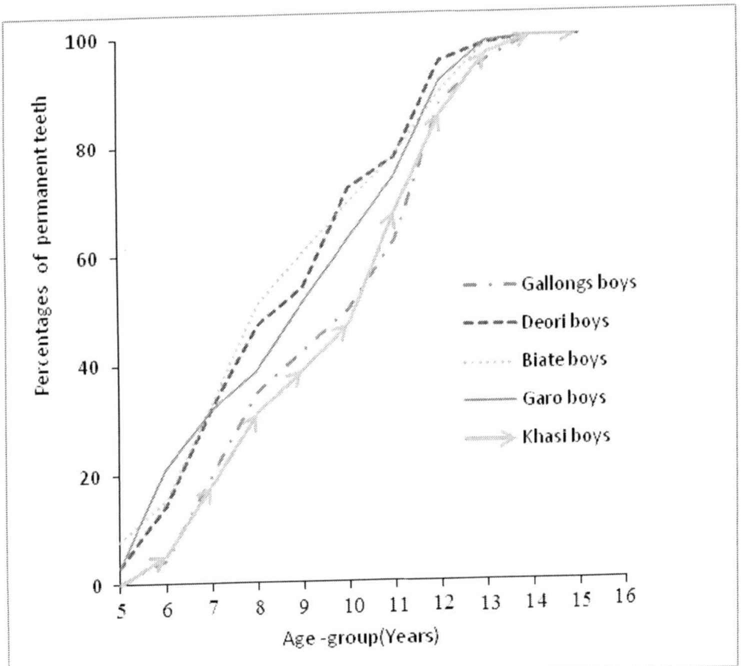


***Fig.17.3: Percentages of Permanent Teeth Eruption in Male Populations.***

Table 17.5 shows the percentages of the erupted permanent teeth (excluding M3) in boys when both the jaws are combined. These teeth erupt early among the Deori, Biate and the Garo boys (five years) and late (six years) among the Gallong and the Khasi. Percentages of the permanent teeth increase with the increase in age. By 14 years of age, eruption completes in almost all the populations excepting the Garo boys. Among the Garo, the eruption of permanent teeth completes at 15 years of age. Fig.17.3 depicts the trend of the eruption of the permanent teeth in some male populations.

**Table 17.5: Percentages of Permanent Teeth in some Mongoloid Male Populations of North East India**

| *Age (Yrs)* | *Populations* | | | | |
|---|---|---|---|---|---|
| | *Gallong (n=494)* | *Deori (n=217)* | *Biate (n=190)* | *Garo (n=287)* | *Khasi (n=1254)* |
| 5 | 0.00 | 3.06 | 7.86 | 3.07 | 0.00 |
| 6 | 4.39 | 14.45 | 15.18 | 21.03 | 5.30 |
| 7 | 19.81 | 31.96 | 32.71 | 31.71 | 17.86 |
| 8 | 35.05 | 47.11 | 50.99 | 39.02 | 31.14 |
| 9 | 42.48 | 54.28 | 60.51 | 51.42 | 38.84 |
| 10 | 49.86 | 72.32 | 69.51 | 63.00 | 47.23 |
| 11 | 62.54 | 77.72 | 78.21 | 74.31 | 67.77 |
| 12 | 87.80 | 95.50 | 89.64 | 91.57 | 85.71 |
| 13 | 95.60 | 98.64 | 98.74 | 98.85 | 96.63 |
| 14 | 100.00 | 100.00 | 100.00 | 99.86 | 100.00 |
| 15 | 100.00 | 100.00 | 100.00 | 100.00 | 100.00 |

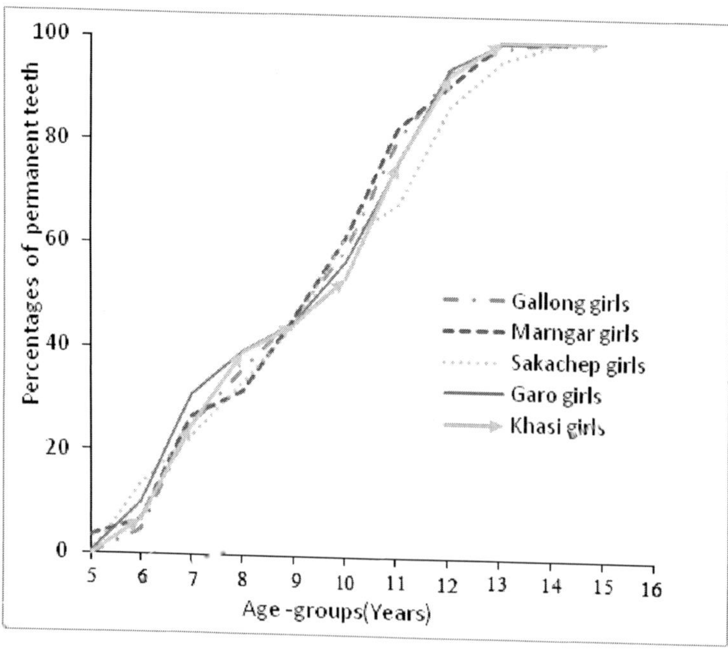


*Fig.17.4: Percentages of Permanent Teeth Eruption in Female Populations.*

Table 17.6 presents the percentages of the erupted permanent teeth among the girls. Among all the permanent teeth emerged, the earliest is in the Marngar and the Garo girls (five years). By 6 six years, all the above populations possess permanent teeth. Eruption completes earliest in the Marngar and the Khasi girls (13 years) followed by the Gallong (14 years). Eruption completes late among the Garo girls i.e., at 15 years. Fig.17.4 depicts the trend of the eruption of the permanent teeth among some female populations.

**Table 17.6: Percentages of Permanent Teeth in some Mongoloid Female Populations of North East India**

| *Age (Yrs)* | *Populations* | | | | |
|---|---|---|---|---|---|
| | *Gallong (n=515)* | *Marngar (n=335)* | *Sakachep (n=77)* | *Garo (n=303)* | *Khasi (n=1263)* |
| 5 | 0.00 | 3.57 | 0.00 | 0.31 | 0.00 |
| 6 | 4.57 | 6.58 | 13.39 | 9.95 | 6.45 |
| 7 | 25.08 | 26.60 | 22.80 | 30.99 | 24.62 |
| 8 | 35.79 | 31.60 | 33.33 | 39.41 | 38,92 |
| 9 | 45.90 | 45.76 | 44.28 | 45.00 | 44.59 |
| 10 | 59.14 | 61.55 | 61.73 | 57.14 | 53.70 |
| 11 | 80.67 | 82.95 | 67.85 | 75.59 | 76.32 |
| 12 | 93.77 | 91.41 | 87.24 | 94.64 | 93.35 |
| 13 | 98.58 | 100.00 | 95.91 | 99.37 | 100.00 |
| 14 | 100.00 | 100.00 | 99.28 | 99.60 | 100.00 |
| 15 | 100.00 | 100.00 | 100.00 | 100.00 | 100.00 |

Comparative study of the sequence of eruption of permanent teeth among some Mongoloid populations of North-East India by jaw and sex is shown in Table 17.7. This table shows that all the mandibular teeth tend to emerge earlier than their maxillary counterparts. Most of the teeth tend to emerge earliest in the Deori boys and late among the Sakachep girls and the Khasi boys. This table also reveals that the Gallong and the Khasi females are markedly advanced in their emergence timing which is reverse in the case of the Garo and the Sakachep.

Table 17.1 further shows that mostly the first mandibular molars ($M_1$) have emerged earlier to all other teeth, followed by the central incisor ($I_1$) and then the lateral incisor ($I_2$). The incisors are followed

**Table 17.7: Median age of Permanent Tooth Eruption among some Mongoloid Populations**

| ***Popu-lations*** | ***Author*** | ***Maxilla (yrs)*** | | | | | | | ***Mandible (yrs)*** | | | | | | |
|---|---|---|---|---|---|---|---|---|---|---|---|---|---|---|---|
| | | $I^1$ | $I^2$ | $C^0$ | $P^1$ | $P^2$ | $M^1$ | $M^2$ | $I_1$ | $I_2$ | $C_0$ | $P_1$ | $P_2$ | $M_1$ | $M_2$ |
| Gallong boys | Limbu (1996) | 7.55 (±0.25) | 8.52 (±0.22) | 11.45 (±0.32) | 10.55 (0.20) | 11.42 (0.26) | 6.52 (0.40) | 12.67 (±0.22) | 6.55 (±0.18) | 7.60 (±0.18) | 9.87 (0.31) | 10.75 (0.20) | 11.32 (±0.15) | 6.35 (0.20) | 11.97 (0.18) |
| Gallong girls | Limbu (1996) | 7.20 (±0.23) | 8.37 (±0.22) | 10.70 (±0.35) | 9.77 (±0.43) | 10.77 (±0.31) | 6.35 (±0.20) | 11.90 (±0.23) | 6.40 (±0.20) | 7.45 (±0.19) | 9.45 (±0.20) | 10.05 (±0.27) | 10.85 (±0.35) | 6.07 (±0.15) | 11.35 (±0.37) |
| Marngar girls | Tsochu (2002) | 7.05 (±0.40) | 7.95 (±0.35) | 10.00 (±0.35) | 10.25 (±0.27) | 10.30 (±0.30) | 6.70 (±0.45) | 11.25 (±0.20) | 6.65 (±0.45) | 7.80 (±0.35) | 10.30 (±0.35) | 10.20 (±0.22) | 10.25 (±0.20) | 6.45 (±0.45) | 11.15 (±0.25) |
| Deori boys | Syiemleih (2004) | 6.90 (±0.05) | 7.00 (±0.45) | 9.60 (±0.05) | 9.40 (±0.05) | 10.20 (±0.45) | 5.90 (±0.05) | 11.00 (±0.05) | 6.40 (±0.35) | 7.00 (±0.45) | 9.80 (±0.45) | 9.90 (±0.05) | 10.20 (±0.05) | 5.80 (±0.40) | 10.40 (±0.06) |
| Biate boys | Lotha (2005) | 6.50 (±0.40) | 7.40 (±0.50) | 9.40 (±0.55) | 9.80 (±0.60) | 10.50 (±0.50) | 5.70 (±0.40) | 11.10 (±1.05) | 6.50 (±0.35) | 7.10 (±0.45) | 9.50 (±0.55) | 9.80 (±0.60) | 10.20 (±0.60) | 5.70 (±0.35) | 10.60 (±0.60) |
| Garo boys | Kasar (2006) | 6.30 (±0.40) | 7.90 (±0.05) | 9.70 (±0.45) | 9.80 (±0.35) | 10.90 (±0.30) | 5.80 (±0.30) | 12.30 (±0.30) | 5.90 (±0.35) | 6.90 (±0.30) | 9.00 (±0.35) | 9.70 (±0.40) | 10.80 (±0.45) | 5.80 (±0.30) | 11.90 (±0.25) |
| Garo girls | Lalram-muana (2006) | 6.60 (±0.20) | 7.80 (±0.40) | 10.70 (±0.35) | 9.80 (±0.40) | 11.20 (±0.14) | 6.60 (±0.35) | 12.10 (±0.40) | 6.00 (±0.30) | 7.10 (±0.25) | 9.60 (±0.25) | 9.20 (±0.30) | 10.70 (±0.20) | 6.20 (±0.25) | 11.50 (±0.35) |
| Sakachep boys | Lotha (2009) | 6.90 (±0.35) | 7.50 (±0.50) | 11.10 (±0.15) | 10.10 (±0.10) | 10.40 (±0.20) | 6.30 (±0.45) | 13.30 (±0.40) | 6.40 (±0.45) | 6.60 (±0.35) | 9.50 (±0.25) | 10.30 (±0.10) | 10.50 (±0.20) | 6.30 (±0.45) | 12.40 (±0.40) |
| Sakachep girls | Lotha (2009) | 7.50 (±0.25) | 8.60 (±0.25) | 11.70 (±0.20) | 10.40 (±0.25) | 10.60 (±0.25) | 6.80 (±0.30) | 12.90 (±0.30) | 7.20 (±0.30) | 7.50 (±0.25) | 9.00 (±0.15) | 10.40 (±0.25) | 10.90 (±0.30) | 6.70 (±0.25) | 12.60 (±0.25) |
| Khasi boys | Present Study | 7.45 (±0.35) | 8.35 (±0.35) | 11.05 (±0.23) | 11.30 (±0.38) | 11.25 (±0.30) | 6.80 (±0.38) | 12.30 (±0.25) | 7.15 (±0.33) | 7.75 (±0.35) | 10.30 (±0.40) | 10.90 (±0.35) | 11.40 (±0.25) | 6.55 (±0.35) | 11.65 (±0.20) |
| Khasi girls | Present study | 7.15 (±0.33) | 7.75 (±0.28) | 10.05 (±0.33) | 10.10 (±5.05) | 10.65 (±5.33) | 6.20 (±3.10) | 12.20 (±6.10) | 6.45 (±0.23) | 6.95 (±0.30) | 9.70 (±0.50) | 10.50 (±0.35) | 11.40 (±0.23) | 5.85 (±0.18) | 11.00 (±0.38) |

by the canines ($C_0$) and then the second molar ($M_2$) which emerges at last. The emergence timing for the third molar ($M_3$) has not considered for the present study as this tooth has a very high variation with regards to its time of emergence from individual to individual.

Both the first mandibular and maxillary incisors ($I_1$ and $I^1$) emerge early i.e., at 5.9 years and 6.3 years respectively among the Garo boys. The mandibular lateral incisor ($I_2$) emerges late i.e. 7.15 years in the Khasi boys and earliest among the Sakachep boys (6.6 years) followed by the Garo boys (6.9 years). The maxillary lateral incisor ($I^2$) emerges earliest in the Deori boys (9.7 years) followed by the Biate boys (7.40 years). In the Sakachep boys, this tooth emerges very late (8.6 years). Among all the populations compared, the Biate boys (9.4 years) show the earliest emergence of maxillary canine ($C^0$) followed by the Deori boys (9.6 years). This tooth appears very late among the Sakachep girls (11.7 years). The mandibular canine ($C_0$) appears advance among the Garo boys and the Sakachep girls (9 years) whereas; in the Marngar girls and the Khasi boys (10.3 years) late emergence is observed. The maxillary premolars ($P^1$, $P^2$) tend to emerge very late among the Khasi and the Gallong boys (11.3 years and 11.42 years) but shows advanced in the Deori boys (9.4 years and 10.2 years). The earliest emergence of the mandibular first premolar ($P_1$) is observed in the Garo girls (9.2 years) and late in the Khasi boys (10.9 years). The earliest emergence timing for mandibular second premolar ($P_2$) was recorded among the Deori and the Biate boys (10.2 years) and late in the Khasi boys and girls (11.4 years). The emergence of the maxillary ($M^2$) and mandibular ($M_2$) second molars in both the upper and the lower jaws was first observed in the Deori boys at 11 years and 10.4 years respectively. These teeth emerge very late among the Sakachep children.

Sexual dimorphism for tooth emergence timing was evident in the Gallong and the Khasi as has been noted by the previous work in other populations (Clements *et al.*,1953; Moorrees,1957; Dahlberg and Menegaz-Bock,1958; Lee *et al.*,1965; Niswander and Sujaka,1960; Nanda and Chawla,1966; Mayhall *et al.*,1978). The salient features of this sexual dimorphism in the Gallong, Garo, Sakachep and the Khasi are as follows: All the permanent teeth in

Gallong and the Khasi emerge at markedly earlier chronological ages than their counterparts. The Khasi and the Gallong females have acquired their permanent teeth in a shorter time span (7.15-7.2 years) than their male counterparts (7.45-7.55 years). As the females showed earlier emergence in all the permanent teeth, it has been suggested by Mayhall *et al.* (1978) that the earliest emerging teeth (particularly $M_I$ and $I_2$) could be considered to be a transition period in which factors controlling emergence of permanent teeth are replacing those that control the emergence of the deciduous teeth. The eruption timing of the permanent teeth among the Garo and the Sakachep is more or less reverse. In both of these tribes, emergence timings of most of these teeth are delayed in the females. The only exception was the second molar of the maxilla (12.3 years), both the mandibular premolars (9.7 and 10.8 years) and the second mandibular molar (11.9 years) which emerge earlier in the Garo females. Among the Sakachep, the second maxillary molar (13.3 years), the mandibular canine (9.5 years) and the second mandibular premolar (10.5 years) emerge early.

## Sequence of Eruption

The sequence of permanent teeth eruption among some Mongoloid populations of North-East India is as follows:

Khasi boys: $M_1 > M^1 > I^1 > I_1 > I_2 > I^2 > C_0 > P_1 > P^2 > C^0 > P_2 > M_2 > P^1 > M^2$

Khasi girls: $M_1 > M^1 > I_1 > I^1 > I^2 > I_2 > C_0 > C^0 > P^1 > P_1 > P^2 > M_2 > P_2 > M^2$

Garo boys: $M_1 = M^1 > I_1 > I^1 > I_2 > I^2 > C_0 > P_1 = C^0 > P^1 > P_2 > P^2 > M_2 > M^2$

Garo girls: $I_1 > M_1 > I^1 = M^1 > I_2 > I^2 > P_1 > C_0 > P^1 > P_2 > C^0 > P^2 > M_2 > M^2$

Sakachep boys: $M^1 = M_1 > I_1 > I_2 > I^1 > I^2 > C_0 > P^1 > P_1 > P^2 > P_2 > C^0 > M_2 > M^2$

Sakachep girls: $M_1 > M^1 > I_1 > I^1 > I_2 > I^2 > C_0 > P^1 = P_1 > P^2 > P_2 > C^0 > M_2 > M^2$

Gallong boys: $M_1 > M^1 > I_1 > I^1 > I_2 > I^2 > C_0 > P^1 > P_1 > P_2 > P^2 > C^0 > M_2 > M^2$

Gallong girls: $M_1 > M^1 > I_1 > I^1 > I_2 > I^2 > C_0 > P^1 > P_1 > C^0 > P^2 > P_2 > M_2 > M^2$

Biate boys: $M^1 = M_1 > I^1 = I_1 > I_2 > I^2 > C^0 > C_0 > P^1 = P_1 > P_2 > P^2 > M_2 > M^2$

Marngar girls: $M_1 > M^1 > I_1 > I^1 > I_2 > I^2 > C^0 > P_1 > C_0 > P^1 > P_2 > P^2 > M_2 > M^2$

Deori boys: $M_1 > M^1 > I_1 > I^1 > I_2 = I^2 > P^1 > C^0 > C_0 > P_1 > P_2 = P^2 > M_2 > M^2$

No sex differences could be observed for the populations compared in the present study since the sequence of emergence in the mandible and that of the anterior teeth of the maxilla ($M^1I^1I^2$) in both sexes is same. The only exception was the Garo females, where the sequence of emergence is observed as $I_1M_1I_2$ and $I^1M^1I^2$. The gingival emergence of the canine relative to the premolars has been ascribed to sexual dimorphism, $C_0P^1$ for females and $P^1C_0$ for males (Adler and Godeny, 1952; Clements *et al.*, 1953). Excepting both the sexes of the Khasi, Garo and the Deori boys, all have displayed the usual predominantly female sequence $C_0P^1$, while, none have shown the mandibular canine-maxillary first premolar ($P^1C_0$) sequence.

Sexual dimorphism with respect to the canine-second premolar sequence in the maxilla ($C^0P^2$ for females, $P^2C^0$ for males) has also been reported (Hurme, 1957; Steggerda and Hill, 1942). The above mentioned predominant female sequence ($C^0P^2$) is absent in all populations. The predominantly male sequence in the maxilla, $P^2C^0$, prevailed only among the Khasi and the Gallong boys.

Data on median ages of emergence for the different ethnic groups of North-East India indicate that the dominant sequence for both sexes is $C_0P_1$ in the mandible (Table 17.7) which is observed only among the Khasi, Garo, and the Deori boys. The $P_1C_0$ sequence has been reported only in the Garo and the Marngar girls.

Table 17.7 further shows that the relative emergence of the mandibular second premolar ($P_2$) to its second molar ($M_2$) may be indicative of dimorphism in the majority of the ethnic groups. The emergence sequence $P_2M_2$ was observed in all the populations and both the sexes. The only exception was the Khasi females. The sequence $P_2M_2$ is relatively ancient, and the reverse ($M_2P_2$) which is present in the Khasi girls is uncommon in modern human species. However, Garn and Lewis (1963) have suggested the possibility of having genetic control of the $P_2M_2$ and $M_2P_2$ sequences. Females at large are evolutionarily more advanced than males. The maxillary sequence, $P^2M^2$, did not reveal sex differences in all the populations compared.

The mandibular first molar - first incisor sequence also seems to show polymorphism. The $M_1I_1$ sequence predominates in both the sexes in many populations. The $I_1M_1$ sequence which is uncommon in human has been reported in the Garo females. That the $I_1M_1$ sequence has not been found in the early Hominids and is only occasionally reported in modern human suggests that the 'field' has shifted mesially to include the first molar (Wallace, 1977). The sequence polymorphism elaborated above has been suggested to be due to the genetically determined differences in the tooth formation timing and can be demonstrated within populations (Garn *et al.*, 1973). The sexual dimorphism for the above sequences observed in various populations is clearly due to evolutionary trends, as early Hominids were also sexually dimorphic in this respect in the time of tooth emergence.

The above sequence of tooth eruption shows that the earliest tooth to be emerged in most of the populations of North East India considered for the present comparative study is the first mandibular molar ($M_1$) followed by the first maxillary molar ($M^1$). Only in the Garo girls, the earliest tooth to erupt is the mandibular first incisor ($I_1$) and among the Sakachep and the Biate boys, it is the maxillary first incisor ($I^1$). Anterior teeth have emerged earlier than their posterior counterpart in all the populations compared. The second maxillary molar ($M^2$) emerges at last in all the populations compared followed by the mandibular second molar ($M_2$). Only the Khasi children deviate from this trend i.e. the last tooth to emerge in the Khasi boys is the first maxillary premolar ($P^1$) and in the girls, it the second mandibular premolar ($P_2$). The eruption timing of the canine and the premolars falls in between the incisors and the molars, however; they do not show any pattern of the eruption. When compared with some Mongoloid populations of North-East India, the Khasi population shows late eruption timing.

## References

Adler, P and E. Godeny. 1952. 'Studies on the eruption of permanent teeth'. *Acta Genetica et Statistica Medica*. 3: 30-49.

Clements, EMB., E. Davies-Thomas and KG. Pickett. 1953. 'Time of eruption of permanent teeth in British children. 1947-1948'. *British Medical Journal*. 1: 1421-1424.

Dahlberg, A and R. Menegaz-Bock. 1958. 'Emergence of the permanent teeth in Pima Indian children'. *Journal of Dental Research*. 37: 1123-1140.

Fisher, RA and F. Yates. 1948. *Statistical Tables for Biological, Agricultural and Medical Research*. Oxford; Oliver and Boyd.

Garn, SM., MN. Jerrold, ST. Sandisky and T. Frederick. 1973. 'Economic impact on tooth emergence'. *American Journal of Physical Anthropology.* 39: 233-237.

Hillson, S., 2002. *Dental Anthropology.* Cambridge; Cambridge University Press.

Hurme, VO., 1957. 'Time and sequence of tooth eruption'. *Journal of Forensic Science.* 2: 377-388.

Kasar, S., 2006. *Eruption of Permanent Teeth and Prevalence af Dental Caries among the Garo Boys of Rangsakona and Dehalbagan Villages of Ri-Bhoi District of Meghalaya and Ambher Village of Kamrup District of Assam.* MSc. Dissertation, Shillong, North Eastern Hill University.

Limbu, DK., 1996. 'Eruption of permanent teeth among the Gallong of Arunachal Pradesh'. *Journal of Human Ecology.* 7: 221-222.

Lotha, T., 2009. *Eruption of Permanent Teeth among the Sakachep Children of Saitsama Village of Jaintia Hills district, Meghalaya.* MSc. Dissertation, Shillong, North Eastern Hill University.

Lotha, Z., 2005. *Eruption of Permanent Teeth and Dental Caries among the Biate Boys of Saipung Village, Meghalaya.* MSc. Dissertation, Shillong; North Eastern Hill University.

Mayhall, JT., PL. Belier and MF. Mayhall. 1978. 'Canadian Eskimo permanent tooth emergence timing'. *American Journal of Physical Anthropology.* 49: 211-216.

Moorrees, CFA., 1957. *The Aleut Dentition: A Correlative Study of Dental Characteristics in an Eskimo People.* Cambridge; Harvard University Press.

Nanda, RS and FN. Chawla.1966. 'Growth and development of dentition in Indian Children.I. Development of permanent teeth'. *American Journal of Orthodontics,* 52: 837-853.

Niswander, JD and C. Sujaka. 1960. 'Dental eruption, stature and weight of Hiroshima children'. *Journal of Dental Research.* 39: 959-963.

Rami Reddy, V., 1986. *Dimensions of Anthropology*, Vol. I, New Delhi; B.R. Publishing Corporation.

Steggerda, M and TJ. Hill. 1942. 'Eruption time of teeth among Whites, Negroes and Indians'. *American Journal of Orthodontics.* 28: 361-370.

Syiemlieh, S., 2004. *Eruption of Permanent Teeth and Dental Caries among the Deori Boys of Mahadevpur Deori villages, Arunachal Pradesh.* MSc. Dissetation, Shillong, North Eastern Hill University.

Tsochu, R., 2002. *Eruption of Permanent Teeth and Dental Caries among the Marngar Girls of Ri-Bhoi district, Meghalaya.* M Sc. Dissertation, Shillong, North Eastern Hill University.

Wallace, JA., 1977. 'Gingival eruption sequences of permanent teeth in early Hominids'. *American Journal of Physical Anthropology.*46:483-494.

Weiner, JS and A. Lourie.1969. *Human Biology: A Guide to Field Methods.* Oxford and Edinburg; Blackwell.

## Chapter - 18

# Buddhism in the Himalaya with Special Reference to Buddhism in Sikkim

—*Manis Kumar Raha*

Buddhism was founded by Lord Buddha himself during fifth century B.C. when Lord Buddha 'preached first sermon and made his first converts on the new site now marked by the Sarnath Stupa' (Waddel, 1976:2). Thereafter this new religion was spread all over North-Western India, and it reached up to Bihar. Then Emperor Ashoka during his time made this religion as a state religion and started promoting it by sending Buddhist missionaries even in the neighbouring countries. So, Buddhism was spread in the countries like Sri Lanka, Myanmar, Afghanistan, Mongolia, China, Japan, Tibet and some other countries.

Buddhism has three dominant strains which are Theravada, Mahayana, and Vajrayana. Of course, there is fourth strain called Zen Buddhism which develops from Mahayana Buddhism.

*Theravada:* There is three basic philosophy of this school which reveals that all worldly phenomena are subject to three characteristics. These are impermanent and transient; unsatisfactory and there is nothing in them which can be called one's own, nothing substantial, nothing permanent. After observing these when perfected insight is reached in a person, i.e. *Nirvana,* that person is a 'worthy person', an *Arhat.* The life of the *Arhat* is the ideal of the followers of this school. Theravada is the most ancient form of Buddhism. It is the dominant school of different countries of South East Asia like Thailand,

Myanmar, Cambodia and Laos. This form of Buddhism (Doctrine of Elders) was transcribed from old literature taught by Buddha. In this form, strong emphasis is laid on the monastic community and on heeding the advice of the wise.

*Mahayana:* Mahayana originated 500 years after Lord Buddha attained enlightenment from Theravada Buddhism. From this form of Buddhism originated different schools, like Tantra or Tantrik Buddhism, Zen Buddhism, Tibetan form of Buddhism, Pure Land Buddhism. It arose from *Mahasanghikas* sect, who was the earliest secede and forerunners of Mahayana. The ideal of Mahayana Buddhism is that of the *Bodhisattva*, a person who delays his or her own enlightenment in order to assist all other beings ultimately attains to the highest *Bodhi*. Mahayana found in Nepal, Tibet, Bhutan, Sikkim, China, Japan, and Korea.

*Vajrayana:* Vajrayana form of Buddhism is a prominent religion in the Himalayan region and found in Tibet, Nepal, Bhutan and also Mongolia. The characteristic of Vajrayana is the ritual use of the *Vajra*, a symbol of imperishable diamond, of thunder and lightning. It is also known as Lamaism as Lama is the main religious figure. Vajrayana has several major lineages like Nymgmapa, Karmapa, Sakyapa, Kargyupa, and also Gelugpa.

In India, there are two forms of Buddhism. These are Hinayana (*Theg-dman*) and Mahayana (*Theg-chen*), Hinayana means modest or lesser vehicle and the meaning of Mahayana is vast or 'great' vehicle. Hinayana appeared in the *Sutras* or Far-reaching Discrimination Awareness *(Prajnaparamita Sutras:* The perfection of Wisdom Sutras). It is the way of expressing the superiority of Mahayana.

The preaching sermons and advice of Buddha were all verbal. These were not written down. His disciples kept these in their memory. Only in the early first century B.C., writing of these was started from the recitations of the disciples. According to *Vaibhashika* version, three *Arhats* recited the teaching from memory. If the assembled members agreed to what these *Arhats* recited was "exactly what Buddha had actually said, and then this would confirm the accuracy of the teachings". These *Arhats* are (i) Ananda recited *Sutras* that is themes of practice, (ii) Upali recited the *Vinaya* (rules of discipline) and

(iii) Mahakashyapa recited the *Abhidharma* that is special topics of knowledge.

These three divisions of Lord Buddha's teaching became *The Three Basket-like Collections* concerning special topics of knowledge. These three baskets are:

1. The *Vinaya* Basket contained teaching of higher ethical self-discipline.
2. The *Sutra* Basket, those on higher absorbed concentration.
3. The *Abhidharma* Basket, the teaching on higher discriminating awareness or higher wisdom.

**Buddhism in the Himalayan Region**

The Great Mountain, the Himalayas spread from North-Western region to North-East region of India via Northern region. This mountainous range received Buddhism at very early years after the Third Council convened by King Ashoka. After this council, he sent five monks, led *Arhat* Majjhima to different areas of Himalayas to spread the *Dhamma.* When Huien Tsiang visited Kulu and its surrounding valleys in the seventh century he found about twenty monasteries and a thousand or so monks of Mahayana sect of Buddhism. Gradually almost the whole of the Himalayas became followers of Buddhism. At present Buddhism is found in different areas of the Himalayas like Ladakh, Zanskar, Lahaul, Spiti, Kinnaur, Mustang, Sikkim and some areas of North East India in the Indian side and also Bhutan, Nepal, and Tibet. Very little ancient traces of Buddhism are also found in Garhwal and Kumaon regions of the Indian Himalayas.

In the Indian Himalayan region, Buddhism is found to be practised by a number of communities inhabiting different areas of this mountain range spreading from Leh in Ladakh to Arunachal Pradesh. In the Western Himalayas Buddhism is found to be present in Ladakh areas of Jammu and Kashmir; in Lahaul and Spiti and Kinnaur districts of Himachal Pradesh. In the Central Himalayas, this religion is practiced by some people of Uttar Kashi, Chamoli and Pithoragarh areas of Uttaranchal. In the Eastern Himalayas also some people of the eight states of North East India (Arunachal Pradesh, Assam, Manipur,

Meghalaya, Mizoram, Nagaland, Sikkim and Tripura) are found embracing Buddhism. Outside the Indian Himalayas Buddhism is also practised in Tibet, Nepal and Bhutan. In this chapter, I shall restrict my discussion on Buddhism only in the Indian Himalayas and also of Bhutan and Nepal. But I have given some emphasis on the Buddhism in Sikkim.

## Buddhism in Ladakh, Jammu and Kashmir

In Ladakh areas, particularly in Leh district, different ethnic groups like the Bhot, Boto, Bhoto, Bhautta or Mangric and also the Gara, Mon, and Beda who are also known as Dolba, are basically Buddhist. In Ladakh Buddhism as a religion and faith was prevailing long before Emperor Ashoka ruled. Ganhar thinks that 'Buddhism was one of the living faiths in the valley in the time of Surendra...... Obviously, Buddhism has prevalent in the territory or was introduced into it in the time of Surendra......Later in Ashoka's time Buddhism spread widely in Kashmir and other territories' (Ganhar, 1956:175).

Buddhism which is prevalent in Kashmir is not a pure form of Buddhism but a mixture of *Bon* or *Pon* religion of ancient Tibet, Tantrism and Mahayana (Mann, 1986:141). Mann further says that the chief concept of the divinity of the Buddhist of Kashmir is defined under three dimensions. These dimensions are Gautama Buddha (*Sangyas*), the religious principles indicated by Buddha (*Chhos Konchok*) and the Lamas who follow these principles (*Gendun Konchok*). Besides, there are other traits like demology and idolatry which are found in the religion practised by the Kashmiri Buddhist (Mann, 1992:425; Ghosh, 1986:141). This Buddhism also known as Lamaism has two distinct sects called Red hat and the Yellow hat. The Red hat sect, who is also known as *Nyimapa*, is the earliest sect, and the practitioners wear red dresses and cap. The other sect, also known as *Gelukpa* (the virtuous), the red hat sect has been originated in the middle of fourteenth century (Ghosh, 1986:143).

In Kashmir, the Buddhist is mainly found in Ladakh area (Leh district). The Buddhists here worship different gods and goddesses and spirits and ghosts. The gods and goddesses are Chemresi, Chamba, Rikoamganbo, Makz or Gaimo, Cham-Shing, Yut-La, Genboo and

Chanlahete. The ghosts are Sinde, Lhu, Lhande etc. The principal god is Sangyas, Shaka Thubba or Gautam Buddha, the originator of Buddhism. Guru Rimpoche, Padma Sambhava or Lobon Rimpoche is also very important gods of these people. Yul-La is the village god. *Gompa* or monasteries are the religious institutions.

## Buddhism in Lahaul and Spiti, Himachal Pradesh

Buddhism is an important religion in the district of Lahaul and Spiti. The majority of the people practise this religion (Ghosh, 2002: 163). This district of Himachal Pradesh received this religion sometimes during eighth century A.D. according to Census Handbook of 1961 of this district. The great Buddhist monk Padma Sambhava is believed to have entered this district sometimes during eighth century A.D. and preached Buddhism. He also constructed the great monastery of Guru Ghantal......(*ibid,* 1992: 442). 'People are some mechanically devoted to Buddhism that prayer in this area has been reduced to a sort of reflex action and prayer wheel is a common sight' *(ibid)*. Drugpa (Red sect) is the prevailing sect. According to Gill (1972:130) and Ghosh (2002:165) some Nwang Mangyal, a missionary sent by the King of Bhutan about 2000 years ago, introduced this sect in this district. In this district, *Gompa* or monastery is found functioning in almost every village. It is the place of worship, prayer and also meditation for the Lamas and the Chomos, and training centre for the trainee Lamas and Chomos. *Padma Bkotana*, an ancient book, has mentioned the name of some countries like Zahor (Tibet or Mandi) and Garzha (ancient name for Lahaul and Spiti) where Padma Sambhava visited (Raha and Mahato, 1985:297).

## Buddhism in Kinnaur, Himachal Pradesh

Buddhism entered Kinnaur district of Himachal Pradesh also during eighth century A.D. through the adjoining district of Lahaul and Spiti.

In Kinnaur, Buddhism is found to be concentrated in Pooh subdivision. Here Buddhism is quite dominant. Buddhism is also present in Kalpa sub-division and found to have co-existed with local Hinduism. As a result, the same family is found to practise both religions (Raha, 1995:86; Raha and Mahato, 1985; 297). Frazer as early as 1820 found the people of Kinnaur following Buddhism (Frazer, 1820:156-257). Thornton about hundred sixty years ago, opined that 'the religion of Koonawar is Brahmanism in the south, in the north Lamaic religion' (Thompton, 1884:518). Here the Kinnaur Buddhism has two sects namely, *Nyingmapa* and *Dukpa*. The numbers of people embracing Gelukpa are only a few. Gerard could also find Gelukpas in a few villages (Gerard, 1845: 117).

In Kinnaur, there is a number of *Gompa* where people go for worship, prayer, and meditation. There young Lamas also get training. In the monasteries, the metal idol of Lord Buddha is found in the middle along with some saints like Sakya Muni, Padma Sambhava, Avolokiteswar and others. Besides these saints, some others like Nam-Chhra, Lagan, Chhog-dak, Tarema or Chhering-ma, Paldan-Lamo, Ningmet-Cheebe and some others are also propitiated (Raha and Mahato, 1985: 299-300).

## Buddhism among the Bhotia of Uttaranchal

In the Central Himalayas, the Bhotia of Uttar Kashi, Chamoli, and Pithoragarh of Uttaranchal are found to have embraced Buddhism. But their Buddhism has been a peculiar blend of Lamaistic Buddhism, Hinduism, and Animism (Prasad, 1989:100). They were getting influenced by the Tibetans when they used to go to Tibet markets for trade. During this time they accepted Tibetan Lamas as their priest. At present, they worship deities like Landey, Manhfaila and others.

## Buddhism in the Eastern Himalayas

The Eastern Himalayas cover eight states of North East India, Bhutan, and Nepal. In North East India, people are the believers of Shaivism, Vaishnavism, Shaktism, Jainism, Tantricism, tribal religion, along with Buddhism (Raha *et al.*, 2016). According to Dutta and Tripathi (2006:16), Buddhism plays a unique role in the religious life of the people of North East India.

In Northeastern states where Buddhism is practised, different sects like Theravada and Mahayana Buddhism.

In Arunachal Pradesh, the Monpas, Singphos, Tikhak Tangsas, Sherdukpens and others of Arunachal Pradesh, the Tai-Phakes,

Tai-Khamyang, Tai-Aiton, Dowaniyas, and a few Shans and Mans of Assam, the Chakmas and Mags of Tripura are found to practise Mahayana Buddhism. The Khamtis and Chakmas of Arunachal Pradesh, and the Chakmas of Mizoram are the followers of Theravada Buddhism. The Khamtis and Singphos of Arunachal Pradesh also practise Theravada Buddhism. According to Mr C. C. Singpho, 'Buddhism is living force of Arunachal Pradesh and is playing a very important role in the flourishing of Arunachal culture' (2006:21-22).

In Assam, the Tai Khamti people were the first to bring Buddhism in Assam. During the Burmese invasion in the eighteenth century, many Buddhist monks helped to spread Buddhism in Assam. Later on, Buddhism entered Mizoram and Nagaland (Raha *et al.*, 2016). Singpho is also of opinion that Buddhism is very popular among various tribes of Arunachal Pradesh and the imprint of Buddhism is found in their socio-cultural life. The monasteries, *stupas,* dances, festivals, arts and crafts give clear proof about these peoples' love, respect, and devotion for Buddhism (Singpho, 2006:21).

In Mizoram, the Chakmas are the only group who practise Buddhism. They have embraced Hinayana Buddhism though it is blended with local religious faith. They celebrate Buddhist festivals like Buddha Purnima, Kathin Chibar Dana, Ashari Purnima, and Bahu Chakma etc along with some non-Buddhist festivals also (Laskar, 2006: 74-76.)

In Tripura, the Chakmas entered in 1840 A.D. to get settled in this area. They are the believers of Theravada Buddhism. But before they accepted Theravada Buddhism, they used to practise Mahayana Buddhism (Poddar, 2006: 65-70).

Besides in different Indian Himalayan states, Buddhism is also found to be practised by the people of Bhutan and Nepal.

## Buddhism in Bhutan

In Bhutan, Buddhism is the state religion. Here a large section of people practices Mahayana Buddhism. Though it is originated in Tibet, the Mahayana Buddhism of Bhutan shows significant differences from that of Tibet in its ritual, liturgy, and monastic organisation. No doubt there are large numbers of monasteries in Bhutan, but the central Monastic Body with 1,000 monks (Lama or Gelong or novices) is situated in Thimpu and also in Punakha. There are also district monastic bodies, each headed by one *Je Khenpo* who is assisted by five *Lopons* or masters. In Bhutan, some of the monks and nuns belong to Gelugpa sect while some others, followers of Ningmapa sect. The Supreme Dharma King or His Holiness of Bhutan created a non-profit organisation in Bhutan called *Menjong Chothun Tsogpa* in 2002, and then another organisation, Buddha Dordenma Foundation in 2004. The main objective of these organisations is to fulfil a prophecy of Guru Padmasambhava 'to bestow blessings on world peace and glorious happiness'. In this mountainous state, Guru Padmasambhava is believed to be the Patron Saint of Bhutan (Raha *et al.,* 2016).

## Buddhism in Nepal

Siddharta Gautama, who after Enlightenment became Lord Buddha, was born in Kapilavastu, a historic town about 250 km from Kathmandu in Nepal in Sixth Century B.C. Still, Nepal is dominated by Hinduism. Only about 26.00 per cent of the total population here are the followers of Buddhism and they belong to three different sects of Buddhism, Theravada, Mahayana, and Vajrayana. While Mahayana is dominated in North Nepal, Vajrayana is important in Kathmandu valley. The Theravada sect has less number of followers, and they are scattered in different pockets.

During Fourth and Fifth Century A.D. Buddhism from India entered Nepal. Buddhism here is influenced by the beliefs and practices of Tantrism. 'Tantrism is a religion of moral percept, meditation, yoga, mantras and a philosophy that believes in interwoven of all things'. Again it is also believed that Buddhism was brought by the Tibetan Lamas of different Buddhist sects who came from Tibet and preached this religion in different places of Nepal. According to Furer-Haimendorf, the historical development of Buddhism in Khumbu and Solu in western Nepal is 'intimately linked with the age of Sherpa civilisation in its present form' (1964:126-127). The Buddhism of these areas associates themselves with the 'Legendary figures of Lama Sanga Dorje, the sixth incarnation of Chagna Dorje

(*Vajra Pani*)'. According to Snellgrove, 'Buddhism was introduced into Khumbu towards the end of seventh century' (1957:213).

## Buddhism in Sikkim

Regarding who actually introduced Buddhism in Sikkim is a point of controversy. Foning's view is that Lama Lhatsun Nangkha Jigma was the first person to introduce Buddhism in Sikkim. During his stay in Sikkim, he contacted Thekung Menoalong, the *bonthing*, also a shamanistic priest. Lhutsun started preaching a new type of Buddhism:

> Lama Lhatsun had taken special care and pain to prepare a treatise for the mode of worship and offering for this newly innovated special act of faith, quite permissible within the ambit of the Mahayana type of Buddhism. This accomplishment in his is no small measure helped the fusion of the native Rongfolk and the Tibetan from Kham resulting in the evolution of a new tribe called the Denjongpas, just as envisaged by the patriarchs, Thekung Tek and Khye Bumsa, long long ago (Foning, 1987:184).

In the long past over a century and twenty years ago, Waddel studied the Lamaism i.e. Buddhism in Sikkim and published a book entitled '*Lamaism in Sikkim*' as early as 1894. In this book, Waddell has discussed various aspects of Lamaism in this mountainous state. According to him, Lamaism or Tibetan Buddhism is the state religion of Sikkim and adopted by a majority of the Sikkim population. Lamaism which is essentially a priest craft may be defined as a mixture of Buddhism with a preponderating amount of mythology, mysticism, and magic; the doctrine of incarnate Lamas and the worship of canonised saints, now many prominent features of Lamaism, are of recent origin (Waddel, 1973:1).

In Sikkim Lamaism was introduced by Lhatsun Chhemba during seventeenth century A.D. when he arrived in Sikkim. The meaning of his name was 'the great revered God', and his Tibetan name was *Kun-zang nam-gyl* meaning 'The entirely victorious Essence of Godness'. People also know him by the name of *Lhatsun na,-kha Jing-med* meaning 'The Revered God who fears not the sky'. This name was given because people believe that he had the power to fly (*ibid:* 8).

In Sikkim 'The religion ousted by Lamaism were the *Pon* (*Bon*), usually identified with Taoism, and the earlier demon and fairy worship of the Lepcha......'. But still, innumerable traces of these two faiths are found to be embedded in the Lamaism of Sikkim. But Lamaism in Sikkim has two sects of the Lamas namely, Nyingma-pa and Kargyupa as represented by the Karmapa.

The Nyingmapa or 'the old school' represents the primitive and unreformed type of Lamaism. The Nyingmapa has three sub-sects, namely, (1) the Lhatsun-pa, (2) the Kartok-pa and (3) the Ngadak-pa. The members of all these sects came to an agreement to accept the creed known as *Dsog-chhen-bo* or 'The Great End'. It is a purely theoretical distinction. The characteristics are three-fold: (a) their special worship of *Guru Rimpoche,* (b) their highest God is *Kuntu Zang-po* (that is *Samantabhadra*), 'The highest Goodness', (c) their special tutelary deity is *Dub-pa kah gye*, (d) their special guardian deity is *Pat-gon de-nga* and (e) with these characteristic features they exhibit, as a class, a greater laxity of living than any other sect of Lamas (*ibid*: 11).

The members of the Nyingmapa sect worship the great wizard *Guru Pema* or *Guru Rimpoche* as 'second Buddha'. He has eight forms and all these eight forms are worshipped. These eight forms are known as *Guru Tsen-gye*, the great worshipful name of the teacher. These eight forms are:

1. *Guru Padma Jungne* (born of a Lotus) for the happiness of the three worlds.
2. *Guru Padmasambhava* (saviour by the Religious Doctrine).
3. *Guru Padma Gyelpo* (the king of three collections of scriptures i.e. *Tripitaka*).
4. *Guru Dorje-Do-lo* (Diamond comforter of all).
5. *Guru Nyima Od-zer* (The Enlightening Sun of Darkness).
6. *Guru Shakya Seng-ge* (the sacred Sakya – the Lion who does the work of eight sages).
7. *Guru Seng-ge-da dok* (the propagator of religion in six worlds–with roaring Lion's voice).
8. *Guru Lo-ten Chhog-se* (the conveyer of knowledge to all worlds).

The Nyingmapa was first to introduce in Tibet by Guru Padmasambhava when he went to Tibet in 817 C.E. at the invitation of the Tibetan king, Trisong Detsen (742-797). Nyingmapa is a unique lineage of Buddhism in Tibet as it is mixed with the Tibetan *Bon* or *Pon* religion. This lineage, i.e. Nyingmapa emphasises a move towards more advanced stages of enlightenment through 'preliminary practice' of belief and practices of Buddhism before the advent of *Tantra* and through the 'higher practices' which involve the attainment of enlightenment through the chanting of magical spells, special hand gestures, and mystical diagrams.

The Kargyupa or Karmapa is one of the oldest sub-sects. This sect was founded by Ranchug Dorje. There are followers of Kargyupa who have retrograded towards Nyingmapa practices (Waddel, 1976: 13). In another place, Waddel has mentioned that this sect was founded by Lama Marpa in the later half of the eleventh century AD (*ibid:* 5). Kargyupa is a lineage of the Kagyu school of Tibetan Buddhism. It was originated and developed by Marpa Chokyi Lodro (1012–1099) and Khyungpo Nyahjor (978–1079). The approach to *Mahamudra,* the unique feature of Kagyu School normally follows through stages of foundation, path, and fruit. The Tantric practices of Kagyu School are the Six Yogas of Naropa, Chakrasambhava, and Mahakala.

In Sikkim, the Buddhists celebrate different festivals which are the symbol of expressing their faith towards their religion. From these festivals, they get enough of recreation, joy and life element. At the same time give them relief from the monotony of life. These festivals offer them the enough of scope to dance, sing and marry making. These also help them to display their arts and crafts. These festivals are celebrated in different months of the year. For these festivals, they spend enough time and money. Some of these important festivals are:

### Saga Dawa

As the Triple Blessed Festival, it is considered as the holiest of the holy Buddhist festival. The day when this festival is celebrated is a very auspicious day as on this day of different years, Lord Buddha was born, achieved Enlightenment and laid down His life after His *nirvana*.

## Lhabab Dhuechen

This festival is celebrated on that day when Lord Buddha descended from heaven of thirty-three gods after visiting His mother (*Lha* = Heaven; *Bab* = descent; *Dhuechen* = festival).

## Losar

The Buddhists of Sikkim celebrate this festival to mark the Tibetan New Year. The Tibetan also joins this festival. Losar is observed during February. One of the interesting parts of this festival is the yak dance by the Tibetan youths.

## Bumchu

The famous Tashiding monastery hosts this festival in the mid-winter (January or February). In this Bumchu festival, the most important part is the opening of the sealed pot containing Holy Water (*Bum* = pot; *chu* = water). Observing the level of water in the pot the Lama understands the nature and rate of the prosperity for the next year. After distributing some holy water from the pot to the assembled persons, the Lama again filled in the post with fresh water from the river or spring and again he seals the pot and keeps it in the monastery for the Bumchu festival to be held in the next year.

## Guru Rimpoche's Trungkar Tshechu

In this festival when the Buddhists of Sikkim pay homage to Guru Rimpoche. They also express their gratefulness to the Guru for providing them a firm base for Buddhism in Sikkim. This festival marks his victory over the vanquishing demons that stood against the establishment and development of *Dhamma* (Raha *et al.,* 2016).

## Drukpa Tsheshi

This festival is celebrated by the Buddhists of Sikkim in order to mark the event of the first turning of the 'wheel of Dhamma' by Lord Buddha. This festival is also indicates Lord Buddha's first sermon (*four noble truth*) given to his five disciples at Sarnath. On the fourth day (Tsheshi) of the sixth month (Drukpa) of the Tibetan calendar i.e. August.

## Phang Lhabsol

The third Chogyal of Sikkim, Chakdor Namgyal actually popularise this festival in Sikkim. This festival is celebrated during the fifteenth day of the seventh month of Tibetan calendar (corresponding to late August). During this festival, local deities are invoked to observe the festival. The main feature of this festival is to worship of the mountain Kanchendzonga and also marked Lama Dance portraying the guardian deity and *Pong-Toed* dance by the monks. A treaty of blood-brotherhood between the Lepchas and the Bhutias by Khye Bumsa and Tetong Tek is portrayed through songs (Raha *et al.*, 2016).

## Losoong

During the end of the tenth month of the Tibetan Calendar year when the harvest season ended, after praying for bumper harvest during the next season, this festival is held. The *Chaam* dance in the monasteries at Palace (*Tsu-La-Khang*) at Phodong and Ramtek is the main feature.

## References

Dutta, S and B. Tripathi, 2006. *Buddhism in North East India*, New Delhi; Indus Publishing Co.

Frazer, JB., 1820. *Journal of Tour through Part of the Snowy Range of the Himalaya Mountains and to the Source of Jamuna and Ganges*, London.

Furer Haimendorf, C.von., 1964. *The Sherpas of Nepal: The Buddhist Highlanders*, New Delhi; Sterling Publishers.

Ganhar, JN and PN. Ganhar. 1956. *Buddhism in Kashmir and Ladakh*, New Delhi.

Gerard, A., 1841. *An Account of Koonauwar in the Himalayas*, London.

Ghosh, SN., 1989. *Census of India, 1981*, West Bengal, Part IX (III), Special Tables for Scheduled Tribes.

Ghosh, TK., 1992. 'Social stratification in Lahaul'. In MK Raha and PC Coomar (Eds): *The Himalayas and the Himalayans*, Calcutta; Anthropological Survey of India.

Ghosh, TK., 2002. *A Profile of the Himalayan Lahaula*, Kolkata; Anthropological Survey of India.

Gill, MS., 1972. *Himalayan Wonderland*, New Delhi.

Mann, RS., 1986. *The Ladakhi: A Study of Ethnography and Change*, Calcutta; Anthropological Survey of India.

Mann, RS., 1995. 'Religious attributes and social change among the Ladakhis'. In MK Raha (Ed): *The People of the Himalayas: Bio-cultural and Ecological Aspects*. Calcutta; Anthropological Survey of India.

Mann, RS., 1992. *Ladakh: Then and Now*, New Delhi; Mittal Publications.

Prasad, RR., 1989. *Bhotia Tribals of India: Dynamics of Economic Transformation*, New Delhi; Gyan Publishing House.

Raha, MK., 1995. 'Society and religion in Kinnaur'. In MK Raha (Ed): *The People of the Himalayas: Bio-cultural and Ecological Aspects*. Calcutta; Anthropological Survey of India.

Raha, MK., 2003. 'Synthesis of Buddhism and Hinduism in western Himalayas: A study of the Kinnauras of Himachal Pradesh'. In NK Das (Ed): *Culture, Religion and Philosophy*. New Delhi; Rawat Publications.

Raha, MK., 2006. 'Buddhism (Lamaism) among the Sherpas of Sikkim'. In S Dutta and B Tripathy (Eds): *Buddhism in North East India*, New Delhi; Indus Publishing Co.

Raha, MK and SN. Mahato. 1985. *The Kinnaurese of the Himalayas*, Calcutta; Anthropological Survey of India.

Raha, MK and PC. Coomar. 2001. 'Some aspects of the Sherpa Religion'. In S Sengupta (Ed): *The Tribes of the Eastern Himalayas*, New Delhi; Mittal Publications.

Raha, MK, PC. Coomar and S. Bhui. 2016. *The Sherpas of the Himalayas*, New Delhi; Concept Publishing Co.

Snellgrove, DL., 1957. *Himalayan Pilgrimage*, Boulder; Prajna Press.

Thornton, EP., 1854. *A Gazetteer of the Territories under the Government of East India Company and Native States on the Continent of India*, London.

# Index

**E**



**F**



**G**

## L



## M

## S